"Ourtown, U.S.A."—about 1870, in the

RK WEEK 66 HOURS   LIFE SPAN 42½ YEARS
WEEKLY PAY $10.00   EDUCATION 3½ YEARS

11773

PN
4121   DIETRICH
.D533   Practical speaking for the
          technical man

11773

PN
4121   DIETRICH
.D533   Practical speaking
          for the technical
          man

NS FEB 10 76   336-34-1187
   APR 24 85   T 49057

©—1958, by

PRENTICE-HALL, INC.

Englewood Cliffs, N. J.

Library of Congress Catalog Card No.: 58-7585

Current printing (last digit):
15 14 13 12 11 10 9 8 7 6

Printed in the United States of America

C-6939

To

John H. Dietrich

One of America's
 foremost public speakers

and

Etta Mierswa Brooks

A courageous
 and respected leader

preface

IN THIS BOOK the authors have made every effort to provide a practical solution to the everyday speaking problems of the technical man. The book is primarily concerned with getting results. It pivots around the listener. Each principle is discussed in terms of how the listener may be made to respond. The speaking situations which receive primary stress are those which the technical man encounters in his life and work. The illustrations and applications are technical in nature. Special attention has been given to the use of visual aids, the oral report, the interview, conference speaking, and the business meeting.

Two unique features, *Apply the Principles* and a *Formula*, will be found at the end of each chapter. *Apply the Principles* provides practical exercises for the purpose of focusing the technologist's attention on the main features of the chapter. The *Formulas*, designed with the technical man in mind, provide a systematic approach to each chapter. They introduce scales for measuring achievement and check lists of major factors in effective speaking.

The book concludes with three appendixes: (1) discussion questions pertaining to each chapter, (2) a speaking effectiveness scale, and (3) a sample speech representing excellence in organization and language.

In essence the book shows the practical procedures of *how to do it.*

At the same time, a sincere attempt has been made to balance the *how* with the *why*. It is our firm conviction that we do things better if we understand why we are doing them.

We wish to thank the Westinghouse Electric Corporation for permission to use the endpaper drawings. We are also indebted to the Battelle Memorial Institute, the Ohio Fuel Gas Company, and North American Aviation, Inc., Columbus Division, for their splendid cooperation in securing the pictorial material; to Henry Moser of the Department of Speech of The Ohio State University for his advice in drawing the mechanical man; to Ethel Rich for her editorial work; to Lois Dietrich for her devoted attention to the original draft; to Laquata Brooks for her assistance in proof reading.

John E. Dietrich

Keith Brooks

table
of contents

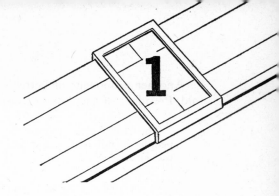

why
speak?

Every professional man needs the art of effective speaking—to sell his services, his product, and his profession. His advancement, his leadership, and his prestige depend largely on his powers of presentation, persuasion, and inspiration.[1]

WHY SHOULD a businessman, an engineer, a doctor, or a machinist want to take a speech course? The speech class of an adult evening school was asked this question, and their replies indicated that they had learned—out on the job—that poor speech was holding them back. One of the students, a top executive with Allis-Chalmers, summed it up this way: "Energy and youth can carry a man just so far, then knowledge and ability take over. One of the real bases of ability is good speech."

This same idea is expressed by Donald H. Menzel, Director of the Harvard College Observatory:

There are only two modes that the scientist has for communicating the results of his research to his colleagues: the written word or the spoken word. And in both of these media the average scientist is almost hopelessly deficient. Good speaking and good writing go hand in hand. Clarity of thought is essential to both. The direct approach, avoidance of circumlocution, is the key to good speaking.

---

[1] D. B. Steinman, Consulting Engineer of New York City.

Another proponent of better communication, Kenneth MacDonald, President of the American Society of Newspaper Editors, says:

> The really crucial problem of the world is communications. If people do not understand one another, then there is little hope for the future.[2]

As long ago as 1930 a study at Purdue University emphasized the importance of good speech.[3] The survey asked successful alumni of this engineering school to check the college courses which they felt were most important. The responses indicated the expected mandatory subjects, such as mathematics, mechanics, and physics, but surprisingly enough they also listed English, economics, and public speaking. Twenty-five years ago top engineers were asking for public speaking in the curriculum! This need has in part been answered. A survey of 122 engineering schools found that 43 per cent require a regular course in speech of all undergraduates.[4] Another 21 per cent require speech training of undergraduates majoring in selected divisions or areas. Less than 5 per cent of the schools reported no training in speech at all.

An anecdote reports that a national business magazine was looking for a science writer. The editor of the magazine wrote to the Du Pont Company asking for a young man who thoroughly understood chemical theory and could make it clear to the average layman. Du Pont is alleged to have written back, "Find us the man, and we'll make him a Vice President!"

SPEECH IN YOUR LIFE

Most speech serves two purposes: (1) the transfer of ideas or information and (2) the control of the listener, the gaining of the desired response. In fact, it may be said with firmness that if the ideas

---

[2] Kenneth MacDonald, "The Press and the New Freedom," *Vital Speeches,* XXII, No. 14 (May 1, 1956), p. 440.

[3] G. C. Brandenburg, "Successful Alumni—What They Do and What They Think," *Studies in Higher Education,* XXXI, No. 3, Purdue University, 1930, p. 19.

[4] Lester Lyle McCrery, "The Status of Speech in America's Science and Engineering Colleges," *The Speech Teacher,* II (September, 1953), p. 183.

are not transferred and the desired response of the listener isn't obtained, the speech is a failure.

Speech in Everyday Life

Stop for a moment and think. How many times during the last twenty-four hours have you made a speech? How many times have you tried to get a response from one or more listeners? If you took part in a discussion in which you held a particular point of view and tried to get others to agree, or if you tried to get a listener to do something for you or with you, you were making a speech.

How did you succeed? Were you able to explain to someone how to tune the new television set or to teach someone how to solve an algebra problem? Did your description of your vacation hold the interest of your audience? Was your explanation of the key play in last night's game as clear as it might have been? If your listeners understood, you succeeded as a speaker; if they didn't understand, you failed.

Speech in the School

Many classes require recitations and reports. Have you ever thought of them as speeches? They are. In the classroom you have a group of listeners and you have something tangible to gain or lose— a good grade. Show me a successful student, and I'll wager that he is a person who can express himself clearly and forcefully. He is not a blowhard or a loudmouth, but rather someone who knows when to speak and how long to speak, someone who has something to say and says it effectively.

The Job Interview

The turning point of your life will be when you look for your first job. How do you convince a prospective employer that you are the well-balanced, congenial, industrious, ambitious young man that he is looking for? Technical competence will not be enough; your academic record and your recommendations will take you only so far. Your ability to express yourself clearly and effectively will be very important.

Conversations with Superiors

After you get the job, you must impress your superiors by your ability. You must continue to sell your ideas and yourself, and again the ability to speak is essential. The man who is unhappy in his job is almost always the man who is not getting along. "Getting along" usually means getting along with others, and adjustment to the society in which one lives is based upon effective human relations and effective communication.

Conferences, Reports, and Meetings

As you move up in your job from the desk in the corner or from your work in the field or shop, your contacts will constantly broaden. Instead of listening at meetings and conferences, you will begin to participate. As you mature, your ideas will count more in deciding the policies of the firm. These ideas will be expressed in conferences on problems of the company and in reports to business meetings. Your success will be measured by your knowledge and, above all, by your ability to communicate that knowledge effectively.

Administration

After you get to the top, almost all your work will be written and oral communication. You will find it necessary to conduct interviews and lead conferences, run business meetings, and make public speeches to technical and lay audiences. Your life will be one of ideas and talk, and your success will be measured by your full and effective use of each.

Community Affairs

As you progress you will begin to take a larger and larger part in community affairs. You will participate in meetings and conferences, make public speeches, and perhaps even make radio and television appearances. Again your leadership will be measured by your ideas and how effectively you present them.

Let us summarize some of the reasons for learning to speak well. First, many men are driven to seek a better control of communication late in life after they have found that this deficiency is slowing them down. Second, thousands of men who are out of school attest to the importance of communication. Finally, examination of many of the phases of a man's life shows that in every instance effective speech is essential to success.

In other words, the young man who says "Who's going to make any speeches?" and receives an answering chorus of "Not me!" is wrong—*dead wrong!* He is going to make thousands of speeches— some informal, some formal, some with big audiences, some with a single listener. Everyone of them will be important because his purpose will be that of getting the *right* responses from his listeners— the responses that *he* wants.

FALSE NOTIONS ABOUT SPEECH

Perhaps you have some false notions about public speaking. Let's put the record straight!

Is Public Speaking for Exhibition?

The answer is no! The speaker who is so concerned with what his listeners think about him that he shifts his attention from his listener to himself is doomed to failure. His speech becomes a performance. He tries to show what he can do, just for the sake of proving what a smooth and facile speaker he is. This type of speaker is an actor who hopes his performance will fascinate the audience; but frequently his dulcet tones and affected mannerisms become overbearing and repugnant. One should *never* permit speaking to become a performance. Speech should always have a purpose and a meaning; the speaker should be merely the agent for transferring facts and ideas.

Does Public Speaking Mean Formal Occasions?

The answer is no! The idea that speech always means a large and formal audience should have been dispelled by previous discussion. Public speaking may imply a somewhat greater formality. You do have to get up on your feet before a group. You will probably be talking on a subject of somewhat greater magnitude than that of the ordinary conversation. You will have to speak for a longer period of time and probably to a larger group of listeners. On the other hand, most of your public speaking will be technical in nature. It will treat subjects about which you have considerable knowledge and confidence and will usually be given before groups of from two to twenty of your co-workers. The formality of the situation should be the least disturbing factor.

Is Public Speaking Radically Different from Private Speaking?

The answer is no! Private and public speaking are similar in most ways: the purpose in speaking and the ideas treated are the same; the basic tenets of good delivery are similar; and the audience is composed of the same human beings. The basic difference is one of amplification. In public speaking you are placed before the group rather than in it, and the group of listeners may be larger. Good private speaking techniques need to be amplified. In public speaking you probably talk for ten to twenty minutes rather than from one to two minutes. This requires careful and sustained preparation and organization of materials.

Does Private Speaking Require Less Preparation?

The answer is no! Probably the greatest misconception of all is that you don't have to prepare when you aren't on a platform. Standing on a platform has nothing to do with it. Think of the important discussions you have had in the last few weeks. Think of the times you have gone home knowing that you didn't make your point or get your way. Did you have sufficient evidence to support your ideas? Was your command of language clear enough to induce understanding? Did you make your purpose and reason sufficiently forceful? If you failed, the answer to each question is no. If you had thought out and worked out your ideas in advance, if you had prepared for the situation, you might have succeeded.

Even if you didn't know the situation was going to arise, the procedures, skills, and techniques of good speech would have helped you get the desired response. The purpose of speech doesn't change from one situation to another. Knowledge and skill will always serve their master.

BREAD-AND-BUTTER SPEAKING

This book is concerned with bread-and-butter speaking. Bread-and-butter speaking may be defined as simple, direct, honest, hard-hitting, straightforward speech. It is the kind of speech that will help you earn your bread and butter; this means speaking in which all your energy is devoted to getting the desired response. Some of the major criteria of good bread-and-butter speaking are listed below.

Straight Thinking

It has been said that "you don't know that which you cannot express." This axiom can be reversed to read "you can't express that which you don't know." In either case good communication is based upon good ideas. Therefore, in this book emphasis is placed on developing ideas which are worthy of expression. And stress will be placed on expressing the idea in a manner that is worthy of the idea.

Good communication actually helps good ideas. You can probably remember an occasion when the attempt to get others to understand an idea implanted it even more clearly and firmly in your own mind. You have probably noticed that when you clearly understand an idea, you are in a much better position to express it.

Thinking on Your Feet

Another essential of good bread-and-butter speaking is the ability to think on your feet. Emphasis will be placed on the kinds of speaking that require constant adaptation of the material to the speaking situation. Most speaking cannot be set or memorized, so the man who learns to think on his feet will be capable of meeting any situation. Of course quick thinking is not a substitute for preparation; it is rather the perfect complement to complete preparation.

Understanding the Listener

Since all bread-and-butter speaking is aimed at getting the desired reaction from the listener, the listener is the most important factor in the speaking situation. The able speaker not only understands what makes the listener respond, but also respects and adapts to the listener's ideas and attitudes. Since satisfactory human relations are based on good communication, knowing the listener will be the first concern of the good speaker.

Recognizing the Situation

The first-rate bread-and-butter speaker recognizes and adjusts to the speaking situation. Speaking is done not only from the platform, but also in the conference room, at the interview, and in the business meeting. Some of the most important speaking takes place on the golf course. Therefore the intelligent speaker will evaluate the situation and adapt his remarks to the spirit of the occasion.

Forceful Expression

Oratory is speaking with an elevated style, careful refinements of language, and a lofty idea. In its best sense it is superb speaking, but in its worst sense it is merely exhibitionism—speaking for the sake of speaking. Although oratory at its best is desirable, this book is not concerned with making orators. Instead the keynotes are simplicity, sincerity, warmth, and directness. If you can express a good idea simply and well, you can be a good bread-and-butter speaker.

A WORD OF ADVICE

At this point you should be aware that good speaking is imperative to your success in life. In addition, you should recognize that good speaking is simple, direct, and purposeful, and that it is based on good ideas and complete preparation.

Before we go further, it should be made clear that no book can teach you to speak. It can at best provide you with tools and a general understanding of how to use them. No instructor can really teach you to speak. He can give you opportunities to try out your speech, and he can point out your strengths and weaknesses; but real improvement is largely up to you. Books, instructors, and classes can help you, but they can't do it for you. In speech as in no other subject you will get out of it exactly what you put into it, and not one iota more.

If you practice good speaking only during class periods or test sessions and drop back into your old habits afterwards, your efforts will be to little avail. You are going to be creating new habits in place of old ones, good habits in place of bad. Since constant awareness and concentration is necessary to build a new habit, you must practice every single time you speak. It is hard work, but the results are worth it.

The need for effective speaking is clear; the rewards are obvious. The technical man must accept and fulfill this responsibility to his job. Eric A. Walker, noted engineering authority and President of The Pennsylvania State University, puts it this way:

> The engineer has at his disposal three methods of communication: Mathematical equations, engineering drawings, and the English language, in either written or spoken form. Unfortunately, his use of mathematics and drawings as a communications channel can only be used when talking with other engineers or other specialists familiar with these languages. Most of an engineer's dealings with his superiors and with those who work with him have to be by means of the English language. Although reports and summaries of reports are powerful tools, the most powerful of all is the short, oral briefing at which an engineer can explain what he is trying to do and how he proposes to go about it. Here he makes his plea for cooperation, either in terms of funds, facilities, manpower or materials to get the job done. It is my opinion that the one truly essential tool is a command of the English language by which the engineer can "put his ideas across."

——Apply the Principles

Learning to speak is done by speaking; therefore throughout this book practical suggestions for application will appear immediately after the principles have been discussed. Try out the following.

(1) Analyze the speeches you have made today. They were probably not formal speeches, but they were important nonetheless. Take each of the criteria for good bread-and-butter speaking and check off the principles you honestly feel you applied. Pay special attention to the principles you overlooked.

(2) Try to analyze your speaking opportunities for tomorrow. Where will you speak and to what purpose? A recitation in class? Solving problems for a friend? An interview with

your instructor? A meeting with your social club? Persuasion of your parents? Decide on your purpose and try to plan how you will go about gaining a desirable response.

(3) Stand apart from yourself when you speak tomorrow. Watch your listener's reactions and try to evaluate your success or failure. Listen carefully to other speeches tomorrow. Try to determine why they succeed or why they fail so that you can profit from analyzing the strengths and weaknesses of the other fellow.

(4) Plan a specific speech to be made in class, on the job, or in any other practical situation. Keep the subject simple and practical. Choose a subject that you know and allow yourself about two minutes. Apply the essentials of good bread-and-butter speaking. Make it a speech to inform. Try to assess your listeners' knowledge of your subject. Tell them something new, yet not so complex that they can't follow it.

(5) Teach your listener or listeners "How to Solve a Problem." Try a simple problem in mathematics, physics, chemistry, mechanics, or construction methods.

FORMULA A

$$WS = U + K - Fn$$

(*WS*) *Why Speak* = (*U*) *Understanding* the importance of speech to you, its part in your everyday life, its function in a successful life; plus (*K*) *Knowledge* that good speaking is simple, direct, purposeful, and requires good ideas and complete preparation; minus (*Fn*) *False notions* about speech.

Now, apply the formula!

UNDERSTAND the *importance* of good speech to you!

> Individual adjustment
> Social acceptance
> Personal advancement

UNDERSTAND the *part* speech plays in your everyday life!

> School
> The job interview
> Conversations with superiors
> Conferences, reports, and meetings
> Administration
> Community affairs

KNOW the *essentials* of good speech!

> Think straight
> Think on your feet
> Understand the listener
> Recognize the situation
> Express ideas forcefully

SUBTRACT *false notions* about speech!

> Public speech is not for exhibitionism
> Public speech does not mean formal occasions
> Public speech is not radically different from private speech
> Public speech needs preparation

CONCLUDE the following:

> Good speaking is imperative to your success in life
> Good speaking is simple, direct, purposeful
> Good speaking needs good ideas and complete preparation

the keys to effective speech

IF A SPEAKER can provide through sight and sound a stimulus that will hold the listener's interest and induce him to understand and approve, he has won the battle. What does the listener see and hear? What excites the listener's interest? What can the listener understand? What can receive the listener's approval? There are questions that every speaker must answer by applying the nine keys to effective speech.

The keys to effective speech are the means by which the speaker communicates his ideas to the listener and gets the desired reaction. These keys will open the doors of response.

Key # 1—Define Your Purpose
Key # 2—Pick a Superior Subject
Key # 3—Know Your Subject
Key # 4—Find Good Material
Key # 5—Develop Clear Organization
Key # 6—Making It Interesting
Key # 7—Choose Meaningful Language
Key # 8—Deliver It Forcefully
Key # 9—Practice Your Speech Aloud

KEY # 1—DEFINE YOUR PURPOSE

Frequently listeners fail to respond because they are unable to determine what the speaker wants from them. Therefore, the first requirement of any speech is that it have a clear purpose.

Everyone has heard the very funny fellow who convulsed his audience. If entertainment was his purpose, then his speech was a success. If the humor was supposed to be the spice added to the basic ingredients of the cake, the condiment has ruined the cake. The humor has attracted so much attention that the real desire, the reason for speaking, has been lost.

Have you ever listened to a speech in which you couldn't decide whether you were merely to understand the subject or whether you were to believe something? A speech on diesel power may be informative, but it may also be persuasive. Perhaps the speaker only wants you to understand the weight to power ratio of the diesel engine. On the other hand, he may want you to recognize the advantages of this ratio and use diesel power. Both informative and persuasive elements may appear in the same speech, but the ultimate response desired by the speaker must be made clear and strong.

Perhaps in an interview with your instructor about a grade you have failed to get the response you desired. Could it have been because the instructor wasn't certain of exactly what you wanted? Many interviews suffer from this lack of definite purpose; probably it is really the lack of a clearcut expression of purpose.

Some sales presentations don't sell. Frequently this is because the salesman doesn't know how to bring about the "closing." That is, he doesn't make his purpose stick with the listener. Instead of making sure that every aspect of his speech is aimed at establishing his point of view, he has allowed the conversation to wander.

Similarly, conferences often don't reach a clearcut understanding. Here, as in no other speech situation, the dangers of an unclear purpose are apparent. The conference ends; the costly time and talents of those conferring have been used; and yet no clear line of development can be found.

Obviously if the speaker doesn't know what his purpose is, he has little chance of achieving it. If he does know what he wants, then he must make certain that the listener is aware of his reason for speaking.

KEY # 2—PICK A SUPERIOR SUBJECT

As a technical man your life will be filled with speeches, interviews, and conversations in which the subjects will be directly related to what you know best—your work. These will be good subjects for you and your listener, because they have arisen out of an apparent need to speak.

At the same time there will be many occasions when you will have to speak on a subject that is not related to your vocation. You will give dozens of speeches which are social, religious, scientific, or political. Some of these will be formal occasions, such as speaking before the civic group, the PTA, the church men's club; however most of them will be less formal situations, such as persuading your neighbors to donate to the blood drive or to give to the Red Cross.

A speech can be prepared without previous knowledge of the subject, but it is a tremendous undertaking. Therefore you are advised to select a subject that you already know something about. Time and again students say "I don't know a thing to talk about" or "I don't know anything that would interest anyone." However, you can't help but know things that others don't. Your experiences in life have been different from those of everyone you know, including your family. You may have shared some experiences with other people, but no one has shared all of your experiences.

The best initial source of speech material is your own knowledge and your own experience. It has been said by psychologists that every man is fascinating once the veneer is penetrated. Search out the events in your life which will be meaningful to an audience.

The second statement—"I don't know anything that would *interest* anyone"—is more likely to be true. An idea that interests you may not always interest others. On the other hand, if it interests you, there is good reason to believe that you can interest others in it. After all they have much the same wants, needs, and desires as you do. The problem is one of fitting the ideas to the particular listeners to whom you are to speak. The reason that most speeches entitled "My Most Embarrassing Moment" or "What I Did Last Summer" fail is that the speaker doesn't consider his most embarrassing moment very embarrassing and doesn't care a whit what he did last summer. If you aren't interested in your subject, you can be reasonably sure that no one else will be.

Occasionally a speaker may misjudge the interest of the audience and be in for trouble. The housewife who wrote the following is an example: "I finish my ironing at 4:00 o'clock and want to watch television. Last Monday your program was entitled 'The Life and Habits of the Woodchuck.' I don't want to know anything about the woodchuck. I have never seen and never expect to see a woodchuck. I am sure that I would not like a woodchuck if I saw him. I think his life and habits are thoroughly repulsive." Thus your job, your hobby, your accomplishments, can make excellent material only if they are in line with the listener's wants. If they aren't, you will immediately become a bore.

The preceding is not meant to frighten you but rather to persuade you that you do know things that will interest others, though selection must be made only after calculating the audience appeal of particular items. In every case the subject must be well adapted to the listener, the time, and the occasion. Sometimes you will know all there is to know about the subject; sometimes you will have to do a lot of research to become an expert. Neglecting to select a good subject is one of the prime reasons for failure in speech.

KEY # 3—KNOW YOUR SUBJECT

Your knowledge of the subject must be adapted to the listener's knowledge of the subject. Remember that you are technically trained and that the jargon of science and engineering comes easily. If your speech is set at too high a level, the audience will soon be lost and begin to doodle. If, on the other hand, your speech is too simple for the knowledge of the audience, they will begin to doodle almost immediately. Donald H. Menzel, Director of the Harvard College Observatory, has this word of caution:

> As for subject matter, the lecturer should carefully consider his audience to determine the level at which he should pitch his talk. Although an audience does not like to be "talked down to," the use of technical jargon may leave a popular audience cold.

Even more frequently the speaker may give the impression that he doesn't know what he is talking about. The listener gets this impression in several ways: (1) There is the possibility that the speaker really doesn't know what he is talking about. (2) The speaker may

have so much material that he appears to or actually does get lost in
the maze. (3) The treatment of the subject matter may be so general
and obvious that the listener loses confidence in the speaker. (4) The
speaker's manner of delivery may be such that the audience feels that
he doesn't know much about his subject. Any one or all of these
problems can cause the audience to distrust the speaker and can result in decreasing the chances for success.

KEY # 4—FIND GOOD MATERIAL

Even though the subject may be superior, the material may be inferior. You cannot afford to depend entirely upon what you know
about a subject, because the material you already have may not serve
your purpose. Is your material clear? In other words, does it really
help the speech? Do your illustrations confuse the issue more than
they clarify it? There are several reasons why material may not serve
its purpose. The material may not be to the point. If it doesn't really
add to your point, don't use it. If the comparison doesn't set up a
clearer relationship, find another. If the statistics you have don't
really help clarify and support, throw them out. If the anecdote is
stale and uninteresting, discard it. If the material doesn't fit the interest and desires of these particular listeners, avoid it. If the material
is not up to date, find some that is.

All of the preceding factors provide clues to what the substance
of your speech should be. The chances are slim that you will have material to meet all of these criteria. Find some that does the job.

KEY # 5—DEVELOP CLEAR ORGANIZATION

Probably more speeches fail because of poor organization than
from any other single cause. Poor organization may give the listener
the feeling that the speaker lacks knowledge of his subject, or it may
result in the listener's not being able to follow the line of thought in
the speech. The impact of a speech can come from the organization
itself. Ideas that are presented in a logical and interesting sequence are
much more clear and more persuasive than ideas which are presented
in a disjointed and rambling way.

The primary purpose of good organization is to make all of the
ideas in a speech fit together in such a way that they are clear and

create a constantly increasing impact. The basic ideas of a speech must be amplified and supported. The amplification and support must be grouped in a logical way. The keystones of understanding will be clusters of material which explain or prove a given point. Destroying the organization destroys the clarity.

Remember that the listener has no chance to sit down and study a speech as he might a book. Since he can't go back and mull the point over, he gets no second chance. Clear organization is the only way in which ideas can be developed so that each one is a stepping stone to the next. Good organization is the only way to make a whole speech out of parts.

KEY # 6—MAKE IT INTERESTING

The only way that the listener can perceive your point is by paying attention to you. You cannot expect the listener to pay attention unless your ideas are more interesting than any of the other stimuli that may be around him. No speaker can compete with a fire engine, a swooping jet, or a jazz band; not just because of the noise, but because each of these disturbances has a sense of excitement about it. However these are not typical distractions. The question is whether you as a speaker can compete with the heat of the room, the hardness of the seat, the thought of the dance to come, the desire to be elsewhere, the weariness at the end of the day. These are the common distractions which the speaker must overcome, and he can overcome them only if his material is interesting and vivid.

KEY # 7—CHOOSE MEANINGFUL LANGUAGE

Words have two qualities. They have an exact dictionary meaning called a denotative meaning, and they have an implied meaning called a connotative meaning. This poses two problems for the speaker. He must select language that has the exact meaning which he intends, and he must choose language that has the desired associations, whether the words are descriptive in order to stimulate the imagination or emotional in order to stimulate a pleasant or unpleasant response.

Even in the best circumstances speaking sometimes fails. More often than not it fails because there has been a breakdown in meaning. This breakdown may be caused by words that do not mean the same to both the speaker and the listener. The word "communist" is an example. Ask the first ten people you meet to define the word. You are in for a surprise. No two of the definitions will jibe in all details, and probably five of the ten will not even seem to be definitions of the same thing. This shows that what one person means by "communist" may not be what the other fellow means and that one must define it to insure meaningful communication.

This problem goes further than the exact meaning. "Communist" also happens to be a word with an emotional bias. For Americans this emotional bias is negative. Therefore, whenever you use it, you will receive a negative response. There are hundreds of other words in the same category, and the good speaker will take care to choose language that is concrete, specific, and easily understood. He will also choose wording that will stimulate pleasant associations with his proposition. The right language is a powerful weapon.

KEY # 8—DELIVER IT FORCEFULLY

Delivering a speech forcefully does not mean making it loud. Forceful delivery is made up of three components: (1) the right mental attitude, (2) animated bodily activity, and (3) a distinct and pleasant voice.

The speaker with the right attitude shows the listener that he has an intense desire to communicate. He is interested in his subject and in his listeners. Since most of us are not good actors, we find it difficult to express something we don't feel. Therefore, sincere belief in the importance of your ideas is basic to successful delivery.

The listener has only two ways to get your point—his eyes and his ears. This means that everything he sees must lead him to the response you desire. Your directness, your posture, your movements and gestures—all have meaning for him. Your activity gives him cues.

Some time ago a young man gave a speech on the subject "The Importance of Discipline in the Armed Forces." The audience saw a seedy young man, suit unpressed, shoes unshined, tie awry, shuffling to the platform with a careless posture, random movements, and ineffectual gestures. His listeners saw the reverse of what good discipline should produce. How could the audience believe this speaker? Very simple—they couldn't and they didn't.

Everything that has been said about visual activity can be said with equal force about voice. Your voice as well as your body must show your desire to communicate your interest in your subject and your listeners.

KEY # 9—PRACTICE YOUR SPEECH ALOUD

There is an old saying that "practice makes perfect." Although this statement makes good sense, it is equally true that "practice makes permanent." It is therefore essential that you practice only good habits and never bad ones. This is one of the best reasons for a course in speaking where you are given opportunities to practice before a discerning audience and a qualified expert. If this situation isn't available to you, practice before any other listener or group of listeners that you can find—your roommate, your wife, your friends. Since they probably won't be thrilled to be practiced upon, they will be highly critical and effective judges of your success as a speaker.

Note the stress laid on practicing before a live audience. This is suggested for two reasons. First, it is absolutely necessary to practice communication rather than just speaking. The live audience will give you a response. A second reason for the live audience is that it will become more difficult for you to allow yourself to become stuck. You will feel obliged to fight your way through the speech. You will get training in thinking on your feet.

Talking in front of a mirror has the advantage of being able to see yourself and possibly correct some of your obvious mistakes in posture, gesture, and so forth. However, there is a very real disadvantage to be considered. When you talk to a mirror, you tend to become extremely conscious of yourself. You grimace and pose and adjust your clothes. In other words, you direct your attention during the process of speaking to the very elements of which you should be unconscious while speaking. Good speech demands that your attention be directed outward to the listener.

Be certain that all of your practice is aloud. Thinking through your speech is useful, but it isn't good speech practice. Thought, while it is subvocal speech, is a short cut process. You can think an idea through without ever clearly expressing it in actual language. When you can't find the way to express an idea, the tendency is to skip on because you know what you mean. However you won't be able to skip ahead when you are on the platform, and you will have to find the language. Thus the difficult process of filling in the gaps is essential and needs practice.

Devote your practice time to real learning. Since effective speaking cannot be learned by rote, practice should never be just a mechanical running over of the material. Think actively as you practice and concentrate on what you are doing; sift out the bad elements and make the good ones permanent.

Finally, try as far as possible to imagine and concentrate upon the actual situation. If you are practicing before a single listener and you know that your real audience will have ten listeners, practice the adjustments that you know will be necessary in the actual speaking situation.

You may not realize it yet, but you will have dozens of opportunities to practice good speaking each day. You will be able to try out your materials, your thought process, your language, and your delivery each time you speak. You must make every conversation, interview, conference, committee meeting, and classroom speech count. *Good* practice makes both permanent and perfect.

These, then, are the keys to effective speech: (1) define your purpose, (2) pick a superior subject, (3) know your subject, (4) find good material, (5) develop clear organization, (6) make it interesting, (7) choose meaningful language, (8) deliver it forcefully, and (9) practice your speech aloud. If you can master these keys to speaking, you cannot fail. Of course, not all speeches are alike in their method of development or presentation; therefore successful application of the keys to effective speech requires an understanding of the types of speaking.

SELECT THE TYPE OF SPEAKING

Speaking situations differ. In some instances there is no time for preparation. In others you are expected to release a copy of your text to the press before or after the speech. These differences in speaking situations lead to four different types of speaking: (1) impromptu speaking, (2) extemporaneous speaking, (3) memorized speaking, and (4) manuscript speaking. Each type has advantages and disadvantages. The speaking situation frequently determines which should be used.

Impromptu Speaking

The impromptu speech—often called speaking "on the spur of the moment" or "off the cuff" or "from the top of your head" or "spontaneous conversation"—is speaking where no special preparation is possible. Therein, of course, lies its greatest disadvantage. Few of us are able to deliver the best speech possible in this situation. (We think of all the funny stories and brilliant witticisms that we ought to have said after we get home.) Nonetheless the situation arises daily, so you must be prepared for it.

Suppose you are sitting quietly at a corner table at the company banquet. The chairman says: "And for his outstanding achievement in company affairs we present this special citation of merit to our good friend, Jim Jones!" Your name . . . Applause . . . Friends urging you from your seat . . . A quickened heartbeat and a flush of blood in your face, as you find your way to the speaker's table and speak. Your full complement of preparation is made as you walk to the platform; your effectiveness depends entirely upon your general background. Your remarks should be simple, sincere, adapted to the listeners, and, above all, brief.

A more typical impromptu situation arises in the conference. "John what do you feel about this policy?" You have absolutely no time to prepare. If you are to succeed in this situation, you must be on your toes. You must be a good bread-and-butter speaker who can think straight at all times and can think on his feet. If you analyze and organize your thoughts habitually, you will have little difficulty. Habitual analysis and organization is the key to effective impromptu speaking; it is the key to success in your everyday life.

Extemporaneous Speaking

In most speaking situations you have time to prepare. Then the question is how much. Should you memorize the speech? Should you write it out and read it? Or should you deliver it extemporaneously? All experts agree that the ideal method is extemporaneous speaking.

Extemporaneous speaking may be defined as speaking which is completely prepared but not memorized. Complete preparation means that the ideas, the organization, and even parts of the wording are all

Big Cash Refunds

DIRECTIONS ON REVERSE SIDE

al Program

($5 refund for each
5,000 sq. ft. purchase
of complete 4-Step
Annual Program or
$1 refund for each
5,000 sq. ft. bag)

plete

ober 31, 1985.
han November 15, 1985.

Scotts® Annual Program

Offer li◼

How to obtain your refund:

1. **Buy** the complete 4-Step Annual Program or any Annual Program Step product.

2. **Save** your cash register receipt(s).

3. **Clip** proof of purchase from each package. Photocopies not accepted

Name_____
           (PRINT CLEARLY)

Address_____

City_____

State_____ Zip_____

Did you have a lawn care service in 1984?
(circle answer)

             YES   NO

If yes, who? _____

S-550 8/84 (11-48, 86) Printed in USA   **Offer expires**

Mail-in Refund Certificate

20 per family or address.

4. Calculate your refund below:

Coverage	Refund Value	Refund Amount
5,000 sq. ft. 4-Step Annual Program (all 4 bags)	$ 5	$_____
10,000 sq. ft. 4-Step Annual Program (all 8 bags)	$10	$_____
15,000 sq. ft. 4-Step Annual Program (all 12 bags)	$15	$_____
20,000 sq. ft. 4-Step Annual Program (all 16 bags)	$20	$_____
or		
5,000 sq. ft. single Step bag(s)	$ 1 ea.	$_____

Total refund (limit $20) $_____
A

5. Mail this certificate, cash register receipt(s) <u>and</u> proofs of purchase to:

> **ANNUAL PROGRAM REFUND**
> **P.O. Box 2014**
> **Marion, OH 43305**
> Allow 4-6 weeks for delivery.
> Offer good only in USA where not prohibited,
> taxed or restricted by law.

er 31, 1985. Must be postmarked no later than November 15, 1985.

Bread-and-Butter Speaking—simple, direct, honest, hardhitting, straightforward, everyday speech. On the job success is dependent on these factors. Do these men mirror any of these factors? (Chapter 1) *Courtesy Ohio Fuel Gas Company.*

The keys to effective speech are the methods by which the speaker can communicate his ideas to the listener and get the desired response. Obviously this speaker is getting the desired response. What are the keys to good speech which have probably led to this response? (CHAPTER 2) *Courtesy Ohio Fuel Gas Company.*

completely in hand. The speaker may or may not use notes, but if notes are used, they should be brief and serve only to jog the memory on the order of the main divisions of the speech.

The advantages of extemporaneous speaking are numerous. In extemporaneous speaking you are thinking on your feet. The vitality inherent in this process alone makes it worthwhile. The speech has a spontaneity and freshness about it. In addition, and this is tremendously important, you are able to adjust your speaking and adapt to your audience as you go along. You can capitalize on every circumstance that occurs during the speech.

For example, suppose that a dog wanders into the room. You can't compete for attention with a dog. Sad as it may seem, the dog will always win. However, if you have the freedom to adjust, which extemporaneous speech provides, you can adapt to the presence of the dog and even capitalize on it. Suppose some of your audience becomes restless or even that one or two drop off to sleep. If you are thinking on your feet, you can change your style and recapture their attention.

You are in control of the speech and the situation with extemporaneous speaking. The excitement of the competition frequently brings your best thinking and your most colorful language into play—but only if you have a disciplined mind and are completely prepared. Lack of preparation is almost always at the bottom of failures in the extemporaneous method. Without adequate preparation your concentration is bound to be focused on straining for the next idea. It should be focused on the listener and concerned with getting him to respond.

Memorized Speaking

Practically the only speakers today who memorize intentionally are orators. The need for elevated style, for perfect and refined language, and for polish makes memorization a requirement. Most modern day oratory is a performance. In many ways it is a performance much in the same sense that an actor performs the role in a play, and frequently the listener reacts more to the performance than to what the speaker has to say. While there is certainly a place for oratory, it won't be a part of your life in science and engineering.

The performance aspect of the memorized speech is exactly what makes it so difficult. The speaker is concerned with putting on a polished show whenever he delivers the speech. Therefore his attention is focused inward upon himself rather than outward toward his audience. His mind is concentrating on remembering the next phrase, adjusting the next gesture, or modifying the vocal quality. These elements are not essential or even desirable in the memorized speech, but they usually do occur. As a result the speech seems "canned"—it sounds memorized—unless the speaker is a good actor.

Just as adaptability is the great strength of the extemporaneous speech, the set pattern is the great weakness of memorized speaking. There can be little change. The mind must stay on the memorized track. If the track is lost, the speaker is lost. So don't memorize your material, because if you do, almost every chance for good bread-and-butter speaking is against you.

Occasionally, particularly with short speeches, the speaker goes over his material so often in preparing it that it becomes memorized. Then the speaker tries to remember how he worded it last time. Try to avoid memorization. Word the speech differently each time you go over it. Refuse to be satisfied with the first expressions you have used. Undoubtedly some of the ideas will find expression during the speech as you have practiced them, but don't devote your energies to making sure that this will happen.

Manuscript Speaking

Certain special situations demand that the speaker read from a manuscript. Usually this is true in radio speaking. Time elements and exactness make a written manuscript imperative. Frequently committee reports which represent the careful agreement of a group of people need to be read. The President of the United States always reads his formal speeches. In these cases hundreds of thousands or even millions of minds scan every paragraph of the speech the next day in the newspapers. The slightest change of emphasis which might result from extemporaneous speaking could have worldwide repercussions.

Reading a manuscript is frequently called oral reading or interpretation of the printed page. Because it involves a situation which the technologist may face, the strengths, weaknesses, and principles of effective reading from manuscript are discussed in Chapter 12.

——*Apply the Principles*

The basic principles which underlie all good speaking have been brought together in a simple form. You have been told *what* makes good speaking without being told in any detail *how* to do it. The *how* will be dealt with extensively in later chapters. Therefore, at this point the application of the principles will depend largely upon your general background—background not only in subject matter but also background provided by years and years of speaking. Following the procedures below will not only help you develop a good speech but will also crystallize the principles discussed in the chapter.

(1) Plan a simple speech *to inform* your listeners. Give yourself about two minutes. Why not try teaching your listeners how to carry out a process or how to perform an operation? Be sure to determine who your listeners will be. Adapt your material to the listener's interest and previous knowledge. There is no sense in explaining something to a person who already knows more than you do about it.

(2) Select a process or operation in which you are interested. Make it a speech on how to do something. Select a subject about which you have a good deal of general preparation behind you. Draw your idea from your skills or accomplishments.

(3) Some examples of things to talk about might be: How to clean a carburetor, hold a golf club, tune a television set, set the points on a distributor, cast a bait, tie a Windsor knot, paint a boat, pour and finish concrete, test for uranium, make ice cream.

(4) Now determine the central idea and the major divisions. The central idea is obviously the process you are explaining. Stick with it; don't get off the track. The major divisions will be the steps in the process. Try to break the process down into not more than three or four steps. Remember that the listener may not carry away with him anything more than the major steps, so be sure they cover the necessary ground.

(5) Having determined your purpose, studied your listeners, selected the subject, and set up the major divisions, draw upon

your own resources for material. Think not only of your knowledge of the process itself but also of the experiences you have had with it which might be interesting to the listener. Thus far you have been able to develop this speech without any outside work. Now try to find one source on the subject—a magazine article, a book, or a newspaper report. Read the source and decide why you think it is worthwhile. Be careful not to throw away all your previous ideas and merely give an oral report on the article. Combine your ideas with those found in the article, giving credit to the author for the ideas you have taken from his material.

(6) Organize the speech on paper. You will need an introduction, a body, and a conclusion. Introduce the speech in some interesting way: tell a short, short story or why the audience should know about the process or use a quotation. The body of the speech will include the major divisions or steps of the process with any amplification which you think necessary for understanding. The conclusion of the speech should have a summary of the major steps and a good strong concluding sentence, perhaps something stressing the importance of the process to the listener.

(7) Finally, practice the speech aloud with a listener. In this speech don't write it out. Let the wording evolve as you go over it. Try to do it without notes. Check the time on it. If you are running long—two minutes will fly by—decide what might be cut without harming the speech. Never try to hurry through it.

(8) You are ready to speak. Good luck!

FORMULA B

$$KGS = (TS + 9KES) (P_1 + P_2)$$

(*KGS*) *Keys to Good Speech* = Taking a particular (*TS*) *Type of Speech* and adding to it the (*9KES*) *Nine Keys of Effective Speech.* Multiply the sum by the quantity (P_1) *Preparation* plus (P_2) *Practice.*

Now, apply the formula!

Prepare and give a five-minute speech. Using the scale below, give yourself a score for each of the eight categories. Also, have several listeners score you by using the same scale. Compare the differences. *The average listener score for each category is your best guide.*

Preliminary Gauge of Speaking Effectiveness		
1–2 Weak	3 Average	4–5 Strong
Category	*Score*	*Explanation of Score*
PURPOSE: Worthy? Justifiable? Clear?		
SUBJECT: Appropriate? Responsible? Adaptable?		
KNOWLEDGE: Thorough? Adaptable? Dated?		
MATERIAL: Supported? Pertinent? Individualized?		

Preliminary Gauge of Speaking Effectiveness (*cont.*)		
1–2 Weak 3 Average 4–5 Strong		
Category	*Score*	*Explanation of Score*
ORGANIZATION: Logical? Effective? Clear?		
INTEREST: Vital? Varied? Appealing?		
LANGUAGE: Colorful? Accurate? Responsible?		
DELIVERY: Forceful? Sincere? Direct?		
Total		

35–40 An excellent start
32–34 Headed in right direction
27–31 Details need attention
23–26 Needs more practice
16–22 Apply the keys
 8–15 Learn the keys

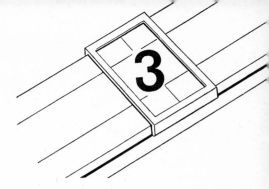

alert your
mental attitude

WHAT THE LISTENER thinks of you as a speaker is closely related to what people think of you generally. Your speech personality is not some magical transformation which you undergo when you rise to speak. It is merely a reflection of your way of thinking, responding, and acting.

Characterize one of your friends. You will find that physical appearance—tall, dark, and handsome—is only part of the picture. The adjectives which describe his personality—dull, stodgy, and listless; or crude, rough, and boorish; or brusque, sharp, and curt; or suave, polished, and smooth; or warm, sincere, and friendly—will be more important. Obviously a man is a mixture of a great number of ingredients, but there are always those which stand out; and these elements are the ones upon which we are prone to judge him. You may ask, "Suppose my personality isn't attractive to others. Am I expected to change it?" While it is not the purpose of this book to reorganize your life, if you do have undesirable personal qualities, you had better deal with them if you expect to succeed, not only in speech but also in life.

Frequently, however, the problem does not run so deep. The speaker's attitude often does *not* reflect the speaker's personality and character. Sometimes the person who is normally warm and friendly freezes up when he speaks; the forthright, honest, sincere man turns

29

into a disorganized mumbler on the speaking platform; the quiet, easy, confident person becomes unbearably aggressive and unfriendly as a speaker. These are simply problems which call for developing the right mental attitude toward speaking.

WHAT CAUSES THE WRONG ATTITUDE?

Nine times out of ten you are unable to express yourself freely because you are afraid. You react timidly, indifferently, or aggressively because you are afraid. Afraid of what? Of whom? Herein lies the confusion. You are probably not really afraid of your listener. Oh, you might be if it is a superior who can influence your future, but that is seldom the real fear.

Reverse your position. Think for a moment of yourself as a listener. What is your attitude toward the speaker? Do you usually dislike him and hope that he fails? Of course not. At worst you are probably indifferent and give him no thought at all. Normally, you are present because you want to hear what he has to say, and you sincerely hope that he says it in a manner that is interesting and understandable. Even if you are antagonistic, except in rare instances it is toward the speaker's subject, purpose, or point of view, not toward the speaker himself. Your own reactions as a listener show that there is little reason for the speaker to fear his listener.

The uneasiness we feel in the speaking situation apparently stems from natural anxieties arising from any new situation. Think of the first time you drove a car. You were tense and excited and uneasy. Think of your first time on the field with the football team or of your first meeting with your advisor; think of the first time you tried to sell a newspaper subscription. Always the same reaction of tension, excitement, and fear from a new situation.

Psychologists advance more than a dozen differing and often contradictory reasons for this fear. It has been said that the fear results from a conflict between a desire to be in the spotlight and a simultaneous desire to remain anonymous. It has been suggested that the anxieties result from the fear of failure in any new situation. Some psychologists feel that it is a fear that we won't get the results we desire. Others think that it comes from lack of skill in emotional control. Still others believe that it is the result of not understanding why we are excited and anxious which merely compounds the fear. Whatever

the reason or combination of reasons for being afraid, it is essential
that we understand the symptoms and characteristics of our fear if
we are to control it.

PERFORMANCE TENSION

Performance tension is not only a universal experience but a perfectly natural state. The new and uncertain situation presents a challenge. Whenever the human being is challenged, his body prepares
itself to meet the challenge. The resultant increase in physical tension
is necessary and desirable.

You have experienced situations in which you couldn't work yourself into the necessary state of mind. You didn't care; you felt sluggish
and indifferent; your performance was poor. Since performance tension is a "gearing up" process, it is essential to a first-rate performance.
On the other hand, think of the times when you have been keyed up
and have done your best. Your mind was crystal clear; your choice of
words was better than usual; your approach and attitude were dynamic. All of these extras came because you were physiologically prepared for the competition.

Performance tension arises primarily in new situations. For example,
the beginning teacher is tremendously excited when he meets his first
class, but the repetition of the situation with the same listeners soon
reduces the challenge and the tensions ease. If the tension and excitement disappears altogether, it will probably be reflected in the quality
of the teacher's performance. Lack of tension and excitement ac-
counts for many a dull lecture period.

The actor and the public speaker, however, face new listeners with
each occasion. Each new situation presents the challenge of catching,
holding, and controlling the new audience. For this reason speakers
always experience performance tension. In an interview with Edward
R. Murrow, Cornelia Otis Skinner expressed it well: "The actor who
doesn't have stage fright is no actor."

THE SYMPTOMS OF PERFORMANCE TENSION

Sparks in the head, feelings of faintness, pounding heart, shaking
knees, shortness of breath, butterflies in the stomach, perspiration,
mouth filled with flannel—these are the symptoms of too much per-

formance tension, which is rightly called fright—stage fright, mike fright, camera fright, and so forth.

How do these sensations occur? What changes take place in the body? When you become aware of the approach of the exciting challenge—this may happen hours before the performance actually takes place—your body needs energy. Food reserves and hormones are dumped into the system by the liver and endocrine glands; fuel is heaped on the fire. Immediately changes begin to take place in the normal balance of your body.

Your heart is stimulated to greater action—thus the noticeable pounding. Blood circulates faster; respiration is stepped up to provide a fresh oxygen supply to the blood—shortness of breath. Faster circulation causes more wastes to be eliminated through the skin—perspirations. Some of the other systems decrease their functions; digestion is slowed down or stopped—butterflies or nausea. Normal secretions dry up—dry mouth. With full tension the body is keyed up, geared up, and has extra energy. Paired muscle groups strain against each other—trembling, knocking knees. The boxer and the runner have an advantage; they can burn up the extra energy. The speaker doesn't need it all, so he fidgets, paces, shifts in his chair—aches.

The body is tensed, pent up, driving for release of energy. The voice also shows the tension. Since the vocal folds are muscles, they tighten up with the rest of the muscles. With great tension these folds may not vibrate properly—cracking voice. With tension the folds are pulled tighter—high pitch. Under tension the entire vocal musculature is strained—strident quality. In extreme cases, the tension goes even farther. This excitement is an emotional response. Generally the intellect functions inversely to the increase in emotion; the more emotional activity, the less intellectual activity—flashes in the head, inability to concentrate, paralyzed memory.

How bad can this state of tension get? Since we have painted a gruesome picture so far, we might as well tell you. It can get so bad that the body refuses to function at all. A few years ago Purdue University's best blocking right halfback—included in some All America selections—rose to make his first speech. He walked to the platform, took a deep breath, and dropped in a dead faint.

What good is performance tension? In small doses the excitement and its attendant tension is useful and desirable. Tension prepares you to meet the challenge; it provides the energy to really strike out toward your goal. The same Purdue halfback learned to control his fear and excitement. He learned to direct his extra energy where it would do the most good, and after a few speeches became an easy and poised speaker. You can do the same.

WAYS TO REDUCE AND CONTROL
EXCESSIVE TENSION

Primitive man, faced with a challenging competitive situation, could do one of four things. First, he could cease to function, as in the case of the young man who fainted. If the shock of conflict is great enough, the body protects itself by withdrawing into an unconscious state. Secondly, primitive man could run away. Withdrawal was a way in which he could avoid the conflict and at the same time release his tension. We find the modern counterparts of withdrawal in the hands-in-the-pockets, eyes-on-the-floor kind of action. Thirdly, he could attack; he could resolve his tensions in violently aggressive action. The modern counterpart of this method is found in the belligerent, aggressive attitude of some speakers. Finally, primitive man could stand his ground, control his emotion, and conquer the situation.

The fourth and final solution is the only desirable way to meet the modern performance challenge. Unconsciousness, withdrawal, or violent aggressiveness are considered unsatisfactory reactions in modern society. Therefore steps must be taken to reduce and control excessive tension.

Direct Your Attention Toward the Listener

One of the disturbing results of fear is a self-conscious attitude. You become *conscious* of your *self;* you find yourself concentrating on your pounding heart, shortness of breath, trembling muscles, and sinking stomach. You become so concerned with your own internal feelings that you are unable to devote full energy to the task at hand. In addition your concentration upon the unpleasant sensations in your body tends to facilitate and increase them. As you know, anyone can increase an emotional experience by dwelling on it; a mild emotional state can be worked into complete panic with the right con-centration.

The solution to the problem of fear is simple to state but difficult to accomplish. You must direct your attention away from yourself. The logical place to direct it is toward your audience. You cannot expect to control your listeners unless you concentrate your energy upon them. You must talk *to* rather than *at* your audience. If you can convince yourself that they are more important than you are, you will automatically satisfy two needs of the speaking situation. First your concentration will be focused where it belongs—on the accomplishment of the task at hand; and second, you will have neither the time nor the energy to indulge in the undesirable practice of studying yourself and your reactions.

Believe in the Listener

Avoid the idea that the listener is an ogre bent on harming you. Recognize him for what he is—a human being like yourself who has come to listen because he may have something to gain. Have some faith in the listener as a person. Recognize that he has the same wants, needs, and desires that you do. Frequently fear is related to the size of the group before which you are to speak. This fear is a fallacious one. All audiences are composed of individuals, each of whom has his own thoughts, his own attitudes, and his own beliefs. You are seldom fearful in a conversation. Realize that the public speaking situation is merely a one-way conversation in which you have all the advantages.

Choose a Subject in Which Your Confidence Is Justified

The man who feels superior is never afraid. If you can select subject matter wherein you are certain that you know more than the listeners, you will feel confident that you have something to offer. Fear is the logical result of not having anything worthwhile to say.

Let us assume that you are a master of the field of electronics. The confidence that is based upon your thorough knowledge is sound. You should be able to speak freely upon the subject with authority and without undue tension.

Look upon Speaking as an Opportunity to Communicate

Enthusiasm for your ideas and a burning desire to share your ideas are incompatible with fear. Look upon speaking as an opportunity to get others to understand or believe or act. Believe that your way, your knowledge, and your understanding will benefit the audience, and you will have accepted the challenge.

Be Thoroughly Prepared

All too often the speaker knows his subject and is enthusiastic about it but still is afraid that he may not be able to put it across. Complete preparation is the only answer. If you know what you are going to do, why you want to do it, and how to do it, the tensions and energies generated by the challenge of the new situation can be put to good use.

Think of Yourself as Worthy

Lack of confidence in what one is and what one has to offer is often the cause of the paralyzing fear that leads to failure in speaking. All the speaker's efforts to insure success—understanding of the audience, complete knowledge and preparation of the subject, interest in putting his point across—can be undermined by an "I'm no good" philosophy. The speaker must forget his failures, real and imaginary, and speak with the assurance of complete preparation. Unless the speaker is sure of himself, he can hardly expect to gain the confidence of his audience.

Set Sensible Goals

The essence of good bread-and-butter speaking is based on the sensible goal. Overambitious dreams are a wonderful way to indulge your fancy in your spare time, but they are not a satisfactory way to meet a specific challenge. Your job is to teach how a turret lathe works, to explain why the tunnel should go through the south side of the mountain, to prove that your electrical switch can be produced more cheaply. Devote your energies to the accomplishment of your specific purpose—getting Jim and his friends to understand, believe, or act. Overambitious expectation can lead to frustration and fear of failure; common sense practical goals can be pursued and achieved.

Apply Reason to Your Fear

It was noted earlier that when the emotional response takes over the intellectual responses are inhibited. Reassert your intellectual dominance. You now know why you are afraid and what the symptoms are. You ought to realize by now that any speaking situation can be controlled. Some years ago the National Safety Council published figures which indicate that the speaking platform is one of the safest places in the world. The number of deaths on the platform annually numbers less than five. No one will harm you.

Keeping an emotion bottled up inside tends to increase it. Talk about your fear. Let your friends share your experience with you before you speak. Objectively decide upon a serene attitude, and the tensions will lessen. Practice relaxation. Many of your muscles are under your control. Consciously relax them.

Overcome Tension by Action

Many of the old adages about breathing deeply, moving strongly, taking a walk, and so forth make good sense. The body is prepared by excitement to engage in a far greater expenditure of energy than is necessary for speaking; therefore activity helps to use up the energy. Most of the suggestions for speakers are made for activity before speaking. The same prescriptions are doubly important during speaking. In Chapter 10 the effective use of the body is discussed in detail.

Accept Every Opportunity to Speak

Never run away. Most people tend to avoid the speaking situation. An invitation to speak brings forth ready excuses for not doing it. "Oh, Joe down the hall knows more about that than I do." "Get Joe, he's a better speaker than I am." "Well, I'm really too busy right now." "Gee, I'd like to, but I can't. Maybe Joe can do it." This unwillingness to even consider meeting a challenge is the old philosophy of "Let Joe do it"—the primitive impulse to run away.

Every time you refuse to speak you accomplish three things—all of them bad. First, you lose the opportunity to practice an art that badly needs practice. Second, you develop the habit of running away which makes each time you have to face the challenge doubly hard. Finally, you lose the chance to make your ideas and personality felt in a meeting with others.

There is no way to learn the skills needed for speaking without speaking. There is no way to satisfy your own desires for advancement without speaking. There is no way to develop confidence in the new and challenging performance situation without speaking. Every time you speak and succeed in gaining the response you desire, you make the next time easier. Only you can establish confidence in yourself. No one can give it to you; it can't be purchased.

WHAT IF YOU FORGET?

Now assume that you have learned to control your tensions. You are speaking easily and, you hope, effectively. You come to the end of an idea or paragraph, and you go blank—nothing, no idea, no next thought. There you are staring at the audience, and they in turn are staring at you. The silence in the room seems unbearable. What do you do? You have a choice between common sense carefully applied and panic. Panic is nothing more than submitting to a great rush of emotion because you are suddenly aware that you are stuck. It happens very fast. A flush, sparks flashing in your head, perspiration, a mounting tension, trembling, pounding heart, no ideas—soon you are completely submerged. What can you do?

Stand Apart from the Situation

Step back immediately—not physically but intellectually. Refuse to indulge in thoughts of anxiety and concern. Avoid the "Woe-is-me-all-is-lost" attitude. Take your time and decide calmly on the method you will use to get back on the track. These suggestions are easy to follow if you will act quickly.

Don't Fight to Remember

"What's the name of that fellow we met last summer? I had it on the tip of my tongue, but it's gone;" and then you spend the rest of the evening fighting to remember. It won't come back no matter how hard you try; but if you drop the attempt to remember, the name pops into your head in a short time.

The same principle works in the speaking situation. If you fight to remember, the cause is lost. Forget about the next point. Take other steps. Before you know it, you will remember the lost idea.

Take Positive Steps to Fill the Gap

Think back to the point you have just covered. You will be able to remember that one. Expand or illustrate that point further. If you can't think of anything further to say on the preceding point, summarize what you have already said thus far in the speech. If you still can't remember, jump ahead to other points farther ahead in the speech. If you keep your head, you should be out of trouble long before this; if you aren't, calmly and simply admit that you are stuck. The audience will not condemn you for it; everybody gets stuck at one time or another. After admitting your position, you can always straight-forwardly restate your specific purpose and conclude your speech graciously. The last four or five steps suggested above will never be needed if you will just "keep your head." Again a little faith enters the picture. Relax, step back, "Think you nothing of itself will come?"

BUILDING THE RIGHT MENTAL ATTITUDE

Perhaps we have approached the problem backwards. We have shown you some of the wrong attitudes and explored the primary cause for them. The ways to eliminate the excessive tensions which promote these attitudes have been discussed. Now look at the elements of the right mental attitude. In some ways they are a summation of the steps which were taken to eliminate the tensions and spend the energies aroused by fear. The right mental attitude is friendly, sincere, and confident.

Be Friendly

'Tis said that "a smile is worth a hundred words." A friendly pleasant person is a persuasive person. Most of us are uneasy with strangers. Some of us are accused of being cold and curt. This lack of friendliness is not a reflection of the attitude we would like to por-tray, but it is hard to be friendly when you are uneasy or afraid. The natural tendency is to withdraw or to be overly aggressive.

The finest salesmen in the world, whether they be salesmen of prod-ucts or ideas, are warm, human, friendly people. We all seek warmth; we all respond to it. The speaker who can be poised, easy, and friendly can encourage a desired response by his attitude alone.

Be Sincere

Everyone hates hypocrisy and artificiality. They immediately set off an unpleasant response. In the same manner a lack of sincerity can be spotted by the listener immediately. His response will also be im-mediate. Emerson once said, "What you are speaks so loudly I can-not hear what you say." What you are, what you say, and how you say it must all tell the listener the same story.

It is generally said that Lincoln was a great speaker but not a polished speaker. His greatest strength lay in his attitude, which was friendly and sincere. If the listener can sense an earnest concern on the part of the speaker, his message will be accepted. One of the most moving and effective speakers I have ever heard was an immigrant mill worker who participated in an adult evening class. His accent was so strong that it was hard to understand him. His choice of lan-guage was crude and awkward. His knowledge of speaking tech-niques was non-existent. Yet in the six speeches he made in the class he never failed to hold his audience. He never failed to get his re-sponse. The key to his success was his sincerity—his simple, earnest, warm, intense desire to communicate his idea to the listeners.

One of the most powerful statements of all time was made by Van-zetti shortly before he and Sacco were executed. Grammatically in-correct, technically unpolished, its sincerity and truth burned their message into the minds of the listeners.

> If it had not been for these things, I might have lived out my life talking at street corners to scorning men. I might have died unmarked, unknown, a failure. Now we are not a failure. This is our career and our triumph. Never in our full life could we hope to do such work for tolerance, for joostice, for man's onderstanding of man as now we do by accident. Our words—our lives—our pains—nothing! The taking of our lives—lives of a good shoemaker and a poor fish-peddler —all! That last moment belongs to us—that agony is our triumph.

Be Confident

In one of Franklin Delano Roosevelt's most famous speeches he told the American people that they had "nothing to fear but fear itself." He expressed his confidence in America and asked all Americans to do the same. Above all he gave the impression of confidence himself. The listeners responded favorably to his strong, forceful, confident attitude.

Don't be misled. Strength is not arrogance. Force is not pomposity. Confidence is not pedantry. Confidence is the simple, straightforward recognition and communication of your own worth and the worth of your subject. Listeners respond to speakers in whom they can have confidence. The leaders you choose are those who give an impression of confidence.

In summary it may be said that the right mental attitude lets the speaker put his best foot forward. It reflects his own personality. It is one in which the tensions due to the performance situation are controlled and directed to the useful end of getting a reaction from the listener. It is an attitude which is appealing to the listener through its friendliness, its sincerity, and its confidence.

Newman A. Hall, Chairman of the Department of Mechanical Engineering, Yale University, found it to be his experience that good speaking is dependent upon the following factors:

> . . . (1) thorough and practical familiarity with one's subject; (2) understanding and appreciation of the viewpoint of one's audience; (3) extensive experience in speaking in order that one may have self-confidence and poise.

Certainly the speaker's mental attitude will be determined and reflected by each of these factors.

—Apply the Principles

At first, mental attitude may seem to be an intangible thing which would be hard to apply. Review the principles and you will find many elements which can be observed in others and yourself. Profit from the strengths and weaknesses of others. Plan and practice the correct attitudes yourself.

Self-Analysis

(1) Think back to the last performance situation in which you were uneasy. Perhaps it was when you had to meet the boss, or went to the company or school tea, or took a new girl on a date, or made a speech.

(2) What kind of an impression did you make? Did you have excessive tension? How did you go about controlling it? Was your attitude appealing—one your listeners would like? If so, why? If not, why not? Did you tend to withdraw? Did you act like a showoff?

(3) How could you have improved your attitude? Can you meet the same situation next time with greater poise? How can you prepare your attitude in advance?

Observation

(1) Watch another person in a performance situation. What clues do you get to his mental attitude? What are his strengths? His weaknesses?

(2) Judge the worth of his performance. Is he friendly? Sincere? Confident? Are there undesirable elements of either withdrawal or aggressiveness in his attitude?

(3) If you were provided with the opportunity to make suggestions, what would they be? How could you approach the problem so that your mental attitude would be so appealing that he would be able to accept the criticism?

(4) Try to help him without being invited to do so. It is a difficult assignment, but it can be done if your own mental attitude is right.

Practice

(1) Prepare a simple speech *to persuade*. Select listeners and an occasion where persuasion is really possible. Allow yourself about three minutes.

(2) Persuade your audience to believe some principle, to accept a new policy, to take some observable action, to become aroused over an injustice, or to buy your product.

(3) Follow steps 3 through 7 in "Apply the Principles," Chapter 2. Use your own knowledge to determine how a persuasive speech differs from an informative speech.

(4) Determine what steps you will take to clearly demonstrate your mental attitude to the listeners. Use your mental attitude as a part of the persuasion.

FORMULA C

$$AYMA = (SC + LC)\ PSP$$

(*AYMA*) *Alert Your Mental Attitude* = (*SC*) *Self-Confidence* plus (*LC*) *Listener Concern*, the quantity multiplied by (*PSP*) *Pleasant Speaking Personality*.

Now, apply the formula!

1. Prepare a speech. Do you expect it to be a success? Will you be accepted by your listeners? Are you enthusiastic? Let's find out what your mental attitude really is.
2. Check the scale below *before* you speak. Your responses indicate your levels of expectation. (Connect the dots and you have a graph)
3. Have your listeners check the scale *after* your speech and record the average of each of their responses on your graph. Use a different symbol or color for the group reaction.
4. Concentrate on those items where a difference appears between the *before* and *after* responses. It is here that you are *not* what you think.

Levels of Expectation Versus Reality					
A Speaker-Listener Graph					
1 No 2 Doubtful 3 Somewhat 4 Probably 5 Definitely					
Criteria	*1*	*2*	*3*	*4*	*5*
SELF-CONFIDENCE:					
Acceptable to listener?	•	•	•	•	•
Enthusiastic?	•	•	•	•	•
Intellectual dominance?	•	•	•	•	•
Serene?	•	•	•	•	•
Desire to share?	•	•	•	•	•
LISTENER CONCERN:					
Favorable response?	•	•	•	•	•
Individual appeals?	•	•	•	•	•
Appropriate vocabulary?	•	•	•	•	•
Worthwhile topic?	•	•	•	•	•
Responsible speech?	•	•	•	•	•
SPEAKING PERSONALITY:					
Relaxed bearing?	•	•	•	•	•
Friendly appearance?	•	•	•	•	•
Sincere quality?	•	•	•	•	•
Graceful movements?	•	•	•	•	•
Mentally alert?	•	•	•	•	•

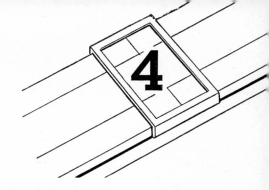

understand
your listener

Eric A. Walker, President of The Pennsylvania State University and past Dean of the College of Engineering and Architecture, recently wrote a humorous article which makes an incisive comment on listening. The article was entitled "The Art and Science of 'O' Filling." This science is a new method of doodling in which the doodler fills the *o*'s on any available typewritten page.

> The art and science of "O" filling is an avocation which has reached a high degree of perfection under the pressure of our modern conference filled, speech listening existence. Whenever a conference is afflicted by a long-winded, monotone-voiced subcommittee chairman equipped with a dull inconsequential report, the audience must find means of amusing itself without revealing its lack of interest to the speaker who, himself, will soon return to his principle posture as listener.[1]

I am sure that either as a listener or as a speaker you are interested in destroying the "Science of 'O' Filling." The fact that such a science exists at all is proof of the need for really good speech, for good speech insures good listening.

The key in any listening situation is the response from the individual

---

[1] Eric A. Walker, "The Art and Science of 'O' Filling," *Engineering Review*, Pennsylvania State University, II, No. 4, 1954, p. 13.

listener. You, the speaker, concentrate your attempt to control upon a single person. Your success is measured by the reactions of that person. It is a one-to-one relationship. This relationship should create a circular response.

THE CIRCULAR RESPONSE

Whenever two persons come into direct social contact, that is, become aware of and respond to each other, social interaction begins. This is exactly what happens in every speaking situation regardless of whether it is a conversation or a public address. The characteristics of social interaction are extremely simple. The first person motivates the action of the second person, who by responding in a particular way in turn motivates the reaction of the first person, and so on. This concept may be expressed graphically in two different ways. In A in Figure 1

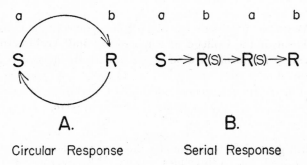

A.   B.

Circular   Response   Serial   Response

Fig. 1. Social Interaction.

the circular response is shown. In B the chain effect of continued interaction may be seen. This chain reaction is called a serial response.

The key to understanding the circular response and the subsequent interaction lies in the realization that the response has the power to act as a *stimulus*. This is easily illustrated in the conversation. Person *a* (see the small letters at the top of the drawing) makes a statement. Person *b* responds. *The response acts as a stimulus which motivates the next action or statement of person a.* The circle of response is complete. Such a chain or series can continue indefinitely with each new response by either party acting as a stimulus until the chain is broken or the desired reaction has been gained.

The one-to-one circular reaction is easily seen in conversation. To illustrate: When you ask your boss for a raise, his reaction to your request determines your course of action. If he says "Yes," the desired reaction has been reached, and you respond by thanking him. If he says "Perhaps in a few months," your next steps are based on his reaction. You either agree, or you propose reasons for its happening now. If he says "No," you offer new reasons for the raise.

In other words, conversation is an alive, dynamic interplay between speaker and listener. In conversation each of the participators alternates as speaker and each acts as a listener at the same time—the speaker listening to himself and the others listening to the speaker.

But let's go to the other extreme of the speaking relationship. You may wonder how the circular response works in the public speech. The listeners in the audience don't respond you say. They may not speak, but they most assuredly do respond. Their responses must be the key to your actions. Listen for them. The listeners may laugh, applaud, nod affirmatively, appear puzzled, or shake their heads negatively. Their responses are constant and dynamic, and you must be able to adapt to them. You affect the listener; the listener in turn reacts. His reaction must be the stimulus to which you respond. Your response affects him, and so on.

The circular response must remain intact throughout your speech. Without it your listener may begin to respond to some other external stimulus or to the internal stimulation of his own thoughts and sensations. You must maintain constant contact with him. This is the reason that we have reiterated that you must speak *to* and *with* your listener, not just *at* or *before* him. Speech is a one-to-one relationship.

THE LISTENER

If the listener is the key to successful speech, Who is he? What is he like? What does he want? What does he approve? What does he disapprove? In a general sense the listener is YOU. He is a human being remarkably like you with the same desires, the same likes and dislikes, the same strengths and weaknesses.

Most of the great principles of life are based on this simple concept. The Golden Rule—Do unto others as you would have them do unto you. Shakespeare—To thine own self be true, and it must follow as the day the night, thou cans't not then be false to any man. Each says the same thing; treat others as you would be treated. Speech is no exception; speak to others as you would like to be spoken to.

How would you like to be spoken to? What do you want from life? Why do you choose at times to listen? What do you respond to? What qualities in a speaker appeal to you? The answers to these questions are directly related to the qualities which make up your being. While these qualities are modified by your intelligence, your nervous make-up, your physique, your age, and your environment, they are essentially the results of the universal basic drives.

THE BASIC DRIVES

Psychologists have long recognized that much of man's activity can be directly related to his attempt to satisfy his fundamental needs. These basic urges have been variously labeled instincts, motives, drives, forces, wishes, prepotent reflexes, and sentiments. Controversies have raged as to whether they are inherited or acquired. Fortunately there is little significance in their name or origin. The important thing is that man's responses and actions are controlled by these basic needs. For the purpose of this discussion we will call these forces basic drives: *basic* because they are fundamental to most of our life action; *drives* because they are dynamic and control and direct our actions.

The different lists of basic drives are as numerous as the names applied to them. Fortunately there is a great deal of uniformity in the listings. One of the most widely accepted classifications includes the drives for security, adventure, recognition, and response.

The Drive for Security

This is the drive which is frequently called self-preservation or preservation of the race. Every man feels an almost desperate urge to be secure; he wants to feel inviolate from attack. He strives to amass wealth so that he may be secure, and he will go to great extremes to protect his family and sometimes even greater extremes to protect himself. He insures his life, his home, his mortgage, his car, and his health, and makes insurance the biggest business in the world. He protects himself against every conceivable type of loss, because he cannot bear to lose that which he has.

Bring the case a little closer to home. Why do you go to school? So that you can know more, make more money, live a better life, and be secure. Why do you go to class? The same reasons. What classes do you cut? The ones which you think won't affect your security. Why are you nice to many people you don't like? Because they can affect your security. We could go on endlessly citing the things that you do, think, feel, and say because you want to be secure.

If these things are true of you, are they not just as true of your listener? They are. Anytime you can show a listener that his understanding something, believing something, or acting in a certain way will provide him with a greater sense of security, you will have found a willing participator in your plan.

The Drive for Adventure

Security is not enough. We must also have adventure. If the only force that drove mankind was security, this would be a dreary world indeed. Luckily there is a drive to match the desire for security—adventure. This drive forces us ahead to accept the new challenge, to take the gamble, to try out our new ideas, to overcome our inertia.

Show a man how he can find excitement, conquer new fields, reach the horizon, and you have a listener. Technologists have been adventurous souls historically. They have been the inventors, the atom busters, the bridge builders. They have dammed waters, tunneled through mountains, and built the machines of peace and war. Even learning can be exciting because of the excitement and adventure in the learning process and the opportunities which the new knowledge can provide.

This is your listener—a man driven to find excitement. One of your jobs as a speaker is to show him how it can be found. Teach him this, and he will do your bidding.

The Drive for Recognition

The desire to get ahead, perhaps ahead of the next fellow, is the desire which is most easy to see in everyday life. It appears as the drive for authority which makes men struggle to the top or as the drive for power to control the lives of others. Other examples of the drive for recognition are the drive for prestige, which produces the master craftsman, and the drive for acquisition, which forces us to "keep up with the Joneses."

In its most desirable form the drive for recognition produces leadership; in its least desirable form this drive produces greed and avarice. American society is based on the concept of competition—competition in strength, competition in intellect, competition in athletics, competition in school marks. Whether this be right or wrong, it is part of the American way of life, and its importance is a frank admission of the drive for recognition. Every speaker, every listener, and every man is first of all for himself. The speaker who can recognize this need and show his listener how he can gain recognition for himself can sway that listener.

Because of this drive everyone is interested in the question, What is there in it for *me?* The answer should be provided by the speaker, whether it is for social gain, cultural gain, spiritual gain, or material gain; for these are the ends man works for.

The Desire for Response

It has been said that no man can live alone because he needs to belong and wants to be loved. This drive is parallel to, but apart from, the desire for recognition. We want to be respected for ourselves alone, not because of what we can do or what we have. Oblivion is one of man's greatest fears. Take away his individuality, his sense of himself, and you kill him. The most timid draftsman in the farthest corner of the office lives by the responses he creates in others. Ignore him, refuse to accept him as a human entity, and he wastes away.

The desire for response is one of the speaker's most powerful tools. By giving the listener his due, by treating him with kindness and consideration, by exposing him to your own warmth, you win his interest and his response.

Everytime a speaker can satisfy one or more of the basic drives, he will get an immediate response from the listener. The listener will study or work late into the night if by learning or doing something he can satisfy one of the urges within him. The listener will believe in any cause which will give him satisfaction. The listener will perform any act which will give him security, adventure, recognition, or response.

A PROFILE OF THE LISTENER

A summary of the forces acting through the basic drives provides you with a general profile of the listener.

1. He wants to protect himself.
2. He wants new and different experiences.
3. He wants to get ahead in the world.
4. He wants to be respected for himself.
5. He wants to learn providing that the knowledge will help him.

These are the core elements in every man's life. They lie at the bottom of every activity in which we engage. All of our actions are motivated by the basic drives, and the successful speaker will use them. However these are only the general forces. The listener whom you will be addressing is a specific individual. His particular experiences and status may make his responses to his basic drives differ from those of another.

To illustrate: A young man may be excited by the thought of owning a motorcycle; yet this thought might not be very appealing to an older man. A woman may be encouraged to learn how to be beautiful and graceful; neither quality would appeal to a man. An educated man may love books which would not excite an ignorant man. One man may love physical exercise; another may hate it. One may be religious; another not. One man may be a liberal; another a conservative. One man may like jazz while another loves the classics.

Since the individual differences among listeners are so varied, the speaker must ascertain what limiting factors are present. Every audience is different. It is this variety that makes speaking such an exciting pastime.

CONTROLLING FACTORS IN THE LISTENING GROUP

Every listening situation is composed of an audience or group of listeners and an occasion. Each of these elements should function as a determinant in the selection of material and the manner of its presentation. The implication in the preceding section was that listeners are diverse in their attitudes and interests. This is true. On the other hand, the fact that a group of listeners has come together tends to cancel out some of the heterogeneous elements. Listeners of the same type, the same background, and the same interests go to hear a single speech.

The committee meeting or conference is almost always composed of workers with the same general characteristics. They have roughly comparable training and generally the same interests; they represent a relatively homogeneous group. In the same way the public address draws a reasonably homogeneous group of listeners. The subject of the speech or its purpose serves as an attraction to the same kind of people. A speech on the sanitation problems of a city will not draw a general audience. A discussion of the trends in modern art will draw listeners with specialized interests. The listeners as a group could not be successfully interchanged for the subjects of sanitation and art.

The *controlling factors* in any audience determine the concentrations of a particular kind of listener. The speaker must know what these concentrations are if he is to adapt his ideas effectively to his particular listener's needs. There are eight of these controlling factors.

1. Age
2. Sex
3. Education and Experience
4. Knowledge of the Subject
5. Occupation
6. Social Habits
7. Special Interests
8. Prejudices and Attitudes

Age

Both the general age level and the variations in age will influence the development of your speaking materials. If your listeners are very young, for example Boy Scouts, you will select material and approach them in one way. If they are oldsters, you will have to change your method. Assume that you are going to speak on how to build a simple radio receiver. The Boy Scouts are curious about electronics; the older people are looking for a new hobby, a way to spend leisure time. Though each group knows nothing about radio receivers, you still must adapt to the characteristics of their age group. The illustrative material should also be adapted to the specific group you are addressing.

A more complex problem arises when there is a large range in age in the audience. Ideas which appeal to a very young person will probably not particularly appeal to an oldster. In such a situation you must appeal to each group during the speech.

Sex

Men and women are startlingly different in the way that they approach a problem—in their manner of response, in what appeals to them, and in their set of values. When speaking to an all male group one set of principles applies. Introduce a single woman into the group and the entire mood of the speaking situation changes. Think of your engineering classes which are made up entirely of fellows and compare them with a class where there is a lone woman engineer.

If the group is predominately women or all women, the standards change again. Your choice of a subject, choice of material, choice of illustrations, choice of appeals—all will be influenced by the dominance of one sex or the other in the audience. Suppose you are to speak on some aspect of the subject of mass production. Your listening group in one case is the Kiwanis Club, in another it is the local Woman's Club. Think through how your speech must change. Your specific subject would undoubtedly be different, you would choose different illustrations, and your appeals would be modified by the interests of your audience.

Education and Experience

Education may come from the formal classroom and frequently does, but you must not overlook the education that comes from broad and varied experiences in life. A grizzled farmer in your audience may have little schooling; yet he may be an almost professional weather forecaster. He may have little knowledge of the scientific instruments and language of meteorology, but his experience in successfully predicting the weather may put the budding meteorologist to shame.

Effective speech is tied to the experiences of the audience. It is adapted to their backgrounds. It judges and uses the listener's education, formal or informal. Be particularly careful when adapting technical materials to the lay audience that you don't depend upon experiences in science and the arts which they have never had.

Knowledge of the Subject

Judging the listener's knowledge of the subject is a particular aspect of their education and experience. A great number of speeches fail on this count. Judging the listener's knowledge of your subject is simply a matter of carefully and accurately setting your sights.

Suppose you are going to try to explain the refrigeration cycle. How would you approach the problem? It is impossible without assessing with considerable care what your audience already knows about it. First, if the listeners already understand it, there is no point in discussing it at all. They will immediately become bored and indulge in the science of "O" filling or sit back and criticize your presentation of the material. Or, at the other extreme, suppose your listeners not only know nothing about the refrigeration cycle but also know nothing about the laws of physics which lie behind it. In this case you must provide simple definitions of these laws before you introduce the refrigeration cycle, or you lose your listeners because they are unable to comprehend.

Occupation

One of the best clues to a man's background, interests, and knowledge is his occupation. Throughout our educational structure from high school to the college or university the course structures are grouped in terms of general occupational interest. For example, in high school the student takes a business course, a liberal arts college preparatory course, or a manual arts course. In college the difference between a mechanical, civil, electrical, or chemical engineer tells us a great deal about the individual and where his interests lie. When formal education is finished, this occupational factor becomes even more decisive. After a person takes a job in a given field with a particular company, his interests are narrowed and his specialized knowledge and dependence upon shop talk increase.

Since listeners represent a considerable degree of homogeneity, occupation frequently is one of the major elements in bringing people together in the listening situation. The problems of adaptation are always the same. You must tie your subject, your material, and your appeals to the listener's knowledge, experience, and interest. Knowing a man's occupation cannot help but strengthen your position.

What the listener thinks of you as a speaker is closely related to what people think of you generally. What do you assume these listeners think of the speaker? What are the factors you observe in this picture which tell you something about the speaker's mental attitude? (CHAPTER 3) *Courtesy North American Aviation, Inc., Columbus Division.*

If all of the aspects of speaking were to be rated, the listener would have to come first. Analyze the listeners in this picture. Discuss their basic drives. Plan a profile of the listeners. What modifying factors are present? What are the influences of the occasion? (CHAPTER 4) *Courtesy North American Aviation, Inc., Columbus Division.*

Social Habits

Next to his job a man's avocation and social habits can probably give the best clue to his way of responding. The sports car enthusiast differs in his reactions from the driver of the black sedan. The fisherman generally has characteristics different from those of the night club patron. The church or social worker has attitudes and interests different from those of the gambler. This is not to suggest that a man can't be both a fisherman and a gambler, but the areas in which he devotes his energies do tell you something about him and how he thinks. More important you can learn a great deal about his interests and adapt your subject and material accordingly. Your interest in him will win you another listener.

Special Interests

Everything which has been written about the basic drives earlier in this chapter could be repeated here. The successful speech is the one which appeals to the listener's wants. However, his wants may take the form of very special interests. These may be related to his job and his hobbies, or they may have a wider scope.

These special interests are frequently related to his personal life, because they are elements which affect him individually. Thus he is interested in his health, for example his habits of eating, smoking, and sleeping, his weight, his age, and his need for exercise. He is interested vitally in those events in his society that may affect him: birth, death, crime, war, peace. Pick up your evening newspaper, and you will find it filled with news of people. Note what you read, and what you omit. In so doing you have defined many of your own special interests.

Prejudices and Attitudes

An attitude is defined as a "tendency to act in a predetermined way." It is a motor set ready to be triggered into action. Attitudes develop because of shocking experiences, or steady association with someone else's attitudes, or because you accept the authority of someone else's point of view. Perhaps you hate snakes; you shiver at the sight of them. Why? Because they might be poisonous? There probably aren't any poisonous snakes in your area. The answer undoubtedly is that you had a shocking experience at one time or another.

Most children love snakes because they wiggle. You picked one up and brought it to your mother. She screamed in terror, smashed it out of your hand, and beat it to death with the nearest weapon. Right there an attitude was formed—a fixed attitude. One that is difficult to change.

You vote Republican or Democratic as the case may be. Why? Because you really understand and believe the principles of that party? Or is it because your father was a Republican and your grandfather before him? "What's good enough for dad is good enough for me." Many of our strongest attitudes and prejudices are formed in just this irrational way. You have an attitude. A fixed one that is difficult to change.

You hate communists. Why? Because you have been told a thousand times that communists are bad. Whether this belief is correct or not is not important here. The point is that you have developed an attitude—a fixed attitude. One that is difficult to change.

Everyone has hundreds of attitudes. Some of them are positive. You like dozens of things without ever having stopped to reason why. You dislike just as many things with no better reasons. The problem of the speaker is that some attitudes are more difficult to change than others, such as intolerance toward other races, creeds, and religions. Such fixed attitudes are a threat to the success of a speaker. Since they are unlikely to be changed by a single speech, it is better to avoid them rather than risk incurring the enmity of the listener. On the other hand, if a speaker can appeal to the fixed attitudes of his listeners, he can put his point across more easily. There is no substitute for a careful study of the listener which not only considers his general needs and wants but also examines all the controlling factors which dictate his response in every situation.

INFLUENCE OF THE OCCASION

The Fourth of July and the church meeting on Christmas Eve are radically different speaking occasions. The mood, the customs, the social situation, and the physical surroundings are all different, and all have a bearing upon the creation and delivery of the speaker. The influence of the occasion may best be stated by suggesting that the speaker must fulfill the expectations of the listeners. On differing occasions the listener has a preconceived notion of what should be said and how it should be said. If the speaker can fit his remarks to the occasion, he is a success; if not, he is a failure.

The Social Situation

Think for a moment of these different occasions and speculate upon the qualities which define the occasion: a labor-management arbitration conference, an explanation to an apprentice in the tool shop, a presentation to the board of directors of a corporation, a speech at the PTA meeting, testimony in court, a discussion in the classroom, an interview with an applicant for a job, remarks given at the funeral of a friend, a conference with a group of high school seniors, an appeal made to the Dean of the college, a sales speech on the golf course.

Each of these situations is different. Some are formal situations, some informal. Some are somber situations; some are joyous. Each has its own special quality. This quality will determine the subject, the material, and the manner of your presentation. Some of the occasions can be prepared for in advance; others will depend upon your sensitivity in catching the tone and responding to it. Nothing is as pitiful as the speaker who is insensitive to the social occasion. The listeners either writhe with embarrassment for him or despise him.

The Physical Surroundings

Control of the physical surroundings is imperative. Many speeches have failed because they were given in the wrong place. You cannot expect your listeners to attend a speech given in a foundry; the distractions are too great. One of the factors which encourages the listener to favorable response is his physical comfort. While you can't dictate what he eats or whether he gets enough sleep, you can provide him with a cool, airy room, a comfortable seat, a room in which the acoustics are adequate, a place from which he can see easily, and a situation where the quiet needed for concentration prevails.

Minimize those things which contribute to listener fatigue. The speaker should insist that distracting influences be removed. If the room has a blackboard, make sure that it is clean; you don't want the listener to spend his time trying to translate the French lesson left by the preceding class. Get rid of animals which mysteriously appear on all football fields and in all lecture halls. Encourage the listener to put down anything which he is doing which may distract; you can't get through to a man who has one eye on a whirring machine or is working a math assignment. If possible arrange the occasion at a convenient time, for you can't persuade a listener who has one eye on the clock. In other words use your common sense. Anything that distracts you will distract a listener.

The Size of the Audience

The size of the listening group is another influential factor. The interview has two—alternating between the interviewer and the interviewee. The committee meeting usually has three to five. The conference may run up to ten. The public speech has an audience of between ten and millions.

What difference does audience size make? The difference, you say, is in numbers. In one sense, yes; in another sense, no. Assume you are trying to convince a conference group that a river should be dammed at a specific point. The question finally comes to a vote. There are six votes for your side and seven votes against. The majority rules, and your proposition fails. However the important factor is that you convinced six individual listeners, and you failed to convince seven other individuals. You were not talking to the committee; you were talking to thirteen individual listeners. Your true success was based on whether or not you could convince each of these listeners.

Most beginning speakers think of the audience as a great, unwieldy, frightening mass. They assume that some new magical formula must be produced. That isn't true at all. An audience is composed of individuals; they react or fail to react as individuals. If anything the members of the audience help each other to react—but we'll talk about that in a moment.

The situation is a sales convention. You are going to try to sell a new packaging process to the members of the group. Your audience numbers a dozen. Now stop and think. Does the audience buy your packaging process? No, the individuals in the audience do the buying. Each listener thinking for himself makes a decision on the basis of your speech. As the representative of his company he must make the decision. Your success is measured by the number of sales to individuals that are made.

In very large and intensely aroused groups some interesting crowd phenomena take place which make it even easier for the speaker. These factors will not be treated in detail because most of you will never have occasion to deal with a crowd. A crowd differs from an audience in that the members cease to think as individuals. Social facilitation and contagion take over. The individual is helped to his response by others around him. Bursts of applause, laughter, and unison chanting or singing weld the members of the crowd together. The individual responds more emotionally; he is more suggestible. This is the type of audience which Hitler addressed; it is not the audience of the scientist or engineer. However even if these crowd factors do operate, they all function in favor of the speaker. Instead of appealing to each of the individuals he appeals to the strong positive individuals; they in turn respond, and the meek are encouraged to do likewise.

The changes caused by size alone are all related to seeing and hearing. With a larger group you may have to speak with greater force and clarity, whereas in the interview you will use a completely conversational tone. The public speech still calls for the conversational impression, but it must be amplified so that it can be heard by the listener in the last row. You may remain seated while talking at a conference, but a larger audience will create a need for standing. Your physical activity may be confined yet forceful in the small gathering. It must be amplified for the larger group.

INSURE GOOD LISTENING

By this time you should have a good understanding of the listener. He is now *your* responsibility. Never again should your listener become anything less than the most important element of the speaking situation. Understanding the listener means doing those things which insure good listening. As a speaker this is your challenge—communicate so that good listening is insured. The factors involved in delivery and organization that will aid you in fulfilling this responsibility will be discussed in later chapters. Right now your challenge involves the handling of your ideas in such a way that they satisfy the basic drives, the controlling factors and the occasion. A leading consulting engineer, D. B. Steinman, says:

> The best address is wasted if it is not attuned to the audience in both interest and clarity. The speaker must make sure that he is applying his presentation to the interests and emotions of his audience,

and that, by clarity and enunciation, every word is reaching his audience. Otherwise the effort is wasted. The favorable response of the listeners is both the objective and the reward.

—Apply the Principles

The principles of analyzing the listener can be applied every day. The extent to which you become acute at judging the needs, attitudes, and interests of others will be a measure of your success in life and in speaking.

(1) Select a subject for an informative speech and tailor the material and development to yourself as a listener. What effect does your new knowledge concerning yourself have in the development of the speech?

(2) Adapt the speech to some listener you know who is radically different in his or her reactions. How will the speech be changed? What additions and deletions of material will be necessary?

(3) Assume that you are going to give the speech in a completely informal situation to a group of men your own age. How will the material be effected? How will the delivery be changed?

(4) Change the audience to a formal occasion with a mixed group of men and women considerably older than yourself. How will you change the speech and its presentation?

(5) Examine your speech carefully for the knowledge of the subject that is necessary to understand it. Where does it break down with listeners who know nothing about it? What about an advanced technical group of listeners? How would you change it?

(6) Re-evaluate your communication after all is said and done. Which portions received the most favorable response? Why? Which portions could have been improved? How? Which aspect(s) must receive special attention in your next speaking opportunity?

FORMULA D

$$UYL = \frac{BD + CF}{O}$$

(*UYL*) *Understand Your Listener* = Adapting to the listener the (*BD*) *Basic Drives* plus the (*CF*) *Controlling Factors* in terms of the (*O*) *Occasion.*

Now, apply the formula!

Develop a five-minute speech for a particular audience and occasion. Do not deliver the speech until you are able to give an affirmative answer to a majority of the questions below.

BASIC DRIVES:

Do my ideas suggest ways toward gaining greater security for my listener?
Do my ideas stimulate thoughts of excitement in my listener?
Do my ideas provide clues for the advancement of my listener?
Do my ideas interest my listener?

CONTROLLING FACTORS:

Are my ideas adapted to the age level of my listener?
Are my ideas adjusted to the sex of my listener?
Are my ideas understandable in terms of the education and experience of my listener?
Are my ideas new, yet tied to the familiar of my listener?
Are my ideas aided by the knowledge of the occupation of my listener?
Are my ideas influenced by the social habits of my listener?
Are my ideas considerate of the special interests of my listener?
Are my ideas sensitive to the prejudices and attitudes of my listener?

THE OCCASION:

Will my ideas fit the situation?
Will my ideas surmount the physical surroundings?
Will my ideas encompass the size of the audience?

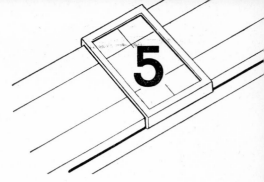

develop
your purpose,
subject, and material

THE THIRD ASPECT of the speech triangle is the speech itself. No matter how effective the speaker may be or how responsive the listener may be, communication is never effective without superior content. Superior content is the first responsibility of every speaker. No one should encourage the communication of emptiness. Our concern here, then, is three-fold: purpose, subject, and material.

1. PURPOSE

A clear-cut purpose is the first requisite of a successful speech. Lack of a well-defined purpose stands as the initial barrier to good communication. The difference between the rifle and the shotgun may suggest the problem. The rifle shoots a single bullet squarely at a desired target, and it hits with terrific impact. The shotgun, on the other hand, sprays small pellets in the general direction of the target on the assumption that if one pellet doesn't hit the target, another will. The impact of the shotgun cannot be compared with that of the rifle; the shotgun may bring down a bird on the wing, but it won't phase a deer on the run. The purpose of a speech must be like a rifle bullet—aimed carefully; it must *hit* the target never *spray* it. Again and again we have said that the target is the response of the listener, that favorable reaction is the only meaningful purpose of a speech. Therefore the exact reaction we wish from the listener must be determined.

Examine the following diagram with care. It illustrates the steps which are necessary in proceeding from the REACTION, symbolized by the big R, through the three general channels of reaction, the GENERAL PURPOSES, to the exact reaction, the SPECIFIC PURPOSE of your speech.

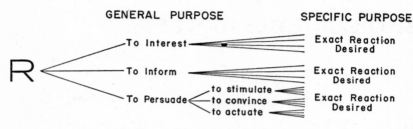

Fig. 2. Selecting the Purpose.

REACTION (THE BIG R)

Nothing more need be said about it. If its meaning isn't emblazoned in your memory, give up the idea of learning to speak.

THE THREE GENERAL PURPOSES

All speaking falls in the three general channels of reaction known as the general purposes. The first decision that the speaker must make, usually before he selects his subject or at least at the same time, is the general purpose. These purposes are statements of the general reaction desired from the listeners.

Clearly it is impossible to prepare a speech which does not have more than one element in it. It would be impossible to interest an audience for long without providing some information. Undoubtedly the persuasive speech will have both interest and information. However every speech must have a *general* purpose or aim. Without it the listener may be confused or misled.

General Purpose I: To Interest the Listener

Many speech authorities call this general purpose to entertain. Entertainment implies being comical. While speeches aimed at this end certainly would be included under the purpose to interest, many other speeches not essentially funny also deserve to be placed here.

There is no doubt that all speeches must interest the audience. However the speaker may not care about gaining understanding or controlling belief or action. He may be concerned only with being interesting. Much after dinner speaking is of this type, as is social conversation, story telling, introductions of speakers, personal incidents, and anecdotes. Speeches of this sort pleasantly while away the listener's time; they relax; they fill out our social experiences. As a technical student you will probably have little occasion to make a formal speech to interest, but you will have hundreds of opportunities in informal social situations.

General Purpose II: To Inform the Listener

In a recent survey of engineering schools the engineers voted overwhelmingly for emphasis on exposition in speaking.[1] Approximately seven out of every ten speeches you give will be to inform the listener. You will speak to employees, to committees, to co-workers and superiors. You will explain problems to technical audiences who know a great deal about the subject and to lay listeners who know little or nothing. This book devotes most of its space to informative speaking.

The speech to inform goes beyond the speech to interest. While it must interest the audience, its primary concern is providing the listener with new information or with a new understanding of information with which he is already acquainted.

A good speech to inform must meet several criteria. First, it must provide information which the listener needs or wants. Second, the information must be adapted to the previous knowledge of the listener. Third, it must provide all of the information necessary to understanding. And finally, the speech to inform must be sufficiently interesting to arouse a desire for the knowledge in the mind of the

---

[1] Louis H. Swain, "The Technical Student Votes for Exposition," *The Southern Speech Journal*, XVII, No. 2 (December, 1951), pp. 130–136.

listener. Speeches to inform fall into two general categories, descriptive and expositional.

A. *Description.* The descriptive speech to inform makes ideas more vivid and graphic for the listener. It draws a picture of ideas, objects, or events. It involves such subjects as description of a television studio, a surveyor's transit, a milling machine, the Pennsylvania Turnpike, precious gems, atomic powered submarines, or the Globe Theatre. In each case the purpose of the description goes beyond that of merely interesting the audience. It should be inclusive and exact; it must inform the listener.

B. *Exposition.* Most technical speeches to inform are expository in nature. They explain the operation or organization of things. The subjects are as wide as man's quest for understanding. They may be technical, such as the working of processes, the operation of machines, the solution of formulas, the definition of ideas. They may range from the natural and social sciences to literature and the arts. The object is always the same—interest and clarity. Success is measured in terms of the listener's complete, exact, and comprehensive understanding. John S. Sinclair reminds us: "Believe constantly in people and in facts, and have faith that, if the former are given the latter, they will eventually reach the right conclusions."[2]

General Purpose III: To Persuade the Listener

Persuasion has already been defined as the process of getting others to *want* to do what you want them to do. In other words persuasion cannot use force, or it ceases to be persuasion. Persuasion is not coercion but rather a process of leading or stimulating. It has been defined as "vitalizing an idea" to the point at which the listener must respond.

Usually the general purpose *to persuade* is divided into three specific aims—to stimulate, to convince, and to actuate. Or they may be expressed—to secure emotional or intellectual stimulation in the listener, to secure the belief or conviction of the listener, and to secure action from the listener. These three types of reaction represent a series of steps. (See Figure 3)

The steps suggest the completeness of the response and the difficulty in obtaining the response. Emotional and rational response must

---

[2] John S. Sinclair, "Are We Mortgaging Our Future Too Much?" *Vital Speeches,* XXII, No. 14 (May 1, 1956), p. 437.

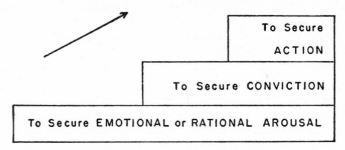

To Secure
ACTION

To Secure CONVICTION

To Secure EMOTIONAL or RATIONAL AROUSAL

Fig. 3. Steps in Persuasive Reaction.

be secured before belief or conviction can be expected. Belief must be obtained before the speaker can lead the listener to act.

The steps are useful in another sense. Frequently a speech stops on the first step or the second. The persuasive purpose may be solely to encourage the listener to think or respond emotionally. Or the purpose may be to secure belief without any concern for action.

A. To stimulate. The speech *to stimulate* differs from the speech *to interest* in that it does more than generate interest. It aims to arouse the listener emotionally and intellectually. Its purpose is to produce profound thought and deep feeling. Essentially the speech to stimulate dwells upon an idea or belief which the listener already knows or holds. It is a speech that intensifies the awareness of faith, people, institutions, customs, and traditions. It is typified by the tribute, the welcome or farewell, the sermon, the inspirational message, and the exploration of values.

On rare occasions the technical man may be called upon to perform these duties. At these times you will be called upon to be more than a bread-and-butter speaker; you ought to be an orator.

B. To convince. In the speech to *convince* you want the listener to agree with you. You don't ask the listener to do anything. The reaction of belief or conviction revolves about two types of propositions, the question of fact and the question of policy.

The question of fact is concerned with whether the proposition is *true* or *not true;* for example, "Atomic power *is* the ideal power." The problem is whether or not this statement is true. A speech on this subject is devoted to proof of the truth of the statement. Note that another speech may be concerned with proving that the statement is *not* true.

The question of policy deals with the problem of whether a given policy *should* or *should not* be carried out; for example, "Atomic power *should* be used on battleships." Again the arguments may be pro or con. The speech is devoted to proof of the policy.

The technical speaker deals with questions of fact or policy endlessly in his working life. You begin by proving that you are the man for the job. You prove that your ideas are the best ideas. You prove that your plans are right. You prove that you should be promoted. You prove that your product is unbeatable. In every instance you succeed if you can lead your listener to believe in your proposition.

C. To actuate. The speech *to actuate* faces the most difficult persuasive problem of all—getting the listener to actually do something. It is much simpler for the listener to agree with an idea or a policy than it is to overcome his natural inertia and do something about it. The speech to actuate is the most complete and the most complex of all the persuasive speeches. It must climb all the steps of persuasive reaction; it must arouse thought and emotion, secure belief, and command action.

Action provoking speeches occur in every aspect of your life. They include informal pleas for action, such as going to the movies, preparing a special breakfast, or bringing in the mail. Some of these simple attempts to control action can be satisfied with nothing more than the plea for action. However if the listener has reasons for not responding, even simple pleas can turn into complex speeches. More formal speeches to actuate strive for varied responses, such as buying —any of a hundred products; voting—in favor of plans, policies, or candidates; giving—money, time, energy, or blood; participating— in games, clubs, and scientific, social, religious, or political activities.

THE SPECIFIC PURPOSE

Re-examine Figure 3 at the beginning of this chapter. You have now traced the general need for reaction through the general purpose and its persuasive subdivisions and arrived at the specific purpose. The specific purpose is the exact reaction which you desire from your listeners. There are as many specific purposes as there are speeches. The importance of the clearly defined specific purpose cannot be overemphasized. Without it you may not be certain of the reaction desired; without it the listener may lose his way. The specific purpose should be embodied in the central idea of your speech. It should usually be expressed clearly and directly for the listener in the form of a purpose sentence.

Let's take a subject and break it down into the general purposes and several possible specific purposes. Take *uranium* as the general subject.

General Purpose	Specific Purpose
1. To interest the listener in—	a. the Lucky Lone Rock mine b. uranium millionaires c. tales of famous prospectors d. the story of Nellie Quemec e. Colorado uranium fields f. etc.
2. To inform the listener about—	a. prospecting equipment b. uranium's fissionable qualities c. kinds of uranium ore d. how to read a Geiger counter e. how to stake a claim f. etc.
3. To persuade: to stimulate the listener about—	a. uranium's contribution to America b. uranium and the atomic age c. the wasting of America's resources d. the lesson of Hiroshima e. uranium and America's future f. etc.
4. To persuade: to convince the listener that—	a. uranium is nature's richest metal b. amateurs should avoid prospecting c. uranium stock is a bad buy d. uranium production should be increased e. uranium should be shipped abroad f. etc.
5. To persuade: to actuate the listener to—	a. go prospecting for uranium b. buy uranium stock c. vote for local control of mines d. buy a Geiger counter e. visit Canada's uranium fields f. etc.

The preceding includes only a fragment of the total number of possible speeches dealing with uranium. Note how the statement of the specific purpose narrows the response to a workable unit. Think of how the specific purpose becomes the central idea of the speech. Since the specific purpose is the exact response desired from the listener after the speech has been concluded, the purpose must be adapted to the listener. In other words the specific purpose must be attainable. The wants, interests, needs, beliefs, desires, and attitudes of the listener should be carefully matched with the specific purpose.

Get in the habit of listing general purpose, subject, specific purpose, listeners, and occasion at the outset. Study them and make sure that they are the best possible combination before proceeding.

General Purpose:	To inform
Subject:	Supersonic jets
Specific Purpose:	To inform the listeners about the latest accomplishments in high speed flying
Listeners:	A group of high school seniors about to enter the armed services
Occasion:	A guidance clinic at the high school
General Purpose:	To persuade—to secure belief
Subject:	Time and motion studies
Specific Purpose:	To convince the listeners that time and motion studies can save money through greater efficiency
Listeners:	Corporation committee on efficiency
Occasion:	Regular weekly committee meeting

Is the best possible match of elements obtained in the two examples given above? Do both the subject and the purposes neatly match the audience and the occasion? Hold the purposes constant and fit other subjects to the listeners and occasions suggested above. What happens if you keep the listeners but change the occasion? Will a more detailed evaluation of the listeners affect the subject and purpose? Careful planning at this point in your preparation will save endless time and grief later.

2. SUBJECT AND TITLE

For some mystifying reason "what to talk about" seems to perplex most speakers. In spite of their training in solving problems and searching out the truth, technologists seem to be no better off than others. Yet all the tools for selecting a good subject are in their hands.

Two problems are basic to selecting the subject: first, you must find a worthwhile general subject; second, it must be limited so that it fits into your speaking situation. By solving these two problems the number of hours you spend pacing with the thought, "What shall I talk about?" can be decreased.

CRITERIA OF A GOOD SUBJECT

A first-rate subject is carefully fitted and adapted to (1) the listener, (2) the purpose, (3) the speaker, (4) the occasion, and (5) the time. If your subject can satisfy all five of these criteria, it should be worth your concentrated effort to develop it.

Fitting the Subject to the Listeners

This criterion should give you no difficulty if you have really assimilated Chapter 4. You know the listener's qualities and characteristics. You understand his basic drives. You recognize the peculiar limiting factors in groups composed of special types of listeners.

From these elements dozens of subjects should occur to you which would challenge the listener and fulfill his needs. Show him how he can gain security for himself, his family, and his job. Give him opportunities for adventure and new experiences, carry him through the excitement of inventions, explain the wonders of the world, provide him with opportunities for personal enjoyment. Teach him the things he needs to know to improve his position, to enjoy his life, to fulfill his ambitions. Show him how he can gain recognition, personally, professionally, and socially. Show him that he is important—needed, loved, and wanted.

Tying the Subject to the Purpose

The relationship of the subject and the purpose should be clear from the preceding discussion. The principle operates in two ways; either the purpose dictates the subject or the subject dictates the purpose. Normally the subject and the purpose are decided upon simultaneously so that they are sure to be matched. For example in a persuasive speech to actuate there is no point in choosing a subject on which the listeners don't have the power to act. It is foolish to appeal for votes if the listeners haven't reached the voting age. It is meaningless to inform an audience on a subject about which they know more than you do. It is absurd to try to interest listeners in social activities of which they disapprove. It is useless to try to convince the members of an audience of the truth of a proposition in which they already believe. It is senseless to stimulate listeners on a subject which makes no appeal to their thoughts or emotions.

Matching the Subject with the Occasion

As we have noted previously occasions influence the listener, the speaker, and the speech. The occasion sets the mood, the quality, the social amenities, the formality of the meeting. Just as the speaker's attitude must match the occasion, so must his subject.

The golf course is hardly the place for an inspirational subject. The church meeting is not the time for a political harangue. Common sense and good judgment should guide you in matching the subject to the occasion.

Adapting the Subject to Your Own Knowledge and Interests

Interest breeds enthusiasm. Knowledge gives birth to confidence. Enthusiasm and confidence are two of the most important ingredients of the speaker. Therefore select material you know about and feel strongly about. Select subjects from your own experiences, accomplishments, profession, hobbies, or social pursuits. Select subjects and propositions which excite you, anger you, please you, frighten you, or perplex you. Select subjects which are close to your wants, needs, and desires. Sell only those ideas you have sold to yourself.

Narrowing the Subject to the Time

During a five-minute speech a young mechanical engineer gave a complete survey of the Pennsylvania Railroad, one of America's most complex transportation systems. How did he do it? First of all he wrote on the blackboard a complete outline of the railroad's table of organization from the board of directors to the man with the sign at the crossing. It filled six eight-foot blackboard panels from top to bottom. He then read the outline off the board. It took him exactly five minutes. Was his speech a success? You guess.

One of the many things wrong with the speech was that the subject had not been narrowed to the time. No one can discuss a subject of such magnitude in five minutes. No one can discuss satisfactorily such a broad general subject in a single speech whatever the length. This speaker didn't understand that the speech idea should be narrowed and made specific and concrete. The broad, general, abstract speech lacks impact.

At the same time keep in mind the actual time limit allowed. How depressing it is to have a fifteen-minute speech become an hour oration. Whatever time is allotted you, it remains your responsibility to stay within its limits. The opening remarks of the Ambassador of Peru in a speech to the Board of Trade in Washington, D. C., were undoubtedly welcomed:

> As I stand here a little proverb that originated in Turkey comes to my mind that goes as follows: "At table keep a short hand, in company keep a short tongue."
> Unfortunately the table you have set today in this old and famed hotel has been so excellent that the first part of this little saying has so far been ignored.
> However, great as is my appreciation at the high honor of speaking on behalf of my Western Hemisphere colleagues at this luncheon, I will do my best to keep to the spirit of the second part of this proverb, as the thought behind it is one with which I doubt anyone here will quarrel—least of all my own and esteemed colleagues.

FIND AND LIMIT A SUBJECT

Assuming that you understand the criteria of a good subject and can judge a subject's worth, you may still ask "How do I find the subject in the first place?" The subject may be found in one of two ways. You may begin with the specific and move toward the general, or you may begin with the general and extract the specifics.

---

[3] Don Fernando Berckemeyer, "A Court of Economic Appeal," *Vital Speeches,* XXII, No. 15 (May 15, 1956), p. 456.

Expanding the Specific Idea

Obviously your original idea may make a satisfactory subject. Frequently, however, the idea which appeals to you may not be extensive enough to make a full speech. For example, you come home one night, put your key in the lock, turn it, and find that the lock won't work. After fiddling with it you climb in a window and call a locksmith. You become interested in locks and decide to make a speech about them. How can you build an interesting speech around a door lock? The idea is too specific and needs expansion. The expansion takes the form of broadening the base from which you look at the idea. Some of the ways in which the specific idea can be more general and inclusive are suggested below.

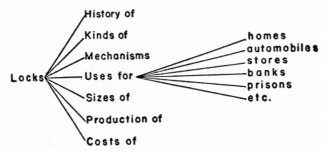

Fig. 4. Expanding the Specific Subject.

The simple idea of a lock is expanded by broadening the classifications. For example, from prison locks you could well go on to consider security systems and ultimately the security of the nation. The story of the lock is not important; moving from the specific to the general is. Starting with the lock an idea has been expanded into dozens of possible speech subjects.

Narrowing the General Idea

The same thing may be done in reverse. This time let's start with a general concept, one much too general for a successful speech, and gradually narrow it until dozens of units begin to appear. The speech subject can readily be extracted from among the units.

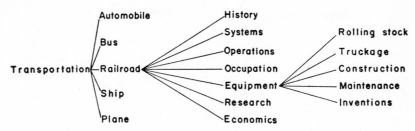

Fig. 5. Delimiting the General Subject.

One single mode of transportation (the railroad), one single aspect of the railroad (equipment), have been traced out. Think of how the chart would look if the same procedure had been used for all of the modes of transportation. Even the final step, breaking down the kinds and problems of equipment, is probably still too broad; but the next step, individual pieces of rolling stock such as cars or engines, provides you with dozens of good speech subjects. You might talk on "The Operation of a Switch Engine," "Dining Car Service," "The Vistadome," "Humping a Freight Car," or "The Railroad Post Office." Usually such an extended analysis is not necessary, but if you are stuck for an interesting subject, this is one way of finding it.

Remember that the two plans of analysis from specific to general and from general to specific operate like a family tree. You can look at it in two ways. You may start with yourself, move to two parents, four grandparents, eight great grandparents, and so on until your ancestors cover the globe and may include a famous king; or you may reverse the procedure and start with a famous king, who had two sons, each of whom had three daughters, and so on until you can prove that you are the descendant of a king along with approximately 10,000 other people.

Applying the Speech Purpose to the Idea

This principle is suggested in the discussion of uranium a few pages back. Given a single subject idea you can treat it in many different ways by modifying the purpose of the speech.

We have examined the criteria of a good subject, and ways to find and expand or limit the subject matter. Please don't ever again say "What shall I talk about?"

WHAT MAKES A GOOD TITLE?

A good title is (1) appropriate, (2) interesting, and (3) brief. Many good speeches have been missed by the listener because the title didn't give him the necessary information and stimulate his interest sufficiently to make him come.

Titles Must Be Appropriate

An appropriate title gives both sufficient information and the right information. Titles should never leave doubt. What would you think if you saw the title "Hiroshima!" The atomic bomb would be a natural association, since that is what the town is most noted for. Or perhaps you would expect a John Fitzpatrick travel talk with slides. The title doesn't tell enough, nor does it give the right information. "Be Prepared." For What? Why? When? Another title that is too brief to give the necessary data. Be particularly careful to make sure that the title doesn't consciously or unconsciously mislead. Quotations, while interesting, can be dangerously misinterpreted. One of the best examples of this is the title of a play *The Children's Hour.* Most audiences think first of Longfellow's little poem about the children's hour where all is warm and quiet and kind. This play, however, is a violent melodrama of a child's viciousness, and the title is deliberately misleading. In a play this kind of surprise may be desirable, but it never is in a speech.

The title should also be appropriate in mood. Avoid placing a comical title on a serious speech or vice versa. "Wee Willie Winkie" is hardly an appropriate title for a speech on the dangers of burglary; yet it has been used. "Nothing's Certain but Death and Taxes" is a poor way to entitle a discussion of methods used by the internal revenue office. "Making A Hi-Fi Pie" is too facetious for the title of a serious discussion of high-fidelity recording.

Titles Must Be Interesting

The title is the first contact that the listener has with your speech. Presumably the title should be sufficiently exciting to make him want to come to the address, or if he is a captive auditor, it ought to arouse his interest in the speech.

Each of the inappropriate titles suggested above are interesting. They create suspense and encourage attendance. Nonetheless they must be rejected. The opposite extreme of these are such titles as "Our Sewage Disposal Problem," "Vote for John P. Jones," "History of Welding," "The Manufacture of Rubber," "Mixing Concrete," "Causes of Juvenile Deliquency." All of these titles are appropriate. In each case they tell you clearly what the speech is about, but they create little enthusiasm or interest. How about: "Sewage Disposal: A Columbus Bugaboo" or "Welding Comes of Age" or "Your Son— Tomorrow's Delinquent."

Titles Must Be Brief

The third and final qualification of a good title is that it should be brief. It should probably not run more than five or six words. All of the titles in the preceding paragraphs are sufficiently brief. Some as we have noted are too brief to be meaningful. The reason for including brevity as a characteristic is that most titles are too long, too labored, and include too much. They sound like the titles of scholarly articles, and they shouldn't. For example, "The Contribution of the Earth Worm to the Agriculture of America," "The Relative Effectiveness of Two Samples of Steel in Withstanding Pressure," "The Social, Cultural, Moral, and Ethical Standards of Prehistoric Man." These titles are relevant; they certainly don't mislead; but they are unimaginative, dull, and much too long. The average listener will not stop to read them; the exceptional person who does suffer through them will certainly not be impressed.

Ideally the title combines the subject and the purpose of the speech in a brief and interesting form. If you can solve this problem, you may be able to equal one of the greatest titles of all time *How to Win Friends and Influence People*. It is interesting. It is tied to the listener's wants. It is reasonably brief. It is appropriate. It is relevant. It gives both the subject and the purpose. It helped sell several million copies of the book.

3. MATERIAL AND SOURCE

With the subject, purpose, and title in hand your next step is to flesh out the speech with the material The various kinds of material and the tests for evaluating it are discussed in detail in later chapters. For the moment it will suffice if you know in general what makes good material and how to find it.

CRITERIA FOR GOOD MATERIAL

Two students were talking about speeches they had to prepare. The conversation went something like this: "How's your speech coming?" "Oh, I've got to find some more material. I've got about three minutes worth, but I have to blow it up to ten." Have you ever had such thoughts? If you have, you are overlooking the function and purpose of material. It is not just a way of filling time.

Material Must Be Representative

The quotations, stories, and statistics that you use must be representative; that is, they must serve the specific purpose of the speech. The material must interest, clarify, stimulate, or convince. The material must be typical of the ideas which can be used to support or prove your point. They should not be tangents from the main core of available ideas. If you set out to prove that a rotary pump should be used for a certain job rather than a suction pump, the materials should be representative of the differences between the two pumps. Only those arguments are valid which clearly demonstrate the advantages of one over the other.

Material Should Indicate a Broad Background

Frequently the speaker stops too soon in his quest for evidence to support his premise. His material is designed to just fill time rather than give broad support to his point. Don't depend upon one source, one article, one expert's opinions. Surround the subject by reading both sides or all points of view. Your own point will be better served if you are really an expert on the subject. Expertness depends upon complete knowledge. Obviously no one can be an expert on all things, but at the same time a minimum of research can broaden the base of your knowledge immeasurably.

Material Should Be Up-to-Date

Your own information and general knowledge may be sadly out-dated. Most fields of knowledge are moving so fast that even slight lags in time may invalidate what you know. For example, television equipment is changing so quickly that a speech on it may be outdated from one month to the next. Think of the major changes—the icono-scope, the image orthichon, the vidicon—all in the space of less than ten years. Make sure that your information is the latest and the best available.

Material Should Be Fair to the Subject

All too often material is not fair. It is either so superficial that it does not give the listener a just impression, or it is so skewed or slanted that the listener does not have a fair chance to judge it. Occasionally it is deliberately misleading or dishonest. The National Food and Drug Act was passed to protect the layman from false claims of ad-vertisers. This type of misrepresentation of subject matter is too ob-vious to warrant further comment.

More common is the lack of fairness that arises from the speaker's selection of only that material which will support his own point of view. Debaters unfortunately frequently treat a subject as though it were either black or white with all the gray tones missing. To them you are either for or against; you can't be partly for and somewhat against. Nevertheless, you will find yourself farther ahead if you are willing to admit the limitations of your ideas.

Still another injustice to material stems from superficial treatment because too little material has been gathered for a clear picture. Scien-tists do not report results without qualifying them. Take the wonder drug cortisone, for example. The medical scientists found that it would help arthritis; at the same time they began to note side effects which were frequently worse than the arthritis. The scientists ex-plained the good result and added the qualifications, but the popular periodicals and press were less just. They publicized widespread claims for cortisone; they aroused the hope of thousands of arthritics who were later doomed to disappointment. It was not a deliberate at-tempt to be dishonest; it was just thoughtless, foolish superficiality.

WHAT ARE THE SOURCES OF MATERIAL?

You are a chemical engineer; your subject is "Soap." Your general purpose is to inform; your specific purpose is to explain how soap cleans. Your listeners are college trained housewives. Your occasion is the meeting of a sanitation institute. Where do you start? First, you plumb the resources of your own experience. Second, you converse and confer with your friends and experts. Third, you turn to magazines and books dealing with the subject of soap.

Use Your Own Experience

One of the reasons that you have been asked to speak or that you have chosen a subject is because you know something about it. Therefore the logical starting point is your own experience. Your own experience may be sufficient, but usually it won't be. Lay out your ideas on the chosen subject. Try to group them into logical headings for your speech. You will find quickly where the gaps in your own information are. After you have drained your own experience, test your ideas. Are they as interesting, clear, and persuasive as they might be? Are your ideas truly representative, broad in scope, up-to-date, and fair? If you can answer both of these questions in the affirmative, you need go no further; the speaker has been perfectly matched to the subject and purpose. Nine times out of ten, however, you will not be able to answer affirmatively. Then you must turn to the next source of material.

Use Conversation, Interview, and Discussion

Your next step is to question your co-workers who know something about the subject or experts in the field whom you may know. If you can stir up their interest, you will quickly find your background being broadened by new knowledge, different points of view, and fresh illustrations and anecdotes. Add this material to that you have already assembled. Fit it into your grouping of material. If there are overlappings, decide whether your original ideas should be supplanted by the new. Or, and this may happen frequently, you may decide to scrap and reorder the entire grouping of your material.

Again note where the gaps occur and turn to the last and major source of material—reading.

Read

Reading not only supplies new material, but even more important, it acts as a constant check upon your own information. Successful reading and research depend upon three factors: (1) how to find the material, (2) how to read it, and (3) how to record it.

HOW TO FIND MATERIAL

An amazing number of people dislike libraries and avoid them unless they are told exactly what book to look for and how many chapters and pages to read. This aversion is usually the result of not knowing how to find quickly and efficiently what they are looking for. We dislike those things we fear, and sometimes the library seems like a maze of confusion. While there is not enough space here to provide a course in how to use a library, one direct line of action can be examined which should produce results.

Use the Library

Before you tackle the library, make certain that you are clear as to exactly what you are looking for because much of the difficulty encountered will come from your own vagueness. Determine what material you want. Classify your needs into logical headings, and think through the different ways your headings might be expressed; for example, what you want to know about radio may be classified under electronics or under engineering. When these steps have been taken, you are ready to approach the library itself.

Use the Catalogues

Every library catalogues its materials by subject and author. If you know the author of a specific work, your shortest road is the author catalogue. If not, look up your headings in the subject catalogue, which provides the names of books and general headings. The catalogue card lists the essential information which is treated in the book.

You should be able to judge quickly whether or not the book will be useful. Draw out only those which seem clearly helpful.

Use the Periodical Indexes

Frequently the information you want can be found in a magazine rather than in a book. In this case the specific article is not listed in the general catalogue. The most useful of the periodical indexes which are maintained to help you is the *Reader's Guide to Periodical Literature*. This guide is like the general catalogue. It lists articles by subject and by author. Since it is published monthly, all of the articles on your subject won't be found in any one guide. Trace your subject through a number of years, selecting those years during which you think the subject would be most actively written about. The *Reader's Guide* starts in 1902. If you are looking for materials prior to that time use *Poole's Index to Periodical Literature* which covers the period 1882–1910. There are also indexes which treat special areas such as *The Industrial Arts Index* and *The Agricultural Index*. The reason for deciding upon the headings under which your subject might be listed will now become apparent. If it isn't listed the way you feel it should be, try related headings.

Use the Reference Desk

Every library maintains a reference desk with a librarian who makes a specialty of helping you find material. Don't go to the reference desk until you have exhausted your own resources, but do feel perfectly free to ask for help when you are stuck. The reference librarian can suggest other sources for you. For example, she will know whether there are specially prepared bibliographies on your subject; or perhaps she will suggest abstracts of articles and theses which may serve as shortcuts. Remember she is there to help you.

Use Newspapers and Current Magazines

The very latest materials will of course not yet be catalogued. For this material go to the periodical room. At the University of Wisconsin's special engineering library, for example, there are more than two hundred engineering magazines of all types. Usually the title of the magazine is self-explanatory; if not, take a little time and browse.

Newspapers provide the latest developments. However unless you know about where to look, they are an unwieldy source. If you have found a story that is applicable, be sure to look up the same story in other papers. The differences in reporting and editorial policy will surprise you. For the most careful and dispassionate treatment look up the story in *The New York Times* or the *Christian Science Monitor*.

Find Other Useful Sources

One good general starting point in filling out a subject is a standard encyclopedia, such as the *Encyclopedia Britannica*, or an encyclopedia which covers a special field, such as *The Encyclopedia of Social Sciences*.

Another source of material is that found in biographical references, such as *Who's Who In America* or *Who's Who In Education*. If you know the name of a great living exponent of the idea, this may be a good place to start.

For statistical references look in the *Statistical Abstract of the United States Government* or the *World Almanac*. For literary references try *Bartlett's Familiar Quotations* or the *Oxford Dictionary of Quotations*.

These then are the general steps which you should take in searching for material in the library. The next question is what to do after you have found something useful.

HOW TO READ MATERIAL

Assume that you have found six or eight books and twenty articles which appear from their titles to deal with your subject. What do you do when you get them?

Read with a Purpose

You must learn to read with a purpose. Without a clearcut purpose you won't be able to select the things in each source which are useful. You will either read much too much or tend to settle for the first likely material that comes along. If you decide too late exactly what your purpose is, you will have to reread much of the material you have already covered.

Learn to use the table of contents and the index of a book. The table of contents can point to your chapter immediately, thereby eliminating your having to look at the fifteen to twenty other chapters. If your material seems to be spread through the book, use the index at the back, where each item in the book will be pinpointed for you.

Learn to scan. Scanning is the process of quickly running over material and picking out the key ideas as you go. Did you know that paragraphs are separated by indentation because they each treat either a new topic or a new phase of a topic? When scanning a chapter which may have material of interest, read just the topic sentence of each paragraph until you hit one that you know is important. Turn back a few pages in this book; note how the key ideas change with each new paragraph. Some are paragraphs involving principles; others are paragraphs dealing with illustrations. In each case just the first line will give the gist of what follows.

The process of looking for material, which is called research, is quite different from reading or studying. If you become involved in reading for the fun of it, you can waste a great amount of time. Even though you leave the library better educated, you will have added little or nothing to the job at hand—your speech. You are reading with a single purpose. Don't spend time on material that does not fit that purpose.

Read a Number of Sources

Don't stop with the first thing that comes along. Certainly make a note of it, but then go on to other things which may be better or different. The broader the base of your speech, the more representative of the subject it will be. Never find a single article and appropriate it in its entirety for your speech. First, since you didn't write the article, you don't have the right to somebody else's work. Second, research went into the article to make it broad and sure, and you must do your own research. Third, whenever you use a substantial number of someone else's ideas, you must give him credit for them. If you are honest and give credit, you will find that you will give up using just one article because you won't want others to know that your speech is so completely dependent upon someone else's thought. Finally, read a number of sources so that you eliminate from your speech any possibility of bias or superficiality.

Read Critically

As you increase the breadth of your background in the subject, your ability to read critically will develop. Some material which you thought was first-rate will begin to pale as you broaden your experience.

Check the sources of your material. There is a strong tendency to accept everything and anything that appears in print as reliable and worthy. This probably stems from the fact that you have leaned on your teachers' experience throughout school, letting them pick out your reading for you. Now that you are doing library research, you will have to sift the good from the bad, the biased from the balanced, for yourself. Everything that appears in print is not automatically excellent. Even the care used by a library in selecting material does not guarantee it. You must check the sources of your material, the freshness of it, the bias in it. Only by critical evaluation can you place it in its proper niche.

HOW TO RECORD MATERIAL

You have gone to the library; found the periodical; located the article; scanned its contents; located the paragraphs that apply; and have before you a very good quotation or idea. Now you must record it correctly.

Faulty recording of material can waste as much time as it would take to do the entire research. It seems laborious, but a little time spent in getting the record straight will save hours later on. Don't jot the ideas down in a notebook; they can't be shifted easily when you organize the speech. Don't use stray slips of paper; they invariably get lost. Don't omit anything when recording the source, or you will have to look it up all over again. Record the item on a 4″ x 6″ card. This size is large enough so that you won't feel cramped. A direct quotation should be put down in quotation marks; any omissions should be indicated by the use of three dots (. . .). If you add ideas for clarity, put the additions in brackets ([   ]). When you want the idea instead of a direct quote, paraphrase carefully so that you don't distort the idea. Record all the information on the source. For books include author's name, title of the book underlined, publisher, place of publication, date, and page numbers; for an article include the author's name, title of the article in quotation marks, name of the periodical underlined, volume number, page numbers, and date of publication. List this information at the bottom of the card. Classify the material at the top of the card. Indicate the subject and the subdivision of the subject; for example, Subject: Locks, Division: Uses of. Remember that if you do it right the first time, you won't hate yourself later.

———Apply the Principles

We have surveyed in considerable detail the first three steps in preparing a speech: choosing the purpose, selecting the subject and title, and finding the material. A summary and review of the principles involved can be found in the following applications.

(1) Reread your daily paper. Find at least two good speech subjects from each of the following pages: the first page, the women's page, the editorial page, the theatre page, the radio-television page, the financial page, the want-ads.

(2) You should now have at least fourteen subjects. Decide upon the best two. Why have you chosen them? Decide upon the listener situation they would serve best. What should the purpose be? Can the subjects serve more than one purpose?

(3) Phrase the two subjects into appropriate, brief, interesting titles. Do the titles suggest the specific purposes? Do they give all of the necessary information? The right information?

(4) Take one of the subjects and do the necessary research for additional material. Watch your procedures in using the library. If you make mistakes or lose time, you should be able to do better next time.

(5) Follow the other steps in speech preparation found in Chapter 2. Deliver the speech in a class or before a group of your friends or colleagues.

FORMULA E

$$DPSM = \left(\frac{SP}{GP} + AS \right) M$$

(*DPSM*) *Develop Purpose, Subject, and Material* = In corporating the (*GP*) *General Purpose* into the (*SP*) *Specific Purpose* plus (*AS*) *Adjusting the Subject.* Multiply the quantity by relevant (*M*) *Materials.*

Now, apply the formula!

1. My general purpose in my next speech is
   To entertain _____
   To inform _____
   To persuade _____
2. My specific purpose is

3. My subject requires the following adjustments:
   To my listener _____
   To my purpose _____
   To the occasion _____
   To my knowledge and interests _____
   To the time _____
4. My subject will be limited to the following phase(s):

   _____

   _____

5. My speech title, which is appropriate, interesting, and brief, will be

   _____

6. My speech materials are
   Representative (*List the pertinent factors to be developed*):

   _____

   _____

   _____

87

Broad (*List the sources*):

_____

_____

Up-to-date (*List the dates of your sources*):

_____

Fair (*List the pros and cons of the pertinent factors*):

Pro	Con
_____	_____
_____	_____
_____	_____
_____	_____
_____	_____
_____	_____

7. Practice the speech aloud and communicate it.

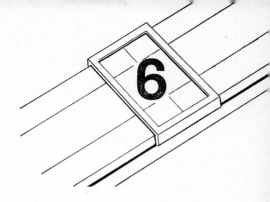

organize
your speech

ORGANIZATION IS ONE of the keystones of successful living. It is an important element in everything you do. You must organize your time *if* it is to serve you well. You must organize your work *if* you are to succeed. You must organize the spending of your money *if* you are to remain solvent. You must organize what you say *if* you are to get the desired response. Notice the *if* factor; organization must answer a need. Without a need you have no direction, no reason for continuing.

W. L. Everitt, Dean of the College of Engineering at the University of Illinois, has this to say:

An engineer is a man interested in action.

Action can seldom be completed by a single individual. In order to translate ideas into useful results, others must be convinced that proposed plans should be put into effect. The only means for persuading others to adopt our ideas or cooperate with us is first to have good ideas, and then present them well by means of our common language. I have found personally that speech training is very helpful in improving ability in the use of language, written as well as spoken. A good speech always involves hard work, which will include attention to organization, to simplicity and brevity, to establishing a bond of mutual interest between listener and speaker, and attention to what information should be conveyed and what action is desired upon the part of the listeners.

THE FIVE E'S TO EFFECTIVENESS

Speech organization in its fullest development fulfills five needs. Each need is satisfied as you organize your material to fulfill the requirement of that need. Although these needs are separate entities in themselves, they are often fulfilled simultaneously. These, then, are the five needs in speech organization:

1. ENGAGE the listener
2. ENLIGHTEN the listener
3. ENCOMPASS the listener
4. ENTHUSE the listener
5. ENLIST the listener

Traditionally we think in terms of three major divisions in a speech —the introduction, the body, and the conclusion. These major divisions have remained the same for more than 2000 years. There have been modern innovators who have renamed the divisions, occasionally even subdivided one or more of them, but the essential structure has remained unchanged. The fact remains that each of these major divisions must answer one or more organizational needs.

The need of the introduction is *to engage* the listener. The needs of the body are *to enlighten, to encompass,* and *to enthuse* the listener. The need of the conclusion is *to enlist* the listener. Figure 6 illustrates these points.

1. ENGAGE YOUR LISTENER

As you rise to speak your listeners begin to form impressions. Certainly with your first words you launch into the job of catching the attention of the listener and creating good will for yourself, your subject, and your purpose. Your first task is to *engage the listener.* This responsibility can be accomplished in three ways.

1. Engage the attention of the listener.
2. Direct his attention to the subject and the purpose.
3. Create good will toward the speaker and the speech.

In some instances you have both the attention and the good will of your listeners at the outset. Then your introduction should be short and to the point. In other instances it may take time to interest the

FIVE E's TO ORGANIZATIONAL EFFECTIVENESS		
INTRODUCTION	BODY	CONCLUSION
Engage	Enlighten Encompass Enthuse	Enlist

Fig. 6. The Organizational Needs.

audience in your material and create good will for yourself and your subject. Then your introduction will be involved.

We have spent a good deal of time discussing the general make-up of the listener and the controlling factors which dictate your overall approach to the listener. But now you have before you a particular listener or a group of listeners. What is their attitude toward you, toward your purpose, toward your subject? These attitudes affect the organizational need of your introduction.

INFLUENCE OF THE LISTENER'S ATTITUDE

Why is the listener here? Did he come voluntarily? Did he feel forced to attend? Was he literally ordered to come? What is his attitude toward me? Does he have any feelings about my subject? Does he in general approve or disapprove of my purpose? The answers to these questions indicate the kind of introduction that will be necessary.

The Interested Listener

Interested listeners are present because they wish to be. They have been impelled by their own desires to hear your speech. They are a voluntary audience. Their reason for coming is based on your subject, your purpose, or you. Perhaps it is your prestige as a speaker; or they may be concerned about the problem you are discussing; or they may be interested but undecided about a plan you offer for approval.

The introduction for the interested audience may be brief and simple. You have their voluntary attention at the outset. Presumably you have their good will. Consequently, your first task—to engage your listener—is minimzed. Your only problem is to direct their attention and good will to your subject and purpose. This may be done without flourishes. A straightforward declaration of why the speech is being given and what the purpose is, will be enough. You may then turn immediately to the body of your speech.

Typical examples of interested audiences might be: your school friends, who wish to hear about your experiences abroad; apprentice employees, who want to learn their job; a civic minded group interested in your solution to a problem; or a partisan political audience attending a rally.

The Indifferent Listener

The indifferent or apathetic listener is more prevalent than the interested one. The uninterested listener is present because he feels that he has to be. He is a member of a committee and his absence from the meeting would be noted. He is part of a class and attendance is taken. He is invited to a conference by his boss and can't refuse. He comes to the meeting because of tradition, social pressure, or because his wife was insistent. By definition he is indifferent. He bears no particular animosity. He neither likes nor dislikes you, your subject, or your purpose. He is a captive listener; captured by reasons not related to your speech. He represents inertia at its greatest.

In this speaking situation the introduction increases in importance. Unless the introduction is effective, the chances for a successful speech are minimized. In order to *engage* your listener each of the three ways must be developed in full. The listeners' attention must be aroused. Since he is inert, the opening must be made particularly strong and exciting. Good will must be created. The listeners don't feel any intense ill will. They just don't feel. Their enthusiasm for you, your subject, and your purpose must be kindled.

This kind of introduction employs as many of the attention devices (see Chapter 8) as possible. It devotes time to motivating the audience. This audience must be shown *why* your subject is important. Each listener must be made to perk up his ears and sense that what is about to happen is significant to *him*. In the speech to inform, for example, the listener may have to be persuaded that the information is important before he will put forth the effort to assimilate it.

The Hostile Listener

The hostile listener is an interested listener, make no mistake about that. He comes to scoff, to jeer, to disagree, to oppose. None of these desires of his may find vocal expression. He may not actually be a heckler, but his mind is just as completely closed as if he were an active and outspoken antagonist.

Before speaking you must find out what the listeners are hostile about. Do they have a personal hostility? For example, are you engaged in the task of persuading personal enemies to stand with you on a problem? Such a task is almost impossible. Is your audience hostile to your principles or the purpose of your speech? Is their animosity a matter of intolerance or is it based upon the listener's individual needs? For example, you may be bumping against a fixed attitude in your listeners about race, creed, or faith. Or you may be proposing a plan which the listener thinks will deprive him of a job or opportunity for advancement. The first is a difficult task; the second is ordinarily less difficult.

The function of the introduction to a hostile audience is *to engage your listeners by opening their minds*. Not to persuade him to your point of view, but to persuade him *to listen* to your point of view. Until his mind is sufficiently open to permit him to judge your proposition fairly, there is no point in going ahead. Special techniques are needed for opening the listener's mind.

A. The Circuitous Introduction. The circuitous or blind introduction is one in which your purpose is not exposed to the listener immediately. Instead he is encouraged to think positively, to feel good will, to open his mind so that he may appraise your proposal impartially.

B. Common Ground. Common ground is frequently called the "you-and-I" technique. It is the process of showing your listener the common bonds that exist between you. Literally it is a matter of showing that you and he stand on a common or shared piece of ground. The politician talks of the problems of labor and identifies himself with the labor movement when he talks to laborers. He speaks of the problems of agriculture and identifies himself with the farmer when he talks to farmers. Most major politicians have farms and love live-stock. They have pictures to prove it.

Successful common ground shows real bonds and above all is honest. Hypocrisy of any kind can make it backfire. Common ground may be used in any speech to secure good will.

C. *The Universal Principle.* The universal principle is that principle upon which everyone must agree. We may disagree on the ways to achieve it, but we must agree with the principle itself. Everyone wants better education for his children. Everyone wants security. Everyone wants a better way of life. Everyone wants freedom. The four freedoms for which we fought World War II are excellent examples of universal principles. The speaker dealing with the hostile audience begins with universal principles. The listener despite his animosity finds that he agrees with the same principles that you do. As a result he may be led to look impartially upon your method of reaching the principle.

D. *The "Yes" Response Barrage.* This technique is a more specific application of the universal principle. The speaker asks a battery of rhetorical questions or he makes a series of statements with which the listener agrees. It has been proved psychologically that every time the listener says "Yes" it becomes that much harder for him to say "No." Hostility can be reduced or eliminated if he is exposed to a battery of principles to which he must agree.

WAYS TO ENGAGE YOUR LISTENER'S ATTENTION

As many a bore knows, attention is easy enough to get if you don't care how you get it. The way you get it is important in a speech, for the introduction must not only get attention but also create good will. Several of the standard ways of beginning a speech are suggested below.

Tell a Story

Everyone responds to a story. In fact some studies suggest that a speech should be nothing more than a series of stories which illustrate the point. Your story must be a carefully selected one. Test it out with the following criteria. Does it relate to the subject and the purpose? Is it interesting? Does it create the right mood for the audience?

Use a Funny Story

Humor has a universal appeal and will invariably catch attention, but it must be used carefully. First of all, your story must be really funny, for there is nothing more embarrassing for both the speaker and the audience than the joke that doesn't come off. Second, the humor must be in good taste; an off-color story may please the majority of the audience, but it may also create a hard core of antagonism in others. Finally, your story must be related to the subject and purpose of your speech; otherwise the attention of the audience may subside with the laughter.

Refer to Your Listeners and the Occasion

Make sincere references to the group before whom you are speaking. Refer to the needs and desires of the listener. Tie your speech to the occasion. Establish common ground by relating your experiences to the listener's experience. The principles which must be followed in this type of introduction are simple. Be honest. Be friendly. Be simple and direct. Avoid platitudes. Avoid flattery. Remember that you are interested in creating good will.

Use a Famous Quotation

The advantage of the well-selected quotation is twofold. It immediately establishes the mood of the speech, and its recognition by the listener establishes the circular response. The rules for selecting the quotation are the same as those for selecting the story.

Use a Barrage of Questions

They may be "yes" response questions, or they may be questions which start the listeners thinking. If you use questions, be extremely careful to make sure that each question counts. The questions should arouse interest in your subject. They should force the listener to respond. The questions may deal with important issues which you will answer later in the speech. Remember that any attentive listener will automatically answer your questions for and to himself. Make sure you know how he will answer them, because you want a unanimous answer or attitude from your listeners.

Use a Startling Statement

This is the shock technique. The startling statement jerks the listener from his lethargy and stimulates his immediate attention. Since it depends on shock several dangers should be considered. The startling statement must be startling. But it must not be too startling, or the listener is liable to remain preoccupied with the statement for too long a period. It must not be so climactic that everything later in the speech pales beside it. The statement must direct attention to the subject and the purpose; otherwise the listener is left in the air with no place to go. The statement must be appropriate; poor taste never creates good will.

These are the standard ways of beginning a speech. These are the standard ways of *engaging your listener.* Your own experience and knowledge of your particular listeners may suggest other courses or combinations.

WAYS TO DIRECT ATTENTION TO THE SUBJECT AND PURPOSE

Each of the preceding methods of gaining attention can and should be used to direct the attention to the subject. There are several additional ways to direct attention to the subject.

Defining the Subject

This is the process of telling the listener what the subject is and what it is not. By using definitions the speaker quickly narrows the subject and pinpoints the treatment which he has planned. Confusion in terms is eradicated. The exact purpose is clarified.

Orienting the Subject

This is the process of relating the subject to the listener. Careful orientation shows the listener his place in the scheme of things and what is wanted of him. The orientation can be done historically by showing the listener how the subject fits into the development of an area or field. It may be done socially by showing the listener how the subject fits into the total social pattern.

Developing the Need to Know

The speaker who wishes to give information and gain understanding is frequently faced with the problem of motivating the listener to desire the knowledge. The speech to inform can't succeed until the listener is aware that the knowledge can be useful to him. Then and only then will the listener expend the energy which is necessary for learning. This part of the introduction is particularly significant when there is reason to believe that the listeners are indifferent.

Backgrounding the Question of Policy or Fact

This special kind of orientation is frequently necessary in the persuasive speech. The question of policy or fact must be examined and evaluated in a particular context. For example, if you are urging universal military training or federal aid to education, not only must the terms be defined, but the relationship of the subject to the listener and his society must be explained. Some recent history of the social and political implications of the subject may be useful.

The Purpose Sentence

The purpose sentence embodies in a single expression the exact response which you want from the audience. Ordinarily it is the concluding statement of the introduction. It focuses your exact intent *before* taking the listener into the body of your speech. Perhaps the examples below will give you the idea.

Preliminary Considerations

I. Subject: U.S. Radar Defense Network
II. General Purpose: To persuade
III. Specific Purpose: To convince the listeners that the U.S. Radar Defense Network should be expanded

Introduction

ENGAGE THE LISTENER

I. (Engaging his attention) You, your family, and your home could be completely wiped out this very minute. Etc. (Directing his attention to the subject and the purpose) The U.S. Radar Defense Network needs to be expanded in order to provide maximum protection. Etc. (Creating good will toward the speaker and the speech) My personal interest in my family and yours compels me to bring you these facts. Etc.

II. (Purpose statement) The safety of America depends on the expansion of our radar defense network.

Or,

Our radar defense network must be increased if America is to survive.

Or,

I propose to prove that your life and the lives of your children depend upon the expansion of the U.S. Radar Defense Network.

In the speech to inform the application is identical.

Preliminary Considerations

I. Subject: The game of chess
II. General Purpose: To inform
III. Specific Purpose: To inform the listeners about the rules of chess

Introduction

ENGAGE THE LISTENER

I. (Engaging his attention) If *you* were a King, would you always make the right move? Etc. (Directing his attention to the subject and the purpose of the speech) The game of chess requires a thorough knowledge of the rules. Etc. (Creating good will toward the speaker and the speech) It is my pleasure to share with you the excitement of learning to play the game of chess. Etc.

II. (Purpose statement) Before you can play chess, you must understand the basic rules of the game. Learning the rules is what we're here for.

Or,

You can play your first game of chess tonight, if you will learn the following basic rules.

Or,

Chess is based upon five simple rules. To understand them is the first step in learning to play chess.

Again the purpose sentence has tied the purpose and the subject to the listener. After you have stated your purpose sentence and are sure that your audience has perceived it, you may proceed to the body of the speech.

As in all good things, there is bound to be an exception. If you wish to reason from a series of specific examples and draw your conclusion at the end of the speech, you will not use the purpose sentence. Statement of the proposition followed by the proof of it is called the deductive method. Beginning with the proof and winding up with the proved proposition is called the inductive method. The use of these two methods is discussed in greater detail in Chapter 9.

In summary, the introduction sets the stage for the body of the speech. The information or arguments which make up the speech do not belong in the introduction. Only those materials which arouse interest and good will, provide the necessary orientation for understanding, direct the attention to the subject and the purpose, and indicate the exact response desired should be included. In other words, only those things which *engage the listener* should be included.

2. ENLIGHTEN, ENCOMPASS, AND ENTHUSE YOUR LISTENER

Having successfully engaged your listener in the introduction of your speech, you are now ready to go into the body (the discussion) of the speech. The body of the speech is the major portion of the speech. It is made up of the main ideas necessary to fulfill the intent of your purpose sentence. The success of the main ideas is dependent on the support provided them. Your main ideas and the support you give them must serve three functions:

1. They must *enlighten* the listener.
2. They must *encompass* the listener.
3. They must *enthuse* the listener.

The information included, regardless of the type of speech, is for the purpose of enlightening the listener. Facts, opinions, theories, relationships, ideas, examples, illustrations—all of these and more are gathered and presented to enlighten the listener. It is not enough to give just any information. It is your responsibility to give that information which clarifies, promotes understanding, supports, enlarges, and inspires. If your information does not enlighten your listener, it has been given in vain.

As this information is individualized, as it is adapted to the interests of the listener, it fulfills another need—it encompasses the listener. Your listener tends to be selfish—and rightly so; he wants to know how your information affects him. Does it concern his individual security? Does it provide adventure for him? Does it afford him recognition? Does it involve a personal response? Your listener must be treated as an individual human being. You must individualize your information. You must *encompass* your listener.

As the individual adaptation of the material affects the listener, as it excites him, it fulfills the next need—to enthuse. Your listener becomes enthusiastic as your individualized information grows in importance. It may offer direction, or hope, or challenge, or inspiration, or a combination of these. It must *enthuse*. This is just as true with the speech to inform as it is with the speech to persuade. In the speech to inform your information should be so organized and presented that your listener becomes vitally interested in listening. In the speech to persuade your information should be so organized and presented that your listener accepts and takes action. These ends are realized as you fulfill the organizational need—to *enthuse*.

These are the organizational needs of the body of any speech. These are your responsibilities to your material and your listener. An excellent example of these needs is found in the body of a speech given by Thomas E. Murray, former Commissioner of the United States Atomic Energy Commission. (See Appendix B, p. 297)

THE ONE-POINT SPEECH

In most of the simple speeches you will give in everyday life the purpose sentence will be the only heading or issue. In this case it is imperative that this single sentence engage the listener. These speeches are known as one-point speeches. The one-point speech consists of a purpose sentence and those illustrations, examples, statistics, testimony, and so forth which amplify or prove it. The five E's to effectiveness are still present. The structure of the one-point speech may be illustrated as follows:

Introduction

I. Purpose statement to *engage* the listener.

Body

I. Main idea to *enlighten, enthuse,* and *encompass* the listener.
   A. Supporting material
   B. More supporting material
   C. More supporting material
   D. Etc.

Conclusion

I. Summary, appeal or ending note to *enlist* the listener.

Main Headings

In more complex speeches the purpose sentence of the introduction is supported by a group of main headings or issues. In the speech to inform, the main headings are the principle divisions of the information. For example, in "The Rules of Chess" the rules are the main headings. In the speech to persuade, the main headings, somtimes called issues, are the major reasons for supporting the purpose sentence. In the illustration of "Expand the Radar Network," for instance, the main headings might be:

1. A complete radar network can provide immediate identification of enemy aircraft. (It is practical.)
2. A complete radar network is cheaper than other forms of defense. (It is economical.)
3. A complete radar network can save your life. (It is desirable.)

Practical, economical, desirable—these are three major reasons. They are the main headings upon which the purpose sentence stands. The organizational needs—the five E's to effectiveness—motivate the development of these main headings.

There are four important considerations in determining your main headings:

1. They must be *major* reasons for supporting the purpose.
2. They must be *mutually exclusive,* that is, each main heading must stand by itself without overlapping any other main heading.
3. They should be *all inclusive,* that is, all of the supporting material must fit under one main heading or another.
4. The main headings should be *limited* in number. If you find you have more than three or four main headings, the ones you have chosen are evidently not the really major supports for the purpose.

Supporting Materials

As in the one-point speech, the supporting materials are the ampli-fication, the evidence, and the appeals which inform or persuade. These supporting materials reflect the organizational needs—to en-lighten, to encompass, to enthuse. Speech is in essence merely two or three one-point speeches strung together in support of a broader pur-pose. The structure of the multi-pointed speech may be illustrated as follows:

Introduction

ENGAGE THE LISTENER

I. Opening remarks
II. Purpose statement

Body

ENLIGHTEN, ENCOMPASS, ENTHUSE THE LISTENER

I. First main heading
   A. Supporting material
   B. More supporting material
   C. Etc.
II. Second main heading
   A. Supporting material
   B. More supporting material
   C. Etc.
III. Third main heading
   A. Supporting material
   B. More supporting material
   C. Etc.

Conclusion

ENLIST THE LISTENER

I. Summary, appeal or ending note

There is no magic in organization. After you have gathered the material for your speech, organization is simply the process of fitting the parts together into a workable whole. In the following sections a number of ways are suggested to put the materials together. The choice of the particular method depends upon the peculiarities of your material.

WAYS TO ORGANIZE MATERIAL

The first step in dividing the material is to examine it for natural groupings. Probably the best procedure for determining the most satisfactory grouping is to look at your subject in terms of the specific purpose. You know what you wish to inform about or what you wish to prove. Now answer the question: How can this material do it? Perhaps there are steps, rules, lists, reasons—these form the natural method of organization. Most material tends to group itself in a natural manner. The relationships which occur most frequently are suggested below.

Arrangement by Time Sequence

Probably the most frequent arrangement is by time. Historical relationships are based on the passage of time. The seasons, a day, a man's life, a football game, and steps in completing many processes are all related to the passage of time. Take your material and try to arrange it in time, moving either forward or backward from a given time. Two examples of how time may act as the basis of organization are suggested below.

History of Iranian Oil

I. In 1901 William D'Archy first drilled for oil.
II. In 1908 the Burmath Oil Company bought out D'Archy.
III. In 1933 the Anglo-Iranian oil company was set up.
IV. In 1951 Mohammed Mossadegh nationalized the oil fields.

The historical time sequence is not only useful for dividing the history of oil, or of a nation, or of mankind; it may also be used to separate ideas or contributions—for example, Einstein's greatest contributions: in 1902 the equation explaining the photo-electric effect; in 1905 the special theory of relativity using time as a dimension; in 1915 the general theory of relativity proposing the curved time-space universe.

Time sequences in a much more limited sense occur in all processes. Woodworking might be divided as follows:

Steps in Woodworking

I. Marking a piece of stock
II. Cutting the design

   III. Planing the stock
   IV. Sanding the surface
    V. Applying the finish

Trace out other processes or operations. The time sequence is always present. Be sure you find the primary divisions in the sequence.

Arrangement by Space

From east to west, from top to bottom, from the inside to the outside, are typical examples of spatial relationships which occur in the grouping of materials. A subdivision could be treated in terms of space. The plantings around a house would be divided by space. A battleship may be divided by decks. Crops, languages, animals, and a host of other materials may be grouped by space. A typical example of space order may be found in a discussion of the atmosphere.

The Earth's Atmosphere

    I. Troposphere
   II. Stratosphere
 III. Ozonosphere
  IV. Ionosphere

Arrangement by Systems

When neither time nor space seems a logical division, try systems. The automobile may be divided best by systems—the ignition system, the cooling system, the fuel system, and so forth. Similarly a house may be described by systems—the heating system, the plumbing system, the electrical system. The human body is a good example:

The Human Body

    I. The nervous system
   II. The skeletal system
 III. The circulatory system
  IV. The digestive system
   V. Etc.

Arrangement by Qualities or Characteristics

Another method of arranging material is by qualities or characteristics. A machine may be discussed in terms of its economy, durability, safety, or efficiency. A man may be evaluated by his personality traits, his physical abilities, or his mental accomplishments. A chemical may be described by its properties. An institution may be examined in terms of the characteristic services it performs. For example, the Red Cross has disaster services, safety services, nursing services, blood-donating services, and international services.

Characteristics of Semi-conductors

I. They can amplify.
II. They can rectify.
III. They can oscillate.
IV. They can limit.
V. They can count.

Arrangement of the Whole and Its Parts

Many large units have their own tables of organization or structure. The United States government may be divided into three parts: the legislative branch, the executive branch, and the judicial branch. A factory may be divided into tooling, foundry, machine shop, sub-assembly, and final assembly. An engineering school may have depart-ments—electrical, civil, mechanical, chemical, mining. These normal divisions provide the best precedure in arranging material.

The Television Station

I. The commercial division
II. The engineering division
III. The programing division
IV. The production division

Arrangement by Structure and Function

Similar to the whole and its parts is structure and function. Any machine could be described in terms of its structure and its function. A police or fire department or any complex organization or organism can be broken down into structure and function.

A Coffer Dam

I. Detail its structure
II. Detail the function of each part

Arrangement by Cause and Effect

Your material may also be divided by showing why something happens; or a situation may be explained and the results described. For example, a water purifying agent might be discussed by showing the results of using it. Causes of the Civil War could be a basis of organization. The same war might also be discussed in terms of its results or effects. The effects of reducing the speed limit could be examined.

Reducing the Speed Limit

  I. Reduces the number of accidents
 II. Reduces property damage
III. Saves lives

Arrangement by Problem and Solution

Many speeches provide solutions to problems. The audience must be aware that a problem exists before they can examine the solution or solutions offered. Therefore one good method of division is to discuss a problem and then explain the solution. The problems in developing the atomic powered submarine can be matched with their solutions. The problem of juvenile delinquency with its solutions may be proposed by the speaker.

Increasing Enrollments

 I. Problem
    A. Increased birth rate since the depression
    B. Increased percentage of students attending college
II. Solution
    A. Train more teachers
    B. Better salaries for teachers
    C. More and better physical plants

Arrangement by Alternatives

The comparison of good and bad—the contrast of the practical with the impractical, the economical with the costly, the safe with the dangerous, the durable with the flimsy, that which will work with that which won't—is another way of partitioning material. Ideas may be compared and contrasted; so may plans or products.

The Advantages of Education

I. The uneducated man
   A, B, C, etc.—His qualities
II. The educated man
   A, B, C, etc.—His qualities

Most of the foregoing illustrations show the arrangement of materials in the speech to inform. The same methods are applicable to the speech to persuade. Think of the discussions you have had that were either informative or persuasive. Try to lay out your ideas in a tightly organized sequence. The organization of those ideas will usually fit into one or more of the sequences suggested above. Choose the best arrangement—the one that best fits the purpose.

3. ENLIST YOUR LISTENER

The conclusion must *enlist* the attention (speech to inform) and/or support (speech to persuade) of the listener. The conclusion is that part in which all of the information or persuasion is brought to a head clearly and forcefully. The conclusion has a "sense" of termination. Speeches do not just end; they must be concluded. If the listener fails to realize that the speech is concluding, the speaker has not fulfilled the purpose of the conclusion; he has not *enlisted* the listener. In other words, he has not gained the listener's attention and support for his summary, his appeal, or his ending note, whichever the case may be.

The Summary

The summary may be used to impress the essential ideas upon the listener's memory. The basis for a good summary is found in the arrangement of material. Look at the illustrations above. In every case the main headings have been listed. These headings make a summary.

If all the listener carries away from the speech is the summary, he will have the knowledge which he needs most. Following is an example of the summary-type conclusion:

> To sum up, the United States is an underdeveloped area in its educational facilities for Asian and African studies. It is an underdeveloped area in its understanding that Asia and Africa can be outlets for our investment capital and products of industry and agricul-

ture. It is an underdeveloped area in its understanding of the political and basic problems of Asia and Africa. It is an underdeveloped area in its understanding of the great eastern spiritual movements which are now an active force in the history of the world and which were the origins of our own spiritual life. The American Academy of Asian Studies was created in order to bring East and West together. All of these things I have outlined above can be done and the Academy offers its unqualified cooperation with your countries in the accomplishment of these objectives. These suggestions are not based on wishful thinking, but are based on a thorough knowledge of conditions as they exist in the United States today. We are imploring the countries of Asia and Africa to take the lead in helping us to overcome these obstacles.[1]

The Appeal

The appeal is most frequently used in the persuasive speech. It is a forceful plea for belief or action; it is the final plea of what the speaker wants his listener to accept or do. If the listener leaves the speech believing as the speaker believed or acting as the speaker persuaded him to act, the speaker has fulfilled the organizational need of the conclusion. He has enlisted the listener's support.

A good example of this is in the concluding remarks of Thomas E. Murray in a speech given at the Golden Jubilee Dinner of Fordham Law School:

All forms of human power over physical nature are in their own way participations in the almighty power of God, whereby the universe is ruled. Christian man is no Prometheus, stealing fire from the heavens against the will of the gods. The God we worship, the God of Abraham, and the Father of Our Lord Jesus Christ, has not set His will against man's possession of fire—or of nuclear energy. It is His positive will that man should have dominion over nature and control of its forces. This is fundamental. It is likewise fundamental that God wills man to use all his power for God's own purposes, which are always creative, never destructive. Freedom, justice, peace—these are God's purposes. His own omnipotence is set in their service. In their service too man must place his present share in God's omnipotence—that is, his possession of the secret of nuclear energy. These are the fundamentals to which a meeting

---

[1] Louise Gainsborough, "An Underdeveloped Area in the United States," *Vital Speeches*, XXII, No. 2 (November 1, 1955), pp. 61–4.

at the Atomic Summit—at Eniwetok—might impel the peoples of the world to return.[2]

The Ending Note

The ending note may be a quotation which is used to heighten the mood; or it may be a story that pulls the ideas of the speech together. If successful, it enlists the attention and/or the support of the listener.

Dr. Ruth Alexander concluded her remarks in a recent speech this way:

> The semanticists and the sentimentalists have pulled out all the stops. Tricked by words, we weep over criminals, while their victims lie unmourned but bloodied. We have compromised with Evil and pampered Evil-doers, and the fearful prophecy of Woodrow Wilson has come true—
> "It will be a sad day for Society, when sentimentalists are encouraged to suggest all the measures that shall be taken for the benefit of the race."[3]

How do you come to the actual stop—the final ending? Always phrase the final statement well. If it can be done with originality, a restatement of the purpose sentence may be in order. Avoid the "thank you" closing. If your speech was good, the audience should thank you; if it was bad, you shouldn't have spoken. Avoid the false stop; nothing is so annoying as to have a speaker seemingly bring his speech to a close and then start in again. Above all, leave the audience wanting more. Never bore the listener with too much, but end with a really thought-provoking sentence.

4. THE OUTLINE

The outline is the final step in organizing the speech. Outlining is nothing more than the process of putting the organization of your ideas into a written form. Why take the time and effort? For the following reasons: Outlining is the only satisfactory way of getting your ideas down in a logical, meaningful sequence. Outlining forces straight

---

[2] Thomas E. Murray, "Some Things The World Should Understand About 'H' Bombs," *Vital Speeches*, XXII, No. 4 (December 1, 1955), p. 110.
[3] Ruth Alexander, "What Price the Fatted Calf?" *Vital Speeches*, XXII, No. 15 (May 15, 1956), p. 467.

thinking; if the ideas don't fit, the outline will show it. Outlining helps teach you the material; learning relies heavily upon visual and motor stimuli, and the mechanical process of putting the ideas down helps you to learn them. Probably most important, outlining immediately shows up the defects in your organization, your material, and your ideas; this tendency to pinpoint weaknesses is why most people dislike outlining. Every hour you spend in working out an outline will be repaid by a better speech.

KINDS OF OUTLINES

There are three types of outlines, each having a different purpose and a different use. The primary differences between them are a matter of completeness.

The Full Sentence Outline

The full sentence outline expresses every idea in the speech in a full sentence. Note that we said every *idea*, not every *statement*. The full sentence outline is not just an indented speech, for the emphasis in every outline is on ideas, not on phraseology. It is the middle ground between brevity, which sacrifices the thoughtful expression of the idea, and profuseness, which blurs the framework of the speech. For example, if you are going to tell a fable about a horse and a donkey to illustrate a point, it might be outlined as follows:

    A. The horse and the donkey are opposites.
      1. The horse is obedient.
      2. The donkey is balky.

Note that you have not told the story in the outline, but have merely indicated the ideas which are embodied in the story. The story will be detailed and colorful; the outline contains only the precise statement of the idea.

The great advantage of the full sentence outline is that it gives you a complete picture of the ideas of the speech. It is complete enough to stand by itself—that is, someone else can read it and understand the development of the speech.

The Key-Phrase Outline

This type of outline is briefer and condenses the ideas into phrases which are meaningful to you. It is useful to show the overall structure of the speech, but it is not effective in communicating the complete ideas. The advantage of the key-phrase outline lies in its brevity; the disadvantage lies in its incompleteness.

The Topic Outline (Speaker's Notes)

The topic outline is really just the jotting of ideas in an organized form and is often called a key-word outline. Only those key words which will jog the speaker's memory are included. The advantage lies in the brevity; the disadvantage is that the notes neither show the complete structure of the speech nor do they express the ideas. Total assimilation of the material must have taken place before such an outline is of any use.

PRINCIPLES OF OUTLINING

Five major principles of outlining are:

1. Logical subordination
2. One idea per symbol
3. A consistent set of symbols
4. Consistent indentation
5. Complete sentences

Each of these principles contributes to the strength of the outline. Elimination or misuse of any one of them decreases the effectiveness and usefulness of the outline.

Logical Subordination

If you can learn the principle of logical subordination, all of the other principles will fall into place, since they are merely methods of graphically indicating the subordination. Logical subordination is the process of showing the exact relationship of ideas; it is a process for arranging the sub-points logically under the main points. Try it out with the following material.

Suppose you are discussing the advantages of the gas turbine engine. After having searched out the material, you might have the following ideas. Examine them carefully and try to pick out the main headings and sub-headings. Avoid looking at the solution to the puzzle until you have tried to do it yourself.

Gas Turbine Aircraft Engines

1. Jet propulsion engine is light in weight.
2. Propeller engine uses less fuel than a ducted fan engine.
3. Ducted fan engine is heavier than a jet engine.
4. Ducted fan engine is best for medium altitudes, medium ranges.
5. Propeller engine is a low speed engine.
6. Jet propulsion engine has poor fuel efficiency.
7. Propeller engine is best for low altitudes, long ranges.
8. Jet propulsion engine is best for high altitudes, short ranges.
9. Ducted fan engine has greater fuel efficiency than the jet.

Are you aware that each step down in the organizational pattern is a result of narrowing the main heading? The sub-headings support the main headings; they are never equal to it. Now look at the organization of the same material below.

Gas Turbine Aircraft Engines

I. Jet propulsion engine is best for high altitudes, short ranges.
   A. It is light in weight.
   B. It has poor fuel efficiency.
II. Ducted fan engine is best for medium altitudes, medium ranges.
   A. It is heavier than the jet engine.
   B. It has greater fuel efficiency than the jet.
III. Propeller engine is best for low altitudes, long ranges.
   A. It is a low speed engine.
   B. It uses less fuel than the ducted fan engine.

If at the end of a heading you can say "for" or "because," you can be reasonably certain that the next idea is subordinate to and related to the preceding heading. Try this test on the outline you made. Now try it on the outline above.

One Idea per Symbol

Each idea must stand as a separate entity. If you combine several ideas in a sentence or paragraph, the framework or structure of the outline is destroyed; for example, in the following passage several ideas are jumbled together:

The Slide Rule

1. The operation of the slide rule can be learned easily because the operations are simple and exact, being based upon the additions of logarithms. They are efficient. The slide rule can be self taught from one of the many good books on the subject. The average college student can learn the C and D scales in a single evening.

Observe how the sense of structure is lost. If one symbol is used for each idea, the flow of ideas becomes much more apparent.

The Slide Rule

I. The operation of the slide rule can be learned easily.
   A. The operations are simple and exact.
      1. They are based on the addition of logarithms.
      2. They are efficient.
   B. It can be self-taught.
      1. There are many good books on the subject.
      2. The average college student can learn the C and D scales in a single evening.

Use a Consistent Set of Symbols

Keep your symbols consistent. The specific set that you use is not important as long as they show a consistent decrease in the importance of the headings. Never change the system of symbols in the middle of the outline. A typical set of symbols is shown below:

I. — — — — — — — — — — — — — — — — —
   A. — — — — — — — — — — — — — — — —
      1. — — — — — — — — — — — — — — —
      2. — — — — — — — — — — — — — — —
         a. — — — — — — — — — — — — — — —
         b. — — — — — — — — — — — — — — —
   B. — — — — — — — — — — — — — — —
II. — — — — — — — — — — — — — —

Use Consistent Indentations

The structuring of ideas is helped by proper indentation. Correct indentation graphically demonstrates the steps in the organization. Al symbols of the same magnitude should have the same degree of indentation.

A sample skeleton of a proper outline appears below:

Preliminary Considerations

  I. Topic:
  II. General Purpose:
 III. Specific Purpose:

Introduction
ENGAGE THE LISTENER

  I. Opening remarks:
  II. Purpose statement:

Body
ENLIGHTEN, ENCOMPASS, AND ENTHUSE THE LISTENER

  I. First main heading:
    A. Sub-heading:
      1. Support:
      2. Support:
    B. Sub-heading:
      1. Support:
      2. Support:
        a. Details:
        b. Details:
  II. Second main heading:
    A. Sub-heading:
      1. Support:
      2. Support:
    B. Sub-heading:
      1. Support:
      2. Support:

Conclusion
ENLIST THE LISTENER

  I. Summary, appeal, or ending note:

Use Full Sentences

Full sentences provide completeness to ideas. They give all of the necessary information. When several subpoints are grouped in support of a heading, try to word them in similar language to help point up their relationship to the heading. Use simple sentences; a compound sentence often means that another division is necessary.

STEPS IN MAKING A FULL SENTENCE OUTLINE

You have decided on your subject and purpose; you have done your research; you have before you more material than you will need; you have worded your purpose sentence. Now you are ready to organize the speech and prepare the outline.

A. Determine your main headings. Start with the body of the speech, leaving the introduction and conclusion until later. Select the main headings which will support your purpose sentence. Remember that these are the issues or arguments in the persuasive speech; they are the main topics of information in the speech to inform.

B. Arrange your main headings. Set up your main headings according to one of the methods of arrangement suggested earlier in the chapter. List each of the main headings on a separate sheet of paper. This will provide ample space for the supporting points. Word the main headings carefully so that they clearly support the purpose sentence. Use full sentences. Assign a set of symbols to the headings. Sort your material into piles under the main headings. Presumably your material will fit. If it doesn't, either the headings are wrong or you have the wrong material.

C. Determine the sub-headings for the first main heading. The procedure is identical to that of fitting the main headings under the purpose sentence. Arrange the sub-headings under the main heading using one of the methods of arrangement. The method may be a different one from that used in organizing the main headings. Word the sub-headings so that they support the main heading, using full sentences. Assign a set of symbols, and repeat the process for each of the other main headings.

D. Arrange the supporting material under each of the sub-headings. This is merely a continuation of the preceding process until all of the material has been fitted into the outline. By this time you should be aware of any confusions in the organization or any gaps in the material.

E. Arrange the material in the introduction and the conclusion. It is easier to develop the ideal introduction and conclusion after you know in detail what you are going to say in the body of the speech. Make sure that the material in the introduction and conclusion leads easily to and from the body of the speech. Check to make sure that the introduction and conclusion both fulfill the necessary criteria.

F. Prepare the final draft of the outline. If you have followed the above steps, you should have the rough draft of the outline before you. Preparation of the final draft involves checking the organization of the material, the wording of the statements, the consistency of the symbols and indentation, and typing the outline in final form.

PREPARING AND USING A TOPIC OUTLINE (SPEAKER'S NOTES)

The topic outline is composed of the main headings and possibly the sub-headings of the speech—nothing more. Speaking notes must not become a crutch to lean upon. They cannot substitute for complete preparation and assimilation of the material. Notes help jog the speaker's memory; they don't supply the information.

The topic outline is prepared from the full sentence outline. Divide the speech into its three major divisions—the introduction, the body, and the conclusion. Select a key word for each of the main headings and possibly the sub-headings. Place them in a logical outline framework with symbols and indentation and type the outline out on 3" x 5" cards. Never write it in long hand or you will find that you can't read it when you need it. Type out any lengthy quotations which you plan to use and read it so that the listener will know that you have it straight. Memorize famous quotations which the listener already knows.

Place your notes on the speaker's stand or put them in your pocket. Refer to them only when you really need to. Never doodle with them. Never try to hide them. Refer to them before you get stuck. Don't let the notes become a barrier between you and the listener. If the speech is long and complicated, you may need them, otherwise throw them away before you start and practice thinking on your feet.

—Apply the Principles

The importance of organization is obvious. It is one of the keystones of successful living. Regular application of the principles will pay daily dividends.

(1) Prepare an introduction to a five-minute speech on a technical assignment recently completed. Keep in mind that your purpose is to engage the listener. Incorporate the three ways of accomplishing this purpose.

(2) Organize the body of your speech on the topic selected above. Keep in mind the organizational needs of the body—to enlighten, encompass, and enthuse. Outline your organization.

(3) Prepare a conclusion for your speech which enlists attention and support for your ideas. Your conclusion may be a summary, an appeal, or simply an ending note.

(4) Outline the manuscript of a speech given by a leader in your field. Does the outline reflect good organization on the part of the speaker? Does the outline show that the speaker fulfilled the organizational purposes? What weaknesses in the manuscript are evident in the outline?

(5) Prepare and outline a one-point speech on a topic you expect to be consulted on tomorrow. Adapt the organizational needs to the listener(s) you expect to have.

No matter how effective the speaker may be or how responsive the listener may be, communication is never effective without superior content. The visual aid above indicates the speaker's content. What is his general purpose? His specific purpose? Under what circumstances will his speech satisfy the five-point criteria of a good subject? Discuss the scope of his material. (CHAPTER 5) *Courtesy Ohio Fuel Gas Company.*

The visual aid is a carefully selected, thoughtfully prepared, forcefully presented support. Discuss this visual aid. Would it be accepted or rejected? Why? (CHAPTER 7) *Courtesy Battelle Memorial Institute.*

FORMULA F

$$OYS = \frac{O}{5E}$$

(*OYS*) *Organize Your Speech* = Incorporating the (*5E*) *Five E's to Effectiveness* into your (*O*) *Outline*.

Now, apply the formula!

Organize and outline a five-minute speech to persuade. Communicate your speech. Have your listeners rate your speech by using the following scale.

Organizational Competence Scale		
Speaker _____	Rater _____	
Subject _____	Date _____	
1–2 Weak *3 Average* *4–5 Strong*		
Criteria	Rate	Comments
INTRODUCTION — ENGAGE THE LISTENER: Attention getting Subject and purpose stressed Good will created	_____ _____ _____	
BODY — ENLIGHTEN THE LISTENER: Main headings Sub-headings Support	_____ _____ _____	
ENCOMPASS THE LISTENER: Appeal to basic drives Modifying factors Individualized	_____ _____ _____	
ENTHUSE THE LISTENER: Challenging Stimulating Favorable response	_____ _____ _____	
CONCLUSION — ENLIST THE LISTENER: Clear Forceful Gain support, attention	_____ _____ _____	

make your
information clear

You are an engineer. You know Newton's first law, the Law of Inertia; Newton's second law, the Law of Acceleration; Newton's third law, the Law of Equilibrium. You can draw an equilibrium sketch. You know about accelerating force and inertia force. You understand the principles of friction. You can diagram the resolution of forces. You can determine the coefficient of friction. The question remains—can you make this information clear?

You are asked to speak before a group of high school girls on the subject "Why a Sail Boat Sails." Can you do it? Now do you see the problem of making information clear? True, this is an extreme example. However it is quite typical of the problem frequently faced by the technical man who must inform a lay audience. If you can understand the problems of informing the person who knows nothing about the subject and has little education, experience, or background, you will be able to adapt your material to the more advanced listener with ease.

THE PRINCIPLES OF CLARITY

Clarity is primarily a process of adapting your information to the listener. It is the process of simplifying, amplifying, and supporting your ideas.

Clarity Depends on Simplification

Simplification is necessary, but not over-simplification. Present the material on the level of the listener, but not below it. There are a number of ways to make an idea easy to understand.

Adapt your material to the listener's experience. Lead your listener from what he knows to that which he doesn't know. *This can be accomplished if the unknown, the new idea, is tied to the known, old ideas with which the listener is acquainted.* A woman may be mystified by an electrical current and how it flows, but she does understand how water runs through a pipe. Relating the new to the familiar can help understanding.

Organize the material so that the significant points stand out. We have discussed organization at great length. It is mentioned here to emphasize that clear organization is one of the best ways to simplify material.

Generalities are seldom clearly communicated. The abstract concept is hard to understand. Therefore always reduce your ideas to the specific and the concrete. Juvenile delinquency is a vague abstract generality. The particulars such as gang riots, youth killings, property destruction, and arson are specific and concrete. They suddenly make the term understandable and give it new meaning.

Clarity Depends on Amplification and Support

The mere statement of a new idea is seldom enough to bring about understanding. *The idea needs to be amplified and supported.* The listener must have the idea explained and defined; he must be given illustrations and examples of what the idea is and how it works. The idea must be compared with other ideas and examined both quantitatively and qualitatively. In other words, the main points or even the minor points of your speech are not enough, the ideas must be filled in. The framework of a house may indicate the structure, but it is not livable until it has been sheathed, sided, insulated, plastered, painted, wired, plumbed, heated, and roofed. So it is with a speech idea; it must be amplified and supported.

THE WAYS TO CLARITY

There are nine ways to simplify, amplify, and support a speech idea:

1. Explanation
2. Definition
3. Illustration
4. Examples
5. Comparison
6. Statistics
7. Testimony
8. Restatement
9. Visual Aids

Seldom will all of the methods be used to support a single idea. However, in the simple, everyday, one-point speech as many as five or six are commonly employed. Each of the materials of clarity must be selected with a view to interest. Special consideration of the methods and material of interest and vividness is provided in the next chapter.

Explanation

Everyone has made hundreds and thousands of explanations. The primary purpose of the explanation is simplification. The prime question to be asked is "Does it really simplify?" A good example of a typical unclear explanation is the set of instructions you got the last time you asked a native how to find that street or house you were looking for. You were given a list of from ten to twenty turns and distances and wound up not understanding any of them. Explanation involves the analysis of a piece of information. It is primarily a problem in organization; the significant units must be isolated. The greatest danger of the explanation is that it may be dull, and for this reason it is usually coupled with other supporting materials.

Definition

Definition is a special kind of explanation which may be used to simplify and clarify abstract ideas. Sometimes it is used as the basic method of organizing the entire speech: for example, "Democracy:

What It Is." More frequently it is used for clarification of terms or single ideas. The technical speech for the inexpert audience often breaks down because of a lack of definition of terms, or a definition which depends for understanding on knowledge and experience which the listener doesn't have.

There are several methods of definition.

A. Definition by description. A flying saucer can be defined by describing its supposed physical characteristics.

B. Definition by listing the elements that compose the term. Art may be defined by explaining the elements of grace, harmony, unity, proportion, and so forth of which it is composed.

C. Definition by purpose. Many ideas can be understood if we understand their purpose. A strange contraption may well become clear once we understand that it is a well-digger, and its purpose is to dig holes in the ground in search of water.

D. Definition by comparison or contrast. Compare or contrast the new idea with an old and familiar one. Fascism may be defined by contrasting it with democracy and communism. The grid in a vacuum tube may be compared to a faucet.

E. Definition by showing what it is not. Most of the other forms of definition have considered what something is. It may also be defined by determining what it isn't: for example, happiness is more meaningfully defined by showing what is isn't than what it is.

F. Definition by synonyms. Jeopardize may be defined as to "imperil or danger." *Commerce* may be defined as "trade, traffic, barter, exchange."

G. Definition by origin. Many words or ideas can be made clear by showing their root or origin. *Persuasion* can be explained by showing its original meaning—"persuasion—by sweetness."

Illustration

Tell a story that at the same time excites the interest of your listeners and amplifies or supports your point. The characteristics of the illustration are the same as those for a story. The illustration is a narrative—a concrete, specific story of a happening that is detailed enough to be vivid and appealing. It may be either factual or fictional, that is, a story of something that *did* happen or something that *might* happen. It has been said that the ideal speech is one made up of nothing but illustrations. This may be true but it just isn't possible because the well developed illustration is a great time consumer; thus you may have time for only one or two good illustrations per speech.

What makes a good illustration? First, it must support your point. If you have to stretch your imagination to make the story illustrate the idea, find another. Second, tie your illustration to the listener's interests and experiences. If the listeners are women, select illustrations from the woman's world. If they are sports enthusiasts, use the sporting world. One of the great advantages of the illustration is that the listener can identify himself with the people and situations which make it up. Third, make sure the illustration is fresh and interesting. We have said that illustrations take time—make sure the time is well spent. Finally, use as many illustrations as time will permit.

If you are going to talk about "Molding Plastics," tell us the story of how a plastic TV cabinet is made. If you are talking about "Friction Materials for Brakes," tell us the story of how the brake was invented. If you are talking about "Fluid Couplings," illustrate with a story of the competition in building the automatic drive. If you are to talk about "High Altitude Testing," interest us with an illustration of the problems of high altitudes. If your subject is the "Panama Canal," tell us the story of the men who built it.

Examples

The example is similar to the illustration with several notable exceptions. The illustration is narrative; the example is descriptive. The illustration is detailed; the example is brief. The illustration is factual or fictional; the example is always factual.

The strengths of the example are the very qualities which differentiate it from the illustration. It is a brief, factual instance, and brevity makes it possible to use a number of examples together. The primary use of the example is to reinforce the illustration. The illustration may be doubted on the basis that it might be the sole instance of the occurrence, but a cluster of examples strengthens the idea quickly. Let's suppose that you are informing your listeners about the lives saved by the metal safety hat. One illustration, detailed and vivid, can tell the story of the safety hat, but the addition of a half dozen specific examples of other men who owe their lives to the safety hat can reinforce the point.

Your subject, "Historic Flights"; your illustration, the story of Icarus; your examples, each of the key attempts to fly. Your subject, "Die-casting Aluminum"; your illustration, die-castings in an outboard motor; your examples, other uses for aluminum die-castings. Your subject, "Spot Welding"; your illustration, the story of aircraft spot welding; your examples, other uses for spot welding. Your subject, "Television in Industry"; your illustration, the story of using television to inspect merchandise; your examples, other applications of television in industry.

Comparison

Comparisons are particularly meaningful in making ideas clear, vivid, concrete, and specific. Comparison leads the listener from one idea, object, or situation to a similar one. Comparisons can also lead the listener from the known and familiar to the unknown and unfamiliar. Comparison can also help the listener by turning the general and abstract principle into an understandable, concrete, and specific point.

There are four criteria for a satisfactory comparison. First, the comparison must be a logical one; that is, there must be some real basis for comparison. Second, the comparison must be meaningful; it must show a relationship which is helpful to the listener. Third, the comparison should help to make the idea more graphic or vital. Finally, the comparison must be fresh and original, not hackneyed and trite.

Suppose you are describing a landing craft which is 300 feet long. Figures are abstract and not very meaningful to most of us. Three hundred feet—most listeners will respond vaguely and not really understand. But suppose you say, "The landing craft is 300 feet in length —exactly the distance between the goal lines on a football field." Immediately the length of the unknown landing craft takes on meaning. Not only does the comparison make it more meaningful, but it also makes it much more graphic. In addition the description fits within the listener's experience.

In contrast to comparisons found in similar fields is the figurative analogy which compares things in totally dissimilar fields. It is used to make ideas more vivid: for example, the human brain can be compared to a telephone switchboard. The criteria for the analogy are the same as for other comparisons.

Statistics

Statistics show relationships. They reinforce ideas by showing numerically that something is "more than," "less than," "equal to," "a great deal," "not so many," "just a few." To the extent that this knowledge is necessary and speed in presenting it is important, statistics are useful.

The dangers of statistics lie in three directions. First, they are abstract; remember the football field. Second, they are dull; they don't set off ideas in our heads. And third, they are confusing; most people don't comprehend figures very well, especially when they get big and complex.

Several suggestions are in order on their use. Use comparisons and analogies to give the statistics concrete footings. One billion dollars— it means practically nothing. It must be tied to something to help the listener grasp its immensity. What will it buy? How far will it reach? What can it do? The answers will make it meaningful. Interpret the statistics in a form which is within the listener's ability to comprehend. One billion, one hundred and thirty-six million, six hundred and twelve thousand, nine hundred and fifty-one (1,136,-612, 951). If one billion was meaningless, this figure is ridiculous. Simplify your figures by rounding them off. State the preceding as "a little over a billion dollars," and always determine the significance of the figure. In figuring tolerances it may be important to carry figures to the fourth decimal place (0.0001). Compare it to make it real. Avoid such complexity unless exactitude demands it.

Testimony

Testimony is the direct quotation of an expert. This expert testimony provides reinforcement. A testing laboratory's measurement of the efficiency of a machine is generally more acceptable to a listener than data you yourself have accummulated. Giving the sources of your data will reinforce it.

Occasionally direct quotations of experts in your field will both provide clarity and lend support to the idea: for example, an expert professional engineer may show that certain steps represent the best solution to a problem. The listener then is satisfied when you choose those steps for your exposition of the problem.

Restatement

Repetition is repeating an idea in the same way; restatement is repeating an idea in a new way. Both repetition and restatement are used to reinforce your ideas. Summaries provide one satisfactory method of impressing your ideas on the listener. They are simply restatements of the most significant points. Psychological studies have shown that both learning and acceptance depend in part upon repetition. The primary advantage of restatement over straight repetition is derived from the interest value of expressing the idea in a new way. On the other hand, if you wish to gain acceptance, use constant repetition of the idea in the same way. The advertising slogans which are on the tip of your tongue demonstrate the value of repetition.

VISUAL AIDS TO CLARITY

As college teachers of speech we have listened to something over 12,000 student speeches. One of the things that most impresses us is that of the 12,000 those speeches which stand out in our memory are the ones which made extensive use of graphic visual materials. In the same vein, it has been demonstrated that television and the training film, both visual mediums, are more effective teaching devices than the radio, which is merely aural. The speaker will find that the use of visual aids will increase his effectiveness.

The visual aid is especially of importance to you, the technical man. You are working with complex materials which frequently defy adequate verbal description. Your natural habitat is the land of the sketch, the diagram, and the model—use them.

Criteria for Visual Aids

The visual aid is something more than a ragged sketch drawn on the blackboard. It is a carefully selected, thoughtfully prepared, forcefully presented support. It must meet certain standards or be rejected. First, it must serve a distinct and real purpose in your speech. It must not be a superfluous addition, but must actually help the understanding or impact of the idea. It must carry the speech forward. Second, the visual aid should create interest and add appeal and impact to the speech. Many poorly selected, sloppily executed, badly presented visual aids act as a severe distraction and confuse the listener. Third, the visual aid must be adapted to the listener; it must be within his range of experience and his ability to comprehend. Fourth, the visual aid must be clear and understandable in and of itself; it will harm the speech if it merely adds confusion. Fifth, it must be large and bold enough to be seen easily, and if necessary, read by all of the members of the audience.

Kinds of Visual Aids

Watch several educational television programs or even commercials. Here is magnificent use of the visual aid. Of course television has the advantage of being able to picture the visual aids in close-up—a fountain pen may be blown up to the size of a baseball bat—but the types of graphic materials and the method of demonstrating them remain the same. There are fifteen to twenty different types of visual aids but they may be classified into those which are three dimensional and those which are two dimensional. The two dimensional visual aids may be broken down into those which are opaque, such as charts, and those which are transparent, such as slides and films.

A. Three dimensional materials—samples, models, and so forth. The mining student wishes to demonstrate the differences between iron ores of different grades. One of the ways of showing the differences is to look at and perhaps touch samples of the ores. The mechanical engineer has a new type of valve. He brings a cut away of the valve to the meeting. The chemical engineer wishes to illustrate a specific chemical reaction which can be seen. He brings the equipment and conducts the experiment. The aeronautical engineer brings a model plane. The civil engineer brings a model of the terrain to show how a pass can be cut through a hill.

These are examples of good visual aids in the sense that they can actually contribute to the understanding of the principles to be covered in the speech. However they still may not be good demonstration materials. Can they be seen? Are they simple enough?

The ore samples mentioned above do help to clarify the point at

issue, and they are simple enough. But they cannot be seen. The only
way to give the listener a good look at them is to pass them around.
As we shall see later, this is undesirable. A better way to demonstrate
the ore samples is to bring enlarged photographs or an enlarged drawing showing the differences. These enlargements can be seen and
understood.

The same principles apply to the valve. It probably isn't big
enough and is undoubtedly too complicated to be understood without close inspection. Here the speaker would be wise to add a very
simple schematic drawing of the operation of the valve.

In regard to the chemistry experiment there is again the problem
of sight and possibly of time; the speech cannot stop while you try
to make it work. The model airplane raises a different question. Does
it really contribute or is it just a nice model plane? The speaker must
use it in his demonstration, or it will merely stimulate interest and
distract from the discussion. The model of the terrain meets all of the
requirements. It can contribute to the idea; it can be seen; it is simple
enough; it is probably the best way to visually demonstrate the idea.

Apply these same principles to any sample, model, or live demonstration. If your material meets the criteria, by all means use it. It
will help the clarity and interest of your speech immeasurably.

B. *Two dimensional opaques—maps, charts, diagrams, graphs, and
so forth.* There is an almost endless variety of two dimensional materials. They include maps, charts, sketches, diagrams, schematics,
blueprints, drawing plates, line graphs, bar graphs, pie graphs, picto-
graphs, cartoons, and photographs. Before using them, you must ask
the questions: Do they really contribute? Can they be seen? Are they
simple enough?

Most commercially prepared maps, charts, and diagrams are unsatisfactory for demonstration purposes. Perhaps some examples of
miserable selection will give you the idea.

The subject was "The Operation of a Milling Machine." The
speaker brought a 3′ by 4′ parts chart. The chart showed a photograph
of the milling machine with arrows indicating the various parts. By
actual count there were two hundred and sixty-four labels indicating parts and their numbers. The chart did not show the operation;
it was not meant to show it. Since nothing of significance could be
seen, the chart only confused and distracted the listeners.

The subject was "The St. Lawrence Waterway." The speaker

brought along a standard road map of the United States. It was about 2′ x 3′ in size. One barely discernable red line showed the waterway. When he stated, "The greatest problems lie at Niagara Falls," his thumb covered most of the state of New York. The map was distracting, hard to see, and very confusing.

The subject was "The Super Heterodyne Circuit." The visual aid was a schematic peeled off the back of a radio set. The results were worse than if it hadn't been used at all—too complex, too small.

The subject was "Homogenized Milk." The graphic material was six 3″ x 4″ photographs. The photographs were plates from two standard sized textbooks. They appeared to the nearest spectator as vague designs; the most distant viewer saw six gray rectangles.

Perhaps the preceding may sound discouraging. It shouldn't. The purpose is to emphasize that care must be made in the selection of materials. You now know the principles of selection—apply them.

C. Two dimensional transparencies—slides, film strips, films, and so forth. Projections are a totally different class of visual material. As they can be enlarged to any given dimensions, they have the advantage of size. They have the advantage of actuality since the listener may be transported to the site of the operation. They have the disadvantage of cumbersome equipment, a darkened room, and the need for an operator. The advantages and disadvantages must be carefully weighed.

Projectors, projectionists, picture screens, cables, darkened windows are all distractions. Therefore, the use of slide and film must be limited to materials that contribute vitally to the understanding of the idea. Well selected, they are magnificent; poorly selected, they destroy the speech.

Select materials which are pertinent but need further explanation and interpretation by you. A doctor was speaking on the subject of cancer. He showed an excellent film on the development of cancer in the human body, which lasted about five minutes. After the film he proceeded to cover exactly the same ground as the film. Since the film did it much better, there was no reason for his talk. In fact the film was so exciting that nothing he could have said would ever have equalled it in audience interest. Here the film did not help the speech; it killed it.

There is a great tendency to overuse projected material. This probably stems from the fact that setting it up is a lot of trouble, and the speaker feels that he might just as well get some use out of it. Don't let your speech become a series of lantern slides with comments. Use the method sparingly to emphasize and dramatize your points.

Making Visual Aids

In most instances you will have to make your own visual aids. In this way you can include exactly what you wish to include and ex-

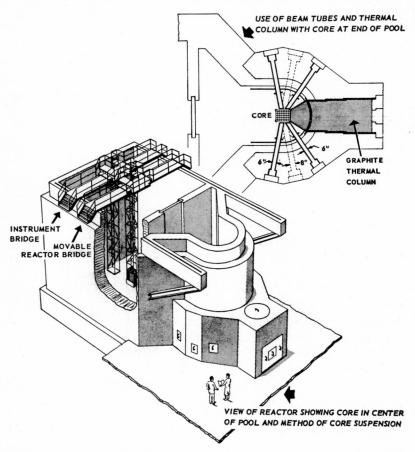

Fig. 7. A Simple Schematic Drawing. Whenever possible always show the complex in a simple schematic drawing. Here is a sample schematic of a portion of the nuclear reactor built by the Battelle Memorial Institute.

clude all elements which don't contribute to your point. Observe the following principles and you will have no trouble.

A. Make it simple. Simplicity is of two types: simplicity of content and simplicity of style and layout. Make the visual aid for the listeners who are going to see it. Include only the elements which are absolutely necessary to get the information across. In a map provide the necessary frame of reference such as the outline of a state and add the information you want to cover. In a sketch, diagram, or schematic (see Figure 7) keep the key elements and discard the superfluous ones. With a graph choose the kind of graph which will best illustrate your information. (See Figure 8) The line graph is most effective for showing trends such as the rise and fall of the stock market. The bar graph is good for simple comparisons such as the number of children in the American family as opposed to the number in the British family. The pie graph is useful in showing the divisions within a whole such as the way your tax dollar is spent. The pictogram or pictograph introduces the additional interest of figures and objects. It is not as exact as the other methods, but it is more attention getting.

The blueprint and drawing plate are almost always undesirable in their native state. Simplify and enlarge them. Simplicity of layout is just as important as simplicity of content. Get rid of the extra frills. Simplify the lines and straighten out the curves; make your demonstration as simple as dollars and doughnuts.

B. Make it large enough to see. Assuming that your material is simple and uncluttered, there is still the problem of making it large enough. You can tell easily enough if something can be seen; just walk away from it to the distance at which the farthest member of your audience will be sitting, and take a look. If you are disappointed with the view, find a larger piece of paper; poster board in 30″ x 40″ sheets is available at most supply stores.

Test out the thickness of your lines. They should be at least ⅛″ wide if they are to be seen at any distance. Remember that as you increase the scale of your drawings, the thickness of the lines must change in scale too. If you use colors, work out color contrasts that will really stand out.

Be particularly careful about labeling the parts of the drawing. The label that can't be seen is worse than none at all. Use as few labels

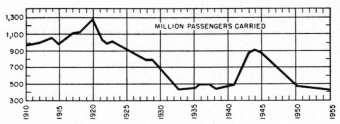

(a) Line graph showing number of revenue railroad passengers by years.

(b) Pie graph showing breakdown of federal income dollar.

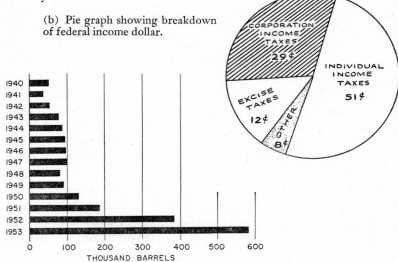

(c) Bar graph showing daily average crude oil production in Iraq.

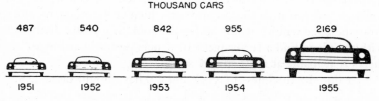

(d) Pictograph showing factory sales of "hard-top" coupes and sedans.

Fig. 8.

Sources: (a) S. J. Lasley and M. F. Mudd, *The New Applied Mathematics,* 5th ed., Englewood Cliffs, N.J., Prentice-Hall, Inc., 1958; (c) Standard Oil Company of New Jersey; (d) *1956 Statistical Abstract of the United States.*

as possible, just enough to orient the parts. Blow up the scale of your labels just as you do the other elements.

Do sectional blowups of complicated units which must be included. This method should fit neatly into your speech organization. You start with the whole and then lead your listener to a consideration of the parts.

C. Make it neat. Every engineer has had a course in mechanical drawing; every engineer has been taught to prepare a report; every engineer has been taught that neatness is mandatory. This training prepares you for constructing and using visual aids. The listeners judge you as much by the kind of materials you use as by the way you look or sound. Companies spend thousands of dollars preparing presentations of their products; you can afford to spend some time on your product, yourself, and your speech.

Using Visual Aids

Good selection or preparation of visual materials can be ruined by poor presentation. Assimilate the following principles before you try your hand at graphic materials.

A. Prepare it before hand. If you are a high speed artist, you may disregard the following. Most of you are draftsmen, not artists; therefore don't try to chalk-talk—it is a specialized art. Think of the miserable art work turned out by most teachers, and you will understand the problem. Sketches dashed on the blackboard are usually worse than none at all. If you must use a blackboard (reasons for not using it in a moment), put your drawings on beforehand and take the time to do them well.

B. Show it only when needed. Bring your visual material into the view of the audience when you are ready to use it, not before. The model or drawing that sits before the audience draws attention to itself and distracts from the speech. If you use a blackboard, cover your material with a blank piece of paper. This will create interest and curiosity, and the listeners will have to wait until you choose to unveil it.

Plan in advance how you are going to display your visual material. Your speech can't wait while you break your thumbnails trying to push thumb tacks into hard wood or wrestle with scotch tape that won't stick to a dirty surface.

C. Position it correctly. Place the visual material so that you can stand beside it or slightly behind it when you speak. This is the most important reason for not using a blackboard. It is almost impossible to demonstrate on a blackboard without turning your back to the listeners.

D. Maintain contact with the listeners. You can get others to look where you look; therefore, if you talk to the visual material, the listeners will look there. If you talk to the listener, he will look at you. Ideally you should look at the model or the graph only when you want the listener to look at it. Many speakers become preoccupied with the visual aid and lose all touch with their audience.

E. Remove it when you are finished with it. After you are through talking about the sample or the sketch, get rid of it immediately. If you don't, both you and the listener will tend to be distracted by it. This is another reason for not using a blackboard; you can't afford the time to erase your drawing.

F. Keep it in your possession. Remember the ore samples we talked about earlier? It might seem like a good idea to pass them around and let the audience have a closer look. But suppose that you pass the the sample to the first member of the audience just as you begin to discuss the structure of the ore. As soon as you start speaking about other things, the sample becomes irrelevant. The trouble is that it will still be moving through the audience, attracting a small circle of attention to itself like a magnet in a field of iron filings. Each time it stops it takes someone away from your speech. The same principle holds with anything else you might consider passing—photographs, outlines, brochures, and the like.

Visual aids can serve to give your speech impact, interest, and clarity. They take time to select and prepare and they demand care in their presentation. Good ones are worth every bit of it.

—Apply the Principles

This chapter has considered ways to make information clear. Nine methods have been discussed. Observe how others use them, and use them yourself.

Observation

(1) Listen to your instructor, your boss, or your friend when

any of them tries to make information clear to you. Are you able to understand? Why? Why not? Was it interesting?

(2) Check the number of illustrations, examples, and comparisons which were used. Were they good ones? Original? Vital? To the point? How might you have done better?

(3) Watch a television demonstration or commercial which employs visual aids (some visual aid other than a pretty girl). Judge the effectiveness. Was the closeup shot needed to make the material visible? How could it have been handled without closeups? Was the material effective? Why? Why not? Did it tell a story? How?

Practice

(1) Try out the principles of clarity in your next attempt to inform. Can they be used in demonstrating how to do a math problem? A physics problem? A history lesson?

(2) Select a subject about which you would like to give information. Make it a one-point speech. Use at least five of the materials of clarity. Introduce at least one visual aid. Give the speech. Test some of your listeners afterward to see whether or not they really got the information.

FORMULA G

$MYIC = 9WC$

(*MYIC*) *Make Your Information Clear* = Developing the (*9WC*) *Nine Ways to Clarity* as they are needed. (Explanation, Definition, Illustration, Examples, Comparison, Statistics, Testimony, Restatement, Visual Aids.)

Now, apply the formula!

Prepare a five-minute speech to inform. Use the check list below as a guide to the clarity of your information.

Guide to Clarity
A Check List

EXPLANATION:

Does it simplify? _____
Does it analyze? _____
Is it organized? _____
Is it interesting? _____

COMPARISON:

Is it logical? _____
Is it meaningful? _____
Graphic or vital? _____
Is it organized? _____

DEFINITION:

Does it clarify? _____
Does it simplify? _____
Is it meaningful? _____
Is it complete? _____

STATISTICS:

Show relationships? _____
Do they reinforce? _____
Are they necessary? ____
Efficiently used? _____

ILLUSTRATION:

Does it excite? _____
Does it amplify? _____
Does it support? _____
Adapted to listener? ____

TESTIMONY:

Does it reinforce? _____
Is it authoritative? _____
Does it clarify? _____
Does it lend support? ____

EXAMPLES:

Is it descriptive? _____
Is it brief? _____
Is it factual? _____
Does it reinforce? _____

RESTATEMENT:

Does it reinforce? _____
Is it pertinent? _____
Does it add interest? ____
Contain newness? _____

VISUAL AIDS:

Does it serve distinct purpose? _____
Does it create interest, appeal, impact? _____
Is it adapted to listener? _____
Is it clear and understandable? _____
Is it clearly visible? _____

make your
information interesting

Third down and goal to go . . . you brace yourself in your seat
. . . the quarterback barks the signals . . . you stare tensely at the
field . . . shift to a single wing to the right . . . you hold your
breath . . . the ball is snapped . . . the fullback squirms through
the off-tackle slot . . . you rise . . . the line backer misses . . . a
tense scream forms in your throat . . . the fullback is smothered
under a mountain of players . . . you hang in mid air . . . the ref-
eree raises his arms . . . you scream, jump, slap your neighbor on
the back . . . then and only then do you relax . . . weariness creeps
over you. This is attention—vital, dynamic, active attention.

Perhaps it is too much to expect this intensity of attention in the
speaking situation, though many great speakers have gripped their
audiences. Nonetheless, without attention your speech will fail. Your
audience may not sit on the edges of their chairs; but they must perceive what you are saying, and without attention perception is impossible. Your information may be beautifully amplified and supported; it may be completely clear. But unless you arouse your listener's interest, you might as well not speak. What is attention? How
does it operate? How can I hold it? You must know the answers to
these questions if you are to succeed.

141

DEFINITION OF ATTENTION

There are three aspects of attention which are of particular importance to the speaker: (1) it is a process of concentration; (2) it lasts for a short time; (3) it is fatiguing.

Attention Is a Concentrating Process

As you sit in the football stadium or the lecture hall, thousands of stimuli impinge upon your system—the heat of the day, the brightness of the light, the idea the speaker is expressing, the tightness of your belt, the hardness of the seat, the weariness after a long day, your tooth that aches slightly, the sound of a distant truck, the sound of the speaker's voice, the itching of your scalp, the movement of the man in front of you, *ad infinitum*. Some of the stimuli are internal sensations; some are external. The sensations are always there, but you are not aware of all of them when you are paying attention. Attention is a focusing process which enables you to select one out of many stimuli for special notice. Which one do you attend? The one which is dominant at the moment. Suppose you're out with the most wonderful girl in the world, and you have a pounding headache. Sometimes you are aware of your throbbing head; during those moments it is the dominant stimulus, and you are not aware of the girl. On the other hand, there will be those times when you pay such attention to your girl that you "forget" the headache. What is the speaker's problem? Simply to make sure that the stimulus of his voice, actions, and ideas is dominant.

Attention Is Brief

How long can you pay absolute attention to the most beautiful girl in the world? An hour? A minute? Ten seconds? The answer is less than ten seconds, probably about three to five. Suppose I were to tell you that your chair was wired for sufficient current to kill you and that you must pay absolute attention to what you are reading or be electrocuted. You wouldn't last very long because you would immediately give your attention to the question of whether what I said was true; that is not paying attention to the reading.

The attention span is very short, but you can recall whole paragraphs from a speech you have never heard before because you have paid attention to the speaker often enough to still be able to fill in the pattern with those things that were missed. Can you think of times you thought you were paying attention and suddenly realized that you didn't know what the speaker was talking about? Your attention hopped around, becoming aware of other stimuli, to the extent that the pattern with those things that were missed. Can you think of times can't hold attention all the time or for more than a few minutes at a time, he must provide a sufficiently powerful stimulus to attract the listener frequently enough to maintain the pattern of his message.

Attention Is Fatiguing

Class periods in school normally run from forty-five to fifty minutes because it is almost impossible to pay attention to one subject for a longer time. Think of how tired you are after you have paid careful attention for any period of time. Paying attention is hard work. You may enjoy doing it sometimes; nevertheless it is wearying. What does this mean to the speaker? First, the briefer his remarks, the better his chance of holding his audience. Second, no speech can afford to be all climax. The most important ideas must be made incisive and impelling; others must be subordinate.

Attention and Interest

Attention and interest are not quite the same thing. Attention is a concentrating process while interest is an attitude. The fact that we are interested in something tends to make it easier for us to pay attention to it. Or in reverse, those things which catch our attention arouse our interest. For our present purposes, however, we will consider the two terms interchangeable.

Psychologists have long since reached comparative agreement on the ways to catch attention and arouse interest. It can be done by: (1) using the psychological devices which attract attention, (2) intensifying the stimulus of your speaking through the use of strong sensory appeals, (3) choosing language which has listener impact. There is, of course, a great deal of overlapping among the methods. For example, one of the ways to appeal to the senses is to select your language carefully. Similarly, strong sensory appeal may include one or more of the psychological devices of attention. In every case the interest device, the sensory appeal, or the language must be associated with and attached to your message or the attention you arouse will not serve your interests.

THE TOOLS OF INTEREST

All those who wish to hold attention, be they speakers, advertisers, sports promoters, or writers, are aware that man attends to certain factors to the exclusion of others. These details are eight in number.

1. Self-interest
2. The animate
3. The familiar
4. The novel
5. The real and concrete
6. The uncertain
7. The controversial
8. The humorous

Self-Interest

In describing the listener we have said that he is primarily interested in himself. Therefore, it is logical that those things which affect him and his well being should be a focal point for his attention. Careful rereading of Chapter 4, "Understand Your Listener," will insure your awareness of the listener's self-concern. The specific devices for appealing to the listener's self-interest are discussed in Chapter 9, "Learn to Persuade."

Suffice it to say here that self-interest is the most powerful weapon in your arsenal for arousing interest and getting the response you desire, whether your speech is to interest, to inform, or to persuade.

The Animate

Anything which has life or movement will catch and hold attention. Whenever the listener is faced with a choice of responding to that which is moving or that which is still, his attention involuntarily fastens on the moving. Two frogs are in a box: one is plaster; the other is alive. Which do you watch? Two watches are in an advertising display: one is strapped to a board; the other is mechanically dunked in a bowl of water. Which do you watch? Two identical new Cadillacs are parked by a stop sign: one is still; the other jumps ahead as the light changes. To which do you attend? A television news program has still pictures and motion pictures—which arouses the most interest?

How can you employ the animate? Your attitude can arouse interest through its vitality and enthusiasm. Your physical forcefulness can hold attention by activity and movement on the platform. Your visual aids can arouse interest, particularly if they show or have movement. The development of your speech content can attract attention if it gives the impression of moving forward.

The Familiar

We like, trust, and are interested in the things we know. We cling to the symbols of the past. We enjoy and revere the legends and the myths of our fathers. We prefer life among those we know rather than among strangers, even though the strangers may be more interesting. The familiar has the appeal of belonging. We are interested in it. The familiar also provides the bases for new knowledge. In discussing the comparison, it was suggested that the known could be the bridge to the unknown. A comparison of the centrifuge to the spin dryer immediately permits most listeners to identify the subject with themselves.

It must be admitted, however, that the familiar may become boring unless it is used well. Worn out, trite, overused, hackneyed, are all terms applied to the familiar when it represents the same old thing done in the same old way. Therefore, apply the familiar with freshness and originality.

The Novel

Freshness and originality were the last words of the preceding paragraph. They imply novelty. The listener is interested in anything that is new and different. Cartoonist Rube Goldberg has made a handsome living from applying a new twist to old ideas. Novelty is the life blood of the entertainment and advertising industries. If you can find new illustrations, comparisons, examples, or statistics and present them in a new way, your audience will respond with rapt attention.

The Real and Concrete

Visual aids lend great impact largely because they are real and tangible. They can be seen and touched. They are actual. They are concrete. Perhaps the following illustration may be meaningful. Some years ago three speeches in three different engineering speech classes dealt with the subject of the motorcycle. In one class the speaker described the motorcycle in glowing detail—his language was well chosen and he held the listeners' interest through language alone. In a second class, the speaker brought an advertising poster which showed the motorcycle in full color. His choice of language was as vivid as his poster. The interest of this audience was much greater than that of the first. In a third class, the speaker rolled in a glistening red four-cylinder Indian Scout. The audience was transfixed. Late in his demonstration the speaker stepped astride the motorcycle and with a single kick started it. The sense of reality was complete as the machine purred before the group.

This is, of course, a somewhat extreme illustration; but the point is clear. Everytime that you can introduce by language or action the real and the concrete in place of the abstract and general you will capture the attention of your audience. Talk about real events; refer to specific people; describe actual occurrences; give the details. Encourage the audience to relive the event because of the reality of its presentation.

Another factor closely related to reality and concreteness is nearness or proximity. Have you ever noticed how the advertiser sets the picture of his product in the foreground of the ad. You feel that you can almost pick it up; it is so near and so real. Reference to the audience was one of the methods suggested for introducing a speech. This technique relies on the interest we have for things close at hand. Reference to the morning paper, the room where you are speaking, the preceding speaker or his topic—all create interest because of their proximity or their timely relationship.

The Uncertain

The motion picture and the play are built on suspense. The excitement stems from your not knowing how it will come out, who will win. To a lesser degree the same device is useful to the speaker. Raise questions in the listener's mind. How can that be? What will happen now? How does the darn thing work?

A word of caution: don't try to arouse curiosity and create suspense unless the material is worth it. There is always the possibility that uncertainty may resolve itself into a "so what?" attitude. Uncertainty can create and heighten interest only if there is a real pot of gold at the end of the trail.

The Controversial

"Fight! Fight! Look! A fight!" Everybody turns to watch. Two cars crash in the middle of the night; in minutes dozens of people appear from nowhere. A fire engine or squad car's siren wails in the distance. Immediately your attention is caught; you think about going; perhaps you jump in the car and go. Why? Because one of the prime movers of interest is conflict.

In the speech we can catch attention by introducing controversy or by relating illustrations and examples which show conflict. Controversy implies disagreement. Disagreement involves conflict. Conflict holds attention. Controversal subjects hold attention. The newspapers merely mention agreements, but they detail controversies. In persuasive speeches controversy has unlimited possibilities. In the speech to inform it may be introduced through illustrations and stories of the struggles and battles behind the inventions and the processes.

The Humorous

Humor was suggested as one of the ways to introduce a speech because it will catch attention and arouse interest. It was suggested that the humor be related to the subject; that it be funny; that it be tailored for the particular listeners; that it be in good taste.

What is humor? Humor is based on incongruity, that is, we are amused by the fitting together of things that don't belong together. The tall man and the short man, the fat lady and her skinny husband, the slip on the banana peel, the pun, the word play of the witticism— all exploit the incongruous.

The actual materials of humor are (1) exaggeration, (2) surprise, (3) superiority, (4) escape. Start with two elements that don't fit, exaggerate them and they become funny. Imagine Jerry Lewis as a boxer. Lead the listener to expect one ending and then surprise him with another. Two men greet each other enthusiastically from a distance, they rush toward and *pass* each other into the arms of two other people. Let the listener feel superior to his superiors. Dorothy Bond's 'Boss' cartoons are based on ridicule. The ever-popular student take-off lampoons the faculty member. Build up the tension in a situation; then let the listener escape and he will laugh.

Let humor be the spice of the speech not the main course. Try to make your attempts at humor fresh and original. Don't tell the story that caused grandfather to kick the slats out of his crib. Remember that humor can be amusing and arouse interest without the belly laugh that shakes the building. Don't over-reach your own capabilities. Play it gently; then if the audience doesn't get it, you won't be hurt.

Integrate the Tools of Interest

Tie the eight tools of interest into your material. Don't use them in isolation from the body of your material. Never try to hold attention, then clarify, then hold attention, and so forth. The method of clarification must be selected and developed so that it includes the tools of interest.

WAYS TO APPEAL TO THE SENSES

Listeners like all other human beings and animals live by their senses. Appeals that stir the listener's sense of sight, hearing, touch, taste and smell catch his attention, hold his interest and stimulate him to respond. Unlike the eight tools of interest, appeals to the senses may be used as isolated bits. Self interest, the animate, the familiar, and so forth—each may be heightened by including an appeal to one or more of the senses.

Direct Appeal to the Senses

Actual sights and sounds, tastes and smells may be introduced into your speech. These are direct external appeals. The listener actually experiences the sensation. For example, if you discuss "Flying a Jet," you might use a sound motion picture of a jet in action as a visual aid. The sights and sounds of the jet plane would make a deep sensory impression on the listener. He could tell from his own sensory experience what it would be like to fly a jet. This is an example of heightening the real (the concrete) by appealing to the senses of sight and hearing.

Appealing to the Imagination

A second and frequently more practical method of appealing to the senses is by stirring the imagination. Through the careful use of vivid language the listener can see in his mind's eye and hear in his mind's ear the actions and sounds of the jet fighter.

Imagination may be defined as "the re-creation of a sensation." Are you aware that you can't imagine anything without having experienced it? "Oh no," you say, "I haven't even been in a jet, yet I can imagine it." Yes, you can; you do it by putting together in a new form sensations you have already experienced. You haven't been in a jet, but you have heard them flying overhead. You have sat in a plane at the movies. You put the old sensations together and synthesize the new imaginative experience. You may be all wrong, but nevertheless you can imagine it. Let's simplify the illustration. Suppose you are asked to picture a "purple cow." You have never seen one, but you can imagine it easily. You have experienced "purple" and "cow." You synthesize or put them together in the new imaginative experience "purple cow." The point of this discussion is that if you expect to stir the imaginations of your audience you must provide them with a basis in experiences either actual or vicarious that they have already had. *Remember! Any of the eight ways to arouse interest can be heightened by including an appeal to one or more of the senses described below.*

A. Imagery of sight. Word pictures which create vivid scenes in our minds are the most frequently used images. Illustrations can be loaded with appealing language which leads the listener to experience in his imagination as deeply as he would in the actual situation. Most engineers think of science and engineering as problems of slide rule and formula, but there is another side. Can you describe the violence and beauty of a Tesla coil? Could you picture for the listener the awesome beauty of Boulder Dam? Could you make the operation of the spectograph interesting and exciting? Pictures in the listener's mind can capture his interest.

B. *Imagery of hearing*. The lonesome whine of a generator; the guttural roar of water rushing through a sluice gate; the strident crackle of a spark gap; the muted groan of a beam under stress; the explosive crack of small arms ammunition—these are living sound pictures. They are the stuff of which science is made. Use vivid colorful language to make your information vital and exciting.

C. *Imagery of touch*. Texture is one form of tactual imagery. Sensations of heat and cold are the other. Frequently we perceive through our imagined touch. Think of the emotional meanings of texture—the slick sheen of satin, the rough feel of tweed. Think of the sensations of heat and cold—the burning glow of the open hearth, the vicious cold of the Arctic. Even in the sense of touch, science and engineering can be manifested.

D. *Imagery of taste*. Describe grandmother's old-fashioned Thanksgiving dinner. Done well, your listener's mouth will water. He can be attracted by the imagery of palatable tastes; repulsed by vile tastes. Search out the language of taste and use it to excite your audience.

E. *Imagery of smell*. Much like the imagery of taste but frequently more powerful, the sensation of smell can also be used to stir up images in your listener's mind.

F. *Imagery of muscle tension*. Known as kinesthetic imagery, muscle tension is not one of the five senses. Yet descriptions of violent activity can be used to actually arouse muscular responses in the listener. With exciting description the listener can be made to empathize, to feel into, to become a part of the experience.

G. *Imagery of internal sensation*. Did you know that an average audience can be so caught up in a description that certain members may be made physically ill? It has been proved. Man is suggestible. He can be made to experience any of the human emotions if the speaker is good enough.

You may say, "Yes, but this for the orators, not for me." Don't fool yourself. With a little care in selecting the language which can forcefully and graphically describe, you can change a dull speech into an interesting one. (See Appendix B for examples of sensory appeals.) Good bread-and-butter speaking depends upon capitalizing on all of the assets of the speech situation; vivid appeal to the imagination is one of the speaker's strongest assets.

Three dimensional materials. How do these titanium metal products serve as a visual aid? What is their contribution to the speaking situation? How do they meet the criteria for visual aids? (CHAPTER 7) *Courtesy Battelle Memorial Institute.*

Two dimensional opaques. What are the advantages and disadvantages of this visual aid? What observations can be made about the speaker? What effect might this visual aid have on the speaking situation? (CHAPTER 7) *Courtesy Battelle Memorial Institute.*

CHOOSING LANGUAGE WITH APPEAL

Your appeal to imagination, your use of the tools of interest, indeed, your entire speech, depends upon the careful selection of language. Your language must communicate; that is, it must mean the same thing to your listener that it does to you. Your language must stimulate; it must set off responses in your listener. Language should be (1) accurate and (2) stimulating.

Use Accurate Language

Language is the science of symbols. Words stand for things; they are not the things themselves. *Dog* is a symbol; it isn't a particular animal. It is a classification which represents all the animals of a certain type. If it communicates meaning to your listener, it does so because he has the same understanding of the symbol that you do; and in this case he probably does. Now try the word *brotherhood*. You and your listener may have more trouble. Your understanding of the word may be quite different from your listener's. His experiences, his training, his background, may be quite different from your own. How can exactness or accuracy be obtained? Complete accuracy can't be attained because your listener doesn't have the same background of experiences that you do. But it can be strengthened.

Adapt your language to your listener's experience. Select words which you have good reason to believe he understands and will respond to as you do. One of the surest ways to accomplish this is to use the language of the five senses. His experiences will be similar to yours.

Adapt your language to your purpose. Make certain that your words always point the way to an understanding of your idea. Stop and define words which may be confusing. Cut out the phrases which sound nice but mean little or nothing. They merely confuse.

Be concrete. Avoid generalities. Talk in terms of the actual and individual rather than the general. Can you sense the difference between *dog* and *doberman pincer?* One is a general class; the other is the symbol for a specific kind.

Be simple. Avoid complex language. Use the two syllable rather than the five syllable word. Use idiomatic language that everyone can understand.

Be careful of slang. Colloquial everyday language, yes—but not slang. It is miserably overused. Slang is so general that it frequently has lost its meaning. "Gee, that's swell!" Stop and think for a moment of what this phrase means. Practically nothing. Another reason for avoiding slang is that it tags you as a speaker who won't go to the trouble to find language that really expresses what you mean.

Define technical language. The jargon of the trade is usable when you are talking to the trade, but only then. Never trip up the unsuspecting layman with technical terms. Avoid them or define them in terms which you know he can understand.

Use Stimulating Language

Language can stimulate in two ways. It may appeal to the senses, and it may set off pleasant or unpleasant associations. Reread the material on appealing to the imagination. The keys to sensory impact lie in the language you choose.

The second type of stimulation comes from the associations which are set off in the listener. He responds positively or negatively to the word because of his attitudes and feelings about it. Words which set off associations are called "loaded" words. The actual meaning of the word is called the denotative meaning; the pleasant or unpleasant association which it causes is called the connotative meaning. For example, we respond favorably to *truth, loyalty, freedom, brotherhood, justice, democracy*. Frequently we don't really understand what they mean, but the association is pleasant. In the same manner we respond negatively to *dictatorship, communism, hyprocrisy, oppression, persecution, intolerance*.

The loaded word is used extensively by the salesman and the advertiser. He tries to choose language which will bring forth a pleasant response to his product. Take the subject of selling coffee. Coffee may be *strong* or *weak*. But most listeners would say that they don't want strong coffee and they certainly don't want weak coffee. The association is unpleasant. The adjectives the advertiser uses are *mild* and *full-bodied*. Here the associations are pleasant. We want our coffee mild and full-bodied. Note that the denotative meanings are similar. It is the connotative meaning which has changed. You must select language which will stimulate the response you desire.

The concluding comments from a speech given by Herbert Hoover represent accurate and stimulating language. It would be difficult, indeed, for his words to result in misunderstanding or confusion.

And there are mighty hopes before us.

The last dozen years have seen advances in science, invention and technology which amount almost to revolution in our life and world relations.

If we maintain free minds, free spirits, and direct our steps aright, still other new horizons and new frontiers will open to us. New scientific discoveries, new inventions and new applications of old knowledge will come to us daily.

These new frontiers give us other blessings. Not only have they taken great burdens from the backs of men and expanded the standards of living of all our people. They have opened new opportunities and new areas of adventure and enterprise. They open new vistas of beauty. They also unfold the wonders of the atom and the heavens. Daily they prove the reality of an all-wise Supreme Giver of Law.[1]

——Apply the Principles

Anyone can catch attention if he doesn't care how he does it. We hope that when you apply the principles of interest, you will avoid the technique used by a student speaker who stepped before the class and said, "I wish to talk today about cherries— cherry bombs, that is." At which point he lit a cherry bomb firecracker and tossed it into the audience. He got the attention of his listeners. Two of them went to the student infirmary with burns. However, he didn't establish much good will and certainly didn't gain his purpose.

(1) Applying the principles of attention, imagery, and language, develop a speech to inform depending upon both description and exposition.

(2) Select as your subject the description of an object or a location. Select your object from either the field of art or science.

(3) Employ some kind of visual aid which will increase the clarity and the impact of your material. Do not bring the

[1] Herbert Hoover, "World Experience with the Karl Marx Way of Life," *Vital Speeches,* XXII, No. 15 (May 15, 1956), p. 470.

object itself. Depend upon verbal stimulation and support
to describe it. The visual aid might be a blowup of a part
of the object, or a chart of the characteristics of the object,
or a diagram showing the use of the object.

(4) Introduce at least four of the tools of interest into the speech.
Heighten these tools of interest by employing three different kinds of imagery. Make your language rich and vibrant.

FORMULA H

$$MYII = \frac{TI}{SA} + ASL$$

(*MYII*) *Make Your Information Interesting* = Incorporating (*SA*) *Sensory Appeals* into the (*TI*) *Tools of Interest* necessary to the speech. Add (*ASL*) *Accurate and Stimulating Language.*

Now, apply the formula!

Have your listeners respond to your next speech by using the Information Barometer below. Your listeners will react to each of the divisions in the body of your speech by placing a dot in the center of the appropriate square. It is your responsibility to make sure that each of your main ideas is all-inclusive. (Example: A dot in the square opposite 9 in the A column indicates a *High* level of development of the tools of interest used. A dot in the square opposite 5 in the C column indicates a *Medium* development of language and so forth.) *Connect the dots with lines and you have an Information Barometer showing the elevations of interest throughout the body of your speech.*

Information Barometer *Elevations of Interest*											
1–3 Low			*4–6 Medium*			*7–9 High*					
SCORE 1–9	Information of First Heading			Information of Second Heading			Information of Third Heading			Information of Fourth Heading		
9												
8												
7												
6												
5												
4												
3												
2												
1												
CRITERIA A B C	A	B	C	A	B	C	A	B	C	A	B	C
Criteria: A = The tools of interest; B = sensory appeals; C = language											

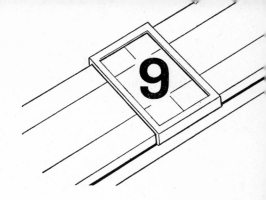

learn to persuade

As a TECHNICAL man, most of your speaking life is devoted to exposition. Yet daily you are faced with the need to persuade. You must sell yourself and your ideas. Your personal and professional needs and desires are such that you must control the thoughts and actions of others. Knowledge of the methods of persuasion will enable you to do it simply and effectively.

The process of leading the listener to want to believe you or do what you ask can be accomplished by two means: (1) by appeal to the listener's reason (logical appeals) or (2) appeal to his emotions (psychological appeals). Some experts define appeal to the reason as argumentation and maintain that persuasion must be limited to appeals to the emotion. Such a definition is too limited for our purposes.

Persuasion may be defined as *the process of getting others to want to believe or do what you want them to by appealing to their reason or their emotions.*

REASON VERSUS EMOTION

The ideal way to persuade is to lead a man to want to believe or do on the basis of facts and logical decision. His decision is based on thought and reason. Such a method is ideal but not very practical. Unfortunately man is not a wholly logical animal. His wants and his desires frequently drive him to make decisions because he *wants* to or *feels* like it.

Therefore persuasion must be a two edged sword. It must appeal to the listener's reason *and* appeal to his emotions. Good persuasion supplies both the logical and the psychological reasons for belief or action. It is upon this premise that the following material on persuasion is divided betwen logical means and psychological means of getting your own way. Do not get the idea that a good proposition cannot appeal to both. The listener may decide both logically and emotionally that he agrees with what you say.

LOGICAL PROOFS

Logical proof of a proposition depends upon facts and opinions. Fact are deeds or acts that have actually occurred. Facts exist; they are not constructed, created, or manufactured. Facts are verifiable. They can be checked up on. They are consistent with other known facts and with normal human experience. For example, that Dwight David Eisenhower was born October 14, 1890 is a fact. That Dwight David Eisenhower will become known as America's greatest president is not established. It is a proposition which must be proved by facts and opinions. Opinions are judgments, personal judgments which we are asked to accept in place of facts or as interpretations of facts. There are two kinds of opinion—opinions expressed by an expert and opinions expressed by a layman. One is called expert opinion and the other common opinion. Obviously we give more significance to expert opinions.

With the facts and expert opinions in hand you are ready to try to prove your proposition to the listener. This may be done by the use of examples, analogies, statistics, or testimony. Note that these are essentially the same devices which were used to amplify and clarify in Chapter 7.

Proof by Examples

The illustration and the example may be used to prove a point. You may either begin with your proposition and support it with numerous factual instances, or you may cite a number of examples and draw a conclusion from them. Suppose you desired to prove that your bulldozer is the best for a job. You could cite instances showing how durable it is. You could give illustrations and examples of its power and its efficiency. Or you could approach the problem in reverse; analyze the job to be performed; and indicate the durability, power, and efficiency that is needed for the job. Then you could draw the conclusion that your bulldozer is right for the job because it has the desired qualities.

Before selecting your illustrations and examples, make certain that they will stand under the tests of a good example. Does the example fit the proposition? Does the example help to prove the premise? Can you show that the example is a typical one? Can you find enough examples so that the listener will accept the proposition?

Proof by Analogies

If we can draw a number of similarities between two objects or situations we have an analogy. For example, Jane and Janet are both girls, both have blonde hair, both have blue eyes, both weigh 110 pounds, both are 5'4" tall. Now we may reason that since Jane wears a size 10 dress; Janet must also wear a size 10 dress. Having noted a number of similarities, we infer that other similarities must exist. Minneapolis, Minnesota, is similar to Columbus, Ohio, in population, expanse, and water supply. Minneapolis successfully uses a particular sewerage disposal system; therefore, Columbus should use the same system.

The strength or weakness of proof by analogy depends almost entirely upon its truth. It may be tested with the following questions. Are the cases well matched? Are the cases matched on relevant items? Do important differences exist? Jane and Janet may be very similar in their physical proportions, but an error would be made if we reasoned that their personalities would be the same. Minneapolis and Columbus may be matched on the items considered, but do important differences exist which would invalidate the conclusion?

Proof by Statistics

Someone once said, "There are lies, damned lies, and statistics." Another man complained, "Figures can't lie, but liars can figure." One part of the preceding is true—figures can't lie. Figures or statistics are facts. Nothing will change them. The place where the lying may come is in the *method* of gathering the statistics and in the *interpretation* of the statistics. Misinterpretation, faulty selection, unfair comparisons—these are the problems of dealing with statistics. Ask yourself the following questions before using them. Are the figures accurate? Many figures have an error value which may change the meaning of them. Do the statistics show what you really think they show? Use the actual figures and interpret them correctly. Avoid loose references such as "statistics prove . . ." or "the records show . . ." The listener is smart if he challenges you with "what statistics?" "what records?" Used well, statistics can do a man-sized job in proving.

Proof by Authority

Each of the other methods leans on facts. Proof by authority depends on opinion—expert opinion. It is simply the process of supporting your ideas with the expert testimony of others. Whether it does the job or not depends on how good the authority is. Apply the following tests to your quotations. Is it an exact and accurate quotation? The meaning can be changed by the dropping of a word or phrase. Be honest. Is the man you quote really an expert? Is he an expert in the field under study? For example, Leo Durocher is undoubtedly an expert in baseball, but he is not an expert on steel trusses. Quote him on baseball only. Avoid the "the-stars-use-it-so-should-you" technique. The fact that a baseball star uses a given razor has nothing to do with how good the razor is. He isn't an expert on razors, nor does he know anything about your beard. Is the expert prejudiced? Don't quote an expert if he has an axe to grind. The United State's Army Chief of Staff is an expert on military affairs, but to quote him to the effect that we should have a larger army is ridiculous. If anybody in the country wants a larger army, it would be the Army Chief of Staff. Is the information first hand? Avoid the rumor chain. By the time ideas have passed through several hands they tend to get changed, so go to the original source and verify it.

Testimony by an authority is one of the most used and most misused methods of proving a point. Expert opinion is very persuasive. Make sure that yours can really be classified as good authority.

Examples, analogies, statistics, and testimony can cause your listener to respond rationally. They help him to reach intellectual decision. At the very same time they may also provide excellent emotional reasons for the decision.

PERSUADE THROUGH PERSONAL PRESTIGE

"What do you think of him?" "He's a nice guy!" "He's a pain." "He'll go places." "Never trust that joker." "Take anything he says with a grain of salt." "I don't know, he bothers me." "I'd give him the shirt off my back." These are human reactions. They are judgments of you. They are representative of the personal prestige which you carry with you. They help to dictate your success or your failure. Your personal prestige is the honor or the stigma which clings to you. Personal prestige is persuasive—either for you or against you.

Personal prestige is of two types. There is (1) the personal prestige which you have already created by your past actions and (2) the prestige which you are able to generate for yourself at any given time because of what you are.

Prestige Is Your Reputation

Once you come in contact with others, you quickly develop a reputation. A reputation for the things you have accomplished, but more important a reputation for what you are. All of the judgments that were quoted a moment ago symbolize attitudes toward your reputation. Answer one simple question. How can a man persuade if people judge him as a pain, as not to be trusted, as an exaggerator? The attitudes of his listeners are predisposed against him. He has a tremendous hurdle to jump. A good reputation, good prestige, works in reverse— you like a man, you have faith in him, you will believe him and do as he asks *because he is what he is.* Unfortunately if you have created a poor reputation, it will take an endless amount of time to change it. But what about the people who don't know you? The people who haven't formed impressions? Listeners who are new to you? You can generate prestige by what you are.

Generating Personal Prestige

When you meet a man on the street, you instantly begin to add up impressions of him. Each time he speaks you add more to the ledger.

You come away from the meeting knowing what you think, and often it is hard to change your mind. What does he think about you? You may be assured that he did the same thing. He formed quick solid impressions which will control his attitudes toward you.

What were the clues that each of you used? How did you make the judgments? They were made on the basis of his looks, his words, and his attitudes.

You judged his looks. Not whether he was handsome or ugly, though too much of either of these qualities may have an effect. Rather you noted how he was dressed; how he carried himself; whether he was clean or dirty, shaven or unshaven, neat or sloppy.

You judged his words. You noted whether he was a "fast talker," "too slick," "confused and disorganized," "an educated man," "a stuffed shirt." You may not have put these into the speech terms of organization, choice of language, and delivery, but you formed the impression nevertheless. You judged his attitudes. We have already talked about this. Reread Chapter 3.

Put together the worst combination of looks, words, and attitudes that you can imagine. Could such a man persuade you? He could not! Put together the best combination. You may not know it, but you are half persuaded before he even makes his point.

Perhaps this seems abstract; therefore let's suggest some things that you can specifically do to persuade the audience through your personal prestige.

A. Show respect for your listener. He too is a thinking, wanting human being. Never talk down to him; that is, don't treat him like a child as though his knowledge or his background is inferior to yours. On the other hand, don't talk up to him either. Be afraid of no man. Stand firmly poised when you talk to any man. The greatest respect that you can show a man is neither arrogance nor deference; it is sincerity and directness.

B. Recognize the identity of others. Recognize and refer to the occasion, the audience, and particularly the individual. Remember a man's name. Learn how to spell it. Nothing proves to a listener that you don't think that he is important faster than the inability to recognize him. He is an individual, who demands recognition if he is to preserve his self-respect.

C. Manifest honesty and fairness to opponents. Give your opponent his due. It is doubtful that his plan is all wrong, all bad. Recognize the strong points and compliment him on them. Then and only then disagree. But disagree in a generous and pleasant way. All but very partisan listeners tend to "side with the under-dog." If you are fair or honest in dealing with your listeners, you need never fear their responses. They will respect you and respect your point of view.

D. *Never get in an argument.* No one ever won an argument. Oh, yes, you may get your way for the moment, but if disagreement has reached the point of argument, the lines are so firmly drawn that your opponent will never be able to surrender his position. Treat a disagreement with dignity and above all poise. The end results will be much more to your liking.

E. *Show your character by your language.* Choose language which is brilliant and trenchant, but avoid habitual overstatement. Once you are tagged as one who exaggerates—and it doesn't take long—your ability to persuade decreases. You can be vivid and powerful without stretching the point.

F. *Show that you have a piercing mind.* Never let your listener characterize you as "the guy with the feather pillow mind." Incisive, straight, analytical thinking is the key to the piercing mind. Carefully organized knowledge of your subject matter gives the impression of strength and clarity. Your listeners will respect you and respond positively.

G. *Be warm, friendly, and human.* We have already talked about this, but let's mention it again. There is no substitute for it. (See Chapter 3.)

H. *Recognize the competence and accomplishments of others.* Most men respond much better to a pat on the back than to a harsh criticism. Give each man his due and he will respect and respond to you.

Now do you see how personal prestige can help you win others to your point of view? What you are counts. If you can be respectful, honest, fair, calm, warm, friendly, human, clear, and analytical, you can't lose in the game of persuasion.

PERSUADE THROUGH THE BASIC DRIVES

Have you seen the insurance advertisement of a mother and her young daughter walking down the street holding hands with a shadow of a man who stands between them. The caption reads, "Could this be you?" This is an appeal to the basic drives. The emotion is fear, the basic drive is security. The purpose of the ad is to sell life insurance.

Have you seen the travel poster with palm trees and pretty girls with motor boats and water skiers, sunlight and water in the background? The caption reads "Florida Is Calling." The emotion is joy; the basic drive is adventure.

Have you seen the advertisement of the endowment plan where the caption reads "For the young man on the way up!" Do you see how this appeal is meant for everyone? Does anyone think of himself as an "old man on the way down?" All of these and thousands more are devoted to the single proposition that the advertiser's purpose be tied to the desires and drives of the listener.

In Chapter 4 we told you the story of the listener. The drives which govern his every thought and action were outlined—security, adventure, recognition, and response. Now your job is to determine how to set the drives in motion. How to tap the potential energy so that it flows into the response you want.

The Specific Desires of the Listener

While every listener is governed by the four major drives, it is important to realize that the particular manifestation of the drives in the individual will depend to a great extent upon his experiences, attitudes, and habits. To some men the amassing of wealth is the most important goal in life. They are sometimes referred to as the "Cadillac crowd." To other men, full appreciation of great literature, music, and art are the goals. The drives are the same, but the manifestations of them are quite different. With this word of warning let's quote some examples where appeals to the four basic drives are used. You can certainly find other appeals in your experience. You may not even agree with the classification. It is not important. Most of our desires are so simple that they can be traced back to either one or a combination of the basic drives.

A. The drive for security. Typical appeals to the listener's desire for security may include security for himself, his family, his friends, his country, his home, his job, his savings, his future, his old age, his freedoms, his beliefs, his rights, his independence.

The listener's desire for the security of his country is appealed to in these words of John Foster Dulles:

There are some who doubt the determination or ability of these free Asian nations to preserve and develop their political independence, and also to make that independence serve to improve social and economic conditions. I do not share that doubt. But I do come back with the strengthened conviction that the United States can help the Asian countries to achieve both of these goals. Also, I feel sure that it is in our own interest to provide that help.[1]

William Benton appealed strongly to the security drive when he informed his listeners of our *lack* of security:

More important than any failure of leadership on your part is that all America now appears to be sleep-walking on the brink, if you will excuse the plagiarism. The American people do not as yet identify the growing educational crisis with their national security.

You have invited me to report on what I learned about education in the Soviet Union, and to suggest what this may mean for America and the free world. Leon Bloy, the French philosopher, once referred to what he called "the good news of damnation." His theory was that none of us might behave as Christians if we were not afraid of perpetual hell-fire. When I finish tonight, I hope you will ask yourselves whether it might not be that the Soviet educational system can prove to be the good news of damnation for American education—the spur which may rouse us and propel us toward salvation.[2]

Bonner Fellers concluded a recent speech with this appeal for security:

The Soviet Union is the base from which emanate all elements and activities dedicated to world Communization. If it is certain that World War III will destroy this base, the Kremlin will never dare to strike.

Only by the immediate creation of overwhelming AMERICAN Air Power can we prevent war and thereby save ourselves and our Allies.

Only Americans can defend America.[3]

---

[1] John Foster Dulles, "The Future Belongs to Independence," *Vital Speeches*, XXII, No. 13 (April 15, 1956), p. 388.

[2] William Benton, "Soviet Education," *Vital Speeches*, XXII, No. 13 (April 15, 1956), p. 391.

[3] Bonner Fellers, "Only Americans Can Defend America," *Vital Speeches*, XXII, No. 13 (April 16, 1956), p. 399.

Certainly Max R. Burnell's observation was meant to focus the attention of his listeners on their personal security:

> In this brief discussion, I have tried to express and to stress my conviction that from the business man's standpoint much more is to be derived from physical exercise than just exercise itself—as important as that is. True, if we can keep that belt in the same notch where it was five years ago, a great deal towards health maintenance has been accomplished. However, as related to the job, a mind relaxed from tensions is as much to be desired as firm abdominal muscles. Equanimity in a world full of stress is an asset of outstanding value to the present-day business executive. No one really wants to be a business casualty. Live each day unto itself—and play a little.[4]

B. The Drive for Adventure. This drive expresses itself in your listener's need for new experiences in his home life, his professional life, his social life, his opportunities to invent, create, build, organize, participate, compete, appreciate, and enjoy.

The listener's need for new experiences in his professional life and opportunities (if he be technically minded) was appealed to by William Benton in the same speech quoted above:

> Let us also study the creation of new kinds of institutions as they may be needed. A few weeks ago I suggested that our government create Technical Assistance Academies, equal in status to the United States Military, Naval, and Air Force Academies—to educate picked young men and women for service overseas as technical specialists. Someone called my suggested Academies "West Points of Point Four." I emphasized that such Academies—and I apply this to all technical or scientific education in our country—should have a curriculum with a strong infusion of the liberal arts, so that our young engineers and scientists can better serve their country overseas. Today how can we expect to persuade the young engineer to serve overseas? If he is well advised he'll go to Topeka or Fargo instead of to Rangoon.[5]

The drive for adventure in the form of a challenge to appreciate was sounded by Rev. Frederick A. McGuire, C.M.:

---

[4] Max R. Burnell, "How Much and What Kind of Physical Exercise Should a Business Man Take?" *Vital Speeches,* XXII, No. 13 (April 15, 1956), p. 408.
[5] Benton, *op. cit.,* p. 395.

What the world needs to know is that we do indeed reject the naturalistic philosophy that denies our dependence on an eternal, omnipotent and loving God. What the world needs to know and what we must tell the world by action as well as by word, is that we see in all men, regardless of color, nationality or creed, the image of God and our brother. If you have principles, prepare to defend them now against the ruthless attacks of a godless enemy and against the personal intellectual laziness that would lull you into imbecilic apathy.[6]

Herbert Brownell, Jr. inspired his listeners with these concluding remarks:

In maintaining the highest professional and citizenship standards, we provide assurance that our form of government shall function as intended by those who fought to create it.

We stand on the threshold of a great era of enlightened dealing between all men. I am confident we will not be lacking in the humanity, wisdom and courage to preserve for our posterity the priceless gifts of our heritage.[7]

Concerning adventure through realizing the opportunities of the future, Charles R. Sligh, Jr., Chairman of the Board of the National Association of Manufacturers, has this to say:

There's no road for us but the hard, level highway we have always trod. The primrose path may be inviting. But it doesn't lead to security, to prosperity, or to any form of economic fulfillment. It runs downhill into ruin—national and individual. The risk—the responsibility—the worry—all of these we must accept.

We must find the ways of stabilizing production and work.

We must do everything humanly possible to eliminate such things as seasonal lay-offs. We must level out the peak and valleys on the sales charts.

In short, we must strengthen jobs—in an expanding economy— because that's the only way we can have a stronger people—a stronger nation—and a stronger industrial freedom.[8]

---

[6] Rev. Frederick A. McGuire, C.M., "The Philosophy of Our Founding Fathers," *Vital Speeches*, XXII, No. 13 (April 15, 1956), p. 403.

[7] Herbert Brownell, Jr., "Federally-protected Civil Rights," *Vital Speeches*, XXII, No. 2 (November 1, 1955), p. 47.

[8] Charles R. Sligh, Jr., "Strengthening Jobs in an Expanding Economy," *Vital Speeches*, XXI, No. 7 (January 15, 1955), p. 989.

C. The drive for recognition. Your listener wants to be recognized and accorded status by his family, his friends, his neighbors, his employers. He wants to be respected for his acquisitions, his authority, his efficiency, his professional contributions, his community service.

The drive for recognition was accorded the teacher in a plea from a speech by William Benton:

> In the development of new and far bigger incentives for talented teachers, I fear we must again turn to the federal government for leadership. Some five or ten years hence, several billion dollars annually will have to be found to add to teachers' salaries. This program, to stimulate our present teachers and to attract new ones, should be launched at once and on a scale into the hundreds of millions, allocated through State Departments of Education to communities which undertake *to attract and keep uncommonly promising teachers.* The federal government must help establish a pattern of standards. This will cause a hue and cry about federal control. We must face up to it.[9]

Christian A. Herter extended recognition of efficiency and authority to the Chicago Council on Foreign Relations in his closing comments:

> If, then, I have offered any suggestions or advanced any ideas which appeal to you as having merit, I hope you will subject them to searching scrutiny. Should you, having done that, still think well of them, let them be given the momentum of your disinterested and bipartisan support. Only through the efforts of thoughtful people like yourselves can we develop a unified response to the enormously difficult and challenging problems confronting us today. Only with such unity can we continue to discharge the responsibilities of world leadership.[10]

Recognition was given the American Legion by John Foster Dulles in the opening remarks of his speech:

> It is an honor and a privilege to speak at this opening of your Convention. You are those who in time of national peril were ready to sacrifice life itself that our country and its principles might survive. And in time of peace, through your conventions and manifold committee and educational activities, you cultivate the spirit of patriotism.[11]

---

[9] Benton, *op. cit.*, p. 394.
[10] Christian A. Herter, "The Outbreak of Amicability," *Vital Speeches,* XXII, No. 13 (April 15, 1956), p. 401.
[11] John Foster Dulles, "International Cooperation," *Vital Speeches,* XXII, No. 2 (November 1, 1955), p. 34.

The contributions of the farm equipment industry were heralded in a speech given by Ezra Taft Benson:

> It is a pleasure, a privilege and an honor to be with you today. Certainly the fortunes of agriculture and the farm equipment industry are closely linked in this choice land of ours.
>
> If there is one thing that has dramatized our agricultural progress, it is the way that our companies, your salesman, and your engineers have given the farmer motorized muscles.
>
> You have helped make the farmer highly productive—some say too productive, and cite our $7 billion inventory of farm products to prove it. But without the products of your factories, the farmer today would be limited in his production by his own muscles and such work as he could coax from stubborn beasts.[12]

D. The drive for response. The listener wants to be loved, wanted, needed, and understood by his wife, his children, his friends, his neighbors, and his employers.

William Benton left no doubt in the mind of his listeners that they were needed and wanted. Benton's speech, you have probably realized by now, is an excellent example in using all four of the basic drives:

> A deep faith in man is the total opposite to the Soviet system which offers a vast technocratic new Sparta. By our standards, their system is more like animal training than the education of human beings. It is without human spirit or soul. It is the state-take-all and let the individual take the hindmost. It is the gospel according to Pavlov.
>
> The peoples of the world are now entering an era when energy comes from rocks and sunlight; when materials for shelter and clothing derive from air, water, and chemicals. Barring war, the aspirations of underdeveloped peoples will soon force industrial and educational development into every cranny of human society. If we of the United States are to meet the new challenge of the world-wide revolt against hunger and disease and ignorance—you who are our leaders in the field of education must march forward in the front ranks. Believe me, however, I do appreciate my difficulties tonight. It is not easy to exhort the professional exhorters.[13]

Richard Lardner Tobin spoke to the University of Michigan Alumni Club of Washington, D.C. He concluded his speech with an expression of affection:

---

[12] Ezra Taft Benson, "Men and Machines," *Vital Speeches,* XXII, No. 1, (October 15, 1955), p. 26.

[13] Benton, *op. cit.,* pp. 395–396.

Indeed, a special sort of heaven must be reserved directly above Ann Arbor (and other cases) for men and women who now must teach what was once taught at the grade-school level in order to prepare the learner with the ability and tools to read and write his way to a liberal education.

I loved the University of Michigan totally when I was there—and I knew it at the time—and I have never loved a place more, nor shall I be able to repay the debt I owe Ann Arbor, and I think it is true of most of us. For most of us, myself included, were likewise taught to read and write, not in the grade and high schools we came from, but in Angell Hall, University Hall, Newberry Auditorium, or the sub-sub-basement of the Romance Language Building.[14]

J. Edgar Hoover responded to the work done by our law enforcement officers in a speech given at the 62nd Annual Meeting of the International Association of Chiefs of Police:

> There is not a law enforcement officer in the Nation who has not has his patience, ingenuity, fortitude and even his faith in human nature put to a severe test while carrying out his sworn duty to make his community a safer place in which to live. We can take real satisfaction from the gradual but steady progress which we have made in recent years, despite the added burdens we have been forced to assume. May I say, on behalf of my associates in the FBI, that we are proud to be associated with so many dedicated public servants.[15]

Examine this list of needs carefully. They are virtually universal. Tie your speech purpose to them.

Methods of Appealing to the Specific Desires

How do you attach your speech purpose to the listener's desires and drives? The process is essentially the same as for logical argument, but the materials are different. Your task is to vitalize the listener's desires. Your job is more than one of mentioning that your purpose will satisfy his need.

You must use illustrations, examples, comparisons, even testimony and statistics. In each case they should be directed to a vivid, appeal-

---

[14] Richard Lardner Tobin, "A Little Learning," *Vital Speeches*, XXII, No. 13 (April 15, 1956), p. 416.

[15] J. Edgar Hoover, "Our Common Task," *Vital Speeches*, XXII, No. 2 (November 1, 1955), p. 41.

ing, even dramatic pointing up of the connection between your proposition and the listener's desire. This can be done by emotional appeal, control of attention, and suggestion.

PERSUADE THROUGH EMOTIONAL APPEAL

The listener's desires and drives can be fanned into the flame of action by appealing to his emotions and his sentiments. We said earlier that we did many things because we wanted to, because we *felt* like it. That is a mild way of putting it; frequently our emotions compel us to act. Fear, anger, love, joy, hate, pride, loyalty, reverence, grief, awe, curiosity, sympathy, respect—these are the emotions and sentiments which cause us to respond.

An enemy approaches our shores. You desire security; you wish specifically to protect your life, the lives of your family, and to preserve our nation. The emotions that make you enlist and fight are fear and anger. Fear, for your security is threatened. Anger, that someone would dare threaten your security. In war the appeals are almost always to one of these emotions, and you respond.

You are offered a new job. You fear the loss of your security; but you want the adventure and the recognition that goes along with it. The man who persuades you to take it appeals to your pride in new accomplishment, your love of adventure, your hate of standing still, your curiosity about what the future may bring. The man who persuades you to stay in the old job appeals to your loyalty to your company, your friends, your town. He may even enlist your sympathy for the old crowd and their great loss. The drives of adventure and recognition on the one hand and security on the other are in conflict.

An injustice develops in your neighborhood. A fine family is losing its home. You act because you hate injustice and wish to right the wrong. You act because you sympathize with your neighbor's problems; you pity his misfortune.

You are persuaded to vote because you are angered at the malfeasance of the present regime. You are persuaded to donate your money because your sympathy and pity have been aroused. You are persuaded to go fishing because enthusiasm for pleasure has been excited. You are persuaded to kill because your fear and anger have been aroused. Emotions are prime movers; arouse them and your listener will respond.

Adapt the Methods of Clarity

How? By vivid stories and vital examples. By dramatic comparisons and by colorful descriptions. By dynamic, loaded language. By stirring appeals to the imagination.

A word of warning: Remember that you are appealing to the emotions not to the intellect. The emotional arousal you desire literally short circuits the mind out of the action. Therefore, you must be subtle; your listener should not see the framework and the techniques. Once he does, your chances of arousing his emotions are gone.

PERSUADE THROUGH CONTROL OF ATTENTION

James A. Winans, a noted speech authority, has said, "Persuasion is the process of gaining fair, favorable, and undivided attention." William James, the psychologist, maintained, "What holds attention, determines action." This is the concept of the exclusive stimulus.

Attention Affects Action

The idea can be very simply explained. Complete concentration and attention results in hypnosis. The concentration on an object or idea is so complete that no other conflicting ideas are able to arise. While you aren't interested in hypnotizing an audience (though many believe that some of Hitler's audiences were actually in a trancelike state), you are interested in attention which is so undivided that no conflicting notion or inhibition to action may destroy your listener's tendency to respond.

Perhaps it may be illustrated this way. Suppose you are simply asked to rise, to stand up, to get on your feet. Your normal response is to respond favorably to this request for positive action. However, before you fulfill the request, a number of conflicting ideas arise. You almost immediately say that you don't want to because you're tired, because you would be conspicuous, because you don't see any reason to rise, and so on. However, if the speaker can get your undivided attention to his proposition, your favorably disposed attention, none of the conflicting ideas or inhibitions will come into your mind, and you will rise.

Attention Can Persist

Attention can persist long after the speech is over. Suppose you have heard a speech which attempts to persuade you to move to Canada, the land of opportunity. If the speech is a truly great one, if your attention has been undivided and favorably disposed toward the proposition, your interest and thought may be devoted to the subject of going to Canada long after the speech is over. In fact, you may continue to devote attention to it until you finally make a decision and move to Canada.

Use the Tools of Interest

In Chapter 8 we discussed in considerable detail the psychological factors which command attention. If these devices can be used to direct the listener's attention in a fair, favorable, and undivided way to your proposition, he will be persuaded. How is it done? By introducing self-concern, animation, familiarity, novelty, reality, concreteness, nearness, uncertainty, conflict, and humor into your illustrations, examples, and comparisons. By appealing to the imagination and directly to the senses by visual aids, you can win your way.

PERSUADE THROUGH SUGGESTION

A few paragraphs back it was noted that when you are asked to rise, your first inclination is to do so. The natural reaction is to respond to any suggestion which is made. Oh, there are "chronic aginners" who seem to respond negatively automatically, but they are the exception.

What is suggestion? Suggestion may be defined as the process of *establishing an idea more or less indirectly, usually in the margins or fringes of attention.* A few examples may be helpful. "Fill 'er up?" asks the gasoline station attendant. The suggestion is made that you buy a full tank of gasoline. Your normal reaction is to do it, unless some conflicting idea arises. If a conflicting idea, such as "not enough money," does arise, the problem has left the margins of attention and becomes the center of it. You stop and think.

Did you know that one of America's largest department store chains found that by providing their saleswomen with a free weekly manicure they encouraged their employees to keep their hair neatly done and be more careful about their clothes? Why? Because a woman with attractive nails feels like a lady, and the suggestion is made that she appear like one in all ways.

If you own a bar and want to get rid of the loud, rough, cheap trade, do you know how to do it? Lay a carpet. It suggests a place which is quiet, refined, and dignified. The results will be apparent. Your customers will talk more softly, conduct themselves with greater reserve, and those who want a place to bellow and guffaw will go elsewhere.

Have you seen the little signs in Marshall Field's department store in Chicago that say "Shall we send it, or will you take it with you?" After the signs were introduced, the number of deliveries of small packages dropped tremendously—a gentle positive suggestion.

Positive and Negative Suggestion

Positive suggestion is simply the process of putting suggestions into a positive form, that is, encouraging the listener to *do*. Negative suggestion urges the listener to *not do*. Negative suggestion depends on the word *don't*.

Suggestion should be positive whenever possible for two reasons. First, we are inclined to respond to suggestion; therefore, it is better to ask the listener to act rather than to ask him not to act. Secondly, negative suggestion may plant the positive act in the listener's mind.

Johnny is standing with his mother on the street corner. Johnny sees a rock in the gutter, picks it up, and examines it. Mother sees him do it and says sharply, "Johnny, don't you dare throw that stone." Throwing the stone has never entered Johnny's mind. But mother implants the idea, so Johnny throws the stone. Had mother said, "John, drop that stone," the chances are that Johnny would have done so.

Select the right phrasing in each of the following instances. In a tool shop—"Don't neglect tools" or "Put tools away." In a disagreement—"Don't give me that stuff" or "All right, let's look at your point of view." In selling a product—"Don't worry about the price" or "Price is an insignificant factor." In teaching a process—"Don't hold your hand that way" or "Hold your hand this way." In a controversy—"Don't tell me that you won't do it" or "Please, hurry along and do it." In every case the negative suggestion tends to encourage resentment. In every case the negative suggestion may implant the very idea you are trying to avoid.

There is one exception to this doctrine—the man who is against anything you stand for. A member of an industrial corporation told me some days ago, "I have finally found out how to get my way with the chairman of the board. He always disagrees with every idea I have. Now I express mild enthusiasm for the very things I don't want, and he goes charging off doing things the way I want them done." A pathetic picture, but a true one. Occasionally you run into people who have to be handled by negative suggestion.

The Methods of Suggestion

Suggestion works in either the individual or the group speaking situation if you handle it right. It is a powerful appeal, whether you want more money for your work or desire your state to bring in a new natural gas line.

A. Let your manner suggest confidence. This is directly related to gaining personal prestige. Your expressions of quiet confidence in your ideas and in yourself are the first major step to suggesting that both you and your ideas are worthwhile. Reread the material on personal prestige.

B. Plant suggestions casually. Most people resent being told what to do. Their almost instantaneous reaction is "Don't push me." Therefore it is essential that suggestion be subtle. Don't let your suggestions move from the margins of attention to the center of it. Conflicting ideas are more liable to get in the way of your response. The magician is a master of suggestion. His patter leads you to look away from the spot where you would see the manipulation of the trick.

C. Avoid crystallizing contrary ideas. In other words avoid negative suggestion. Plant affirmative ideas. Avoid setting up negative arguments merely for the sake of knocking them down. The argument may never have occurred to the listener. You set it up. He examines it. You try to knock it down. He judges your success in dealing with it. If you fail, you are worse off than if you had never suggested it in the first place.

D. Suggest ideas that fit the listener's drives. Probably the greatest effectiveness comes from the suggestion that ties your proposition to the listener's desires and drives. Remember the drives, desires, and attitudes of the listener are tendencies to action. They are dynamic, ready to be set in action. The right suggestion gets them going.

E. *Use positively loaded words.* If every word you choose leads the listener toward your desired response, he can be moved. Always choose language that brings forth positive associations with your idea. His emotions can be stirred by them. Positively loaded words should be associated with positive propositions; negatively loaded words with propositions you wish to have him reject. For example, if you wish to sell a car, select the words that set off his wants about it. Show that it is safe, powerful, economical, comfortable. Choose language which best expresses these ideas. If you wish to have him fear the enemy, associate the negative language of fear with your idea.

F. *Use symbols.* Symbols are loaded just like individual words. In addition, they have the power to catch attention and are usually related to the listener's desires. The symbols of the flag, the cross, and the scales of justice are all positively loaded. The symbols of the swastika, John Bull, and the hammer and sickle are negatively loaded. Each transfers emotional feeling to the listener. They suggest good or bad. Associate your ideas with good.

Many organizations have positive prestige. Get the approval of the Red Cross, the Boy Scouts, the American Legion, or the City Fathers for your ideas and tie your proposition to their approval. The good will which these organizations have will transfer itself to your proposition.

G. *Please and satisfy the listener.* Tell the listener what he wants to hear. Compliment him, but don't flatter him. Remember that a man pleased is a man half persuaded.

—*Apply the Principles*

The tools of persuasion should serve two purposes. They should help you to become more persuasive, but probably even more important, they should provide you with the knowledge necessary to recognize the persuasion of others. Observe other speakers. Determine when they use psychological arguments which will stand the test of time and when they use psychological or emotional appeals which may stir you for the moment but are based purely on appeals to your desires.

Much of the advertising to which you are exposed each day is loaded with emotional appeal which you can detect. When others try to get you to believe or do, examine their arguments. Don't let yourself be moved unless there are good logical reasons behind the appeal. Persuasion is all around you. Try out your new knowledge.

Observation

(1) Pick up a magazine and turn to a full-color, full-page advertisement. Start with the pictorial layout. What appeals do you find? How does the ad hold attention? What emotions are aroused? What suggestions do you see in the pictures? Make a list of the devices employed.

(2) Now examine the copy, that is, the use of language. Do they use illustrations, examples, comparisons, statistics, testimony? Do these devices pass the tests set up for them? Pick out the positively loaded words; then the negatively loaded ones. How does the promotion attach the product to your desires? Which desires? How does the ad employ suggestion?

Practice

(1) Pick a persuasive opportunity from your own everyday existence. Clearly phrase your purpose and your purpose sentence. Analyze your listener. Select his most powerful desires and drives. How can you tie your purpose to those drives? Now how can you implement your idea. Select an illustration, an example, and so forth. Make them serve both a logical and an emotional purpose. The best persuasion is that which incorporates both sound logical reasons and good emotional appeals. Try out your persuasion.

(2) Analyze your success or failure. If your listener won't buy or believe, ask him why. Pick your presentation apart and find out from him how he responded to each of the elements. Find the flaws, correct them, and try again. If your listener was persuaded, by all means find out what caused his positive

response. Check his reasons for acting and decide how much was logic and how much was emotion.

(3) Prepare a persuasive speech for a group. Try to make it a real situation rather than an artificial one. Prepare your speech with care. Make sure it is organized clearly. Select materials and language which have impact. Attach every possible desire of the listener to your proposition. Hit him hard with both logic and emotion.

FORMULA I

$$LP = \frac{SW{:}LW}{A_r A_e}$$

(LP) Learn to Persuade = Getting the *(SW) Speaker's Wants* to become the *(LW) Listener's Wants* by *(A_rA_e) Appealing to the Reason and/or the Emotions* of the listener.

Now, apply the formula!

Prepare a speech to persuade. Have your listeners react to your speech by using the scale below. Compare your listeners' reponses and concentrate on those criteria where the scores are average and below.

Speech to Persuade Scale		
Speaker _____ Rater _____		
Topic _____ Date _____		
1–2 Weak *3 Average* *4–5 Strong*		
Criteria	*Score*	*Comments*
PERSONAL PRESTIGE: Respect Complimentary Recognition Honesty-Fairness Language Argumentative Thought		
LOGICAL PROOFS: Examples Relevance Analogies Typical Statistics Acceptable Authority Accurate		

179

Speech to Persuade Scale (*cont.*)

1–2 Weak	*3 Average*	*4–5 Strong*	
Criteria		*Score*	*Comments*
EMOTIONAL APPEALS: Security Adaptation Adventure Vital Recognition Vividness Response Appeal			
SUGGESTION: Positive Encouragement Negative Confidence Casualness Adaptation Satisfaction Pleasantness			
CONTROL OF ATTENTION: Affects Action Animation Persistence Novelty Favorableness Concreteness Undivided Humor			
General effectiveness			

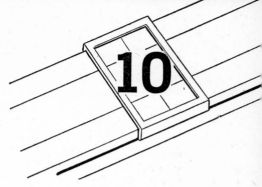

be visually
forceful and direct

ONE OF TELEVISION's crack announcers said, "Frequently my product is sold or unsold before I say a word." What did he mean? The instant that his picture is flashed on the screen, the television listeners see him and form an impression. If the impression is good, his product is sold. If the impression is bad, no amount of talking can sell the product.

Ralph Waldo Emerson once said, "What you are speaks so loudly, I cannot hear what you say." The impression that you make by your attitude and your appearance is so forceful that no words can change it.

Did you know that if you are forced to make a choice between that which you hear and that which you see, what you see will win every time?

All of this leads to an important question. What does the listener *see* when he talks with you and when he looks at you on the platform or across the conference table? What effect does what he sees have upon your chances of success?

WHAT DOES THE LISTENER SEE?

A. The listener sees what you are. We have mentioned this before in reference to your attitude when speaking and your personal prestige. Your listener sees you for good or ill. Trace what he sees. He sees your dress and judges you on it. He sees your walk to the platform and forms a judgment of you by the way you move. He sees your carriage and posture and decides whether you are a strong person or not. He sees your facial expression and judges whether you are enthusiastic or afraid. He sees your movement and decides whether you are forceful or tend to withdraw. He sees your gestures, your hand movements, and reads into them an impression of you.

Above all, he either likes or dislikes what he sees. He forms an impression, a first impression. Then whether you like it or not he judges each new cue and clue that comes to him in terms of the *first* impression. Remember that. He never goes back to the beginning and starts over again. In fact, he finds it hard to say, "I was wrong in my first impression." Usually it is just the opposite; he looks for the elements which will substantiate his first impression. Therefore, what he sees both at the outset and during your entire speech is tremendously important.

B. The listener sees your interest in him. Your listener will be interested in you only if you can give him substantial evidence that you are interested in him. If he knows that you are doing it for him, he will perk up and listen. But if he suspects that you don't care about him, he will tune you out. He judges your interest in him by the directness with which you address him. He judges your interest by your vitality, by the set of your body, by the forcefulness of your bodily activity.

C. The listener sees your interest in your subject. Your speech is made up of both visual and vocal stimuli. Thus the listener must see as well as hear you. The emphatic points of your speech must be brought home through the eye as well as the ear. The listener sees and hears the excitement and enthusiasm which you have for your material. Above all, he judges whether the body belies the voice or the voice speaks differently from the body. A vital, enthusiastic voice with a dull, flaccid body leaves the listener confused because he knows that enthusiasm is a total response.

D. The listener actually responds to your physical vitality. If you are active and enthusiastic, it is difficult for the listener to remain immobile. The stimuli which strike him impel him to respond. He becomes aroused and stimulated because you are aroused and stimulated. He sees enthusiasm, and he becomes enthusiastic. All of the suggestions which are communicated by your manner and your activity tend to lead him positively toward the response you desire.

WHAT DOES BODILY ACTIVITY DO FOR YOU?

A. Bodily activity aids vocal expression. Expressing an idea is a total process, vocal and visual. Not only are voice and action helpful in perceiving an idea, they are both also essential to its expression. Think of the times you have tried to work out an idea. How do you do it? Probably by moving about, gesturing as you talk, and emphasizing the key elements of each idea. The actions of your body actually help in the vocal expression of the idea. So it is on the platform, at the conference table, or in the office. Bodily activity helps straight thinking.

B. Bodily activity helps emphasize ideas. Vocal expression is not enough. Can you conceive of a forceful speaker who never moves a muscle except those used for sound? Of course not. Have you ever watched a radio announcer or actor read his script? The vocal emphasis which you hear over your speaker is accompanied by physical emphasis which you may never see. The ideas expressed would be more forceful if you could see it. Again we say that speaking is a total expression. The listener needs the impact of the eye as well as the ear to get the entire message. Your job of speaking will be easier if you let your body help you.

C. Bodily activity helps relieve tension. Performance tension is a normal part of the speaking situation. Bodily activity provides you with an opportunity to work off the tension. Not only work it off, but use it to help you get your point across. The excess energy and tension can build itself into panic without overt activity. With activity you sense that you are on your way: with activity you can reach out to your listeners; with activity you can work your thought into language; with activity you can emphasize your ideas. Each of these vital needs helps you gain your purpose and at the same time releases the tensions which disturb you.

WHAT IS GOOD BODILY ACTION?

A. Good bodily action is purposeful. Activity, movement, animation of any kind attract attention; therefore your activity must attract attention to your subject. If for any reason your activity is random or purposeless, it will distract from your subject. Some speakers, for example, use up their excess nervous energy in twisting, turning, pawing, pacing, and shifting. This movement certainly attracts attention, but it tells the listener of the obvious nervousness of the speaker. It actually distracts from the ideas of the speech.

B. *Good bodily activity is forceful.* Since the listener judges you and your subject matter partly by what he sees, it is essential that your bodily activity reflect the forcefulness of your ideas. Evasive, half-hearted activity belies your strength of purpose. It points you out as being wishy-washy, without interest in your subject, without conviction. Good bodily activity is firm and dynamic.

C. *Good bodily activity is direct.* Your speech is aimed at the listener. It is created for the listener. It should embrace the listener. Your bodily activity must do the same. Every thought and similarly every action must be directed to the listener. Actions which are not aimed at the listener lack purpose, lack force, and destroy the circular response.

D. *Good bodily activity is genuine.* It is honest. It stems from your desire to communicate. It gives the impression of real enthusiasm because it is a manifestation of real enthusiasm. It gives the listener the feeling of the first time, of a genuine spontaneous desire on your part to communicate your ideas. Never plant or compose bodily activity. Never decide to move here or gesture there; it won't work. You are not an actor; you cannot represent that which you are not. Therefore let your action come from your honest, sincere enthusiasm for your idea.

E. *Good bodily activity interprets.* Good action tells the story. It tells the story you want told. It facilitates and strengthens understanding. It creates the mood of your material. It encourages physical responses from your listeners. It shows your concern for your ideas. It livens up your talk. Show me a good speaker who can talk without activity. It can't be done. Activity is part of the total responsiveness which is speech.

You understand the need for bodily activity. You have studied the criteria. How can it be done? What are the steps in building it?

MAKE FIRST IMPRESSIONS COUNT

As you rise to speak two elements impress the listener—(1) your appearance and (2) the way you move to the platform.

A. *Apparel and Appearance.* What about dress? Dress to fit the occasion. If it calls for blue jeans, wear blue jeans, but if it calls for a suit and tie, wear a suit and tie. More speakers get into trouble at the outset, particularly classroom speakers, because they haven't gone to the trouble to assess the situation. Remember: it is not a question of getting "dressed up"; it is a question of dressing to fit the occasion. You don't want to be noticed for the elegance of your dress; you want to be "inconspicuously dressed." Your dress should not call attention to itself at all.

The other elements of your appearance go without saying. If you look like a slovenly person, you will be judged as one. If you appear clean, neat, and efficient, you will be judged as clean, neat, and efficient.

B. *Moving to the Platform.* The second basis for the first impression you create is the way you go to the platform, or move to the head of the conference table, or move into the office for your interview. The rules are simple. Carry yourself forcefully. Not as a soldier on parade, but as an efficient, purposeful, poised, confident carrier of an important message. Every eye is on you; every mind is adding up the score; make your entrance a sincere and honest one. Don't rush to the platform as though you were being chased by an angry dog. Don't drag or shuffle to the platform as though you didn't care what happened. Move firmly, move easily, move efficiently to the speaker's stand.

After you get to the speaker's stand, look your audience in the eye for a moment. It may be hard to do, but it's worth it. Wait until they settle down and are ready, then begin. Never fuss with papers; never begin before you get to the stand; never shy away from your audience. Be purposeful, forceful, direct, and genuine.

Just a word about last impressions. You can strengthen or spoil a speech by the way you finish and leave the platform. Remember: we said earlier that speeches are concluded; they don't just stop. So finish your speech on the appropriate note. Look your audience in the eye. Look down. Pick up your notes if any and leave. You need not thank the audience. They should thank you. Don't leave before your speech is finished. Many speakers literally deliver the last few words of their speech while they are on the way down the aisle. Don't. After you have finished, move to your seat in the same deliberate, efficient manner with which you went to the platform.

ESTABLISH VISUAL CONTACT

Visual contact is an extremely simple process yet a tremendously important one. It is the process of *looking your listeners directly in the eye*. When there is more than one listener it means talking directly to one listener for a few moments then talking directly to another. If you have a large audience, you talk to one group until you establish contact with them, then turn to another group. Remember when you were in school and volunteered to recite? The teacher pointed to you, and you rose only to find that everyone else around you had also thought the teacher meant him. Eye contact is such that in large groups the listener feels you are talking to him even though you may actually be talking to a person in front or behind or at one side.

Advantages of Good Contact

What are the advantages of visual contact? First, it brings you into direct communication with your listeners. They know that what you have to say is meant for them. You are talking *to* them rather than *at* them. Secondly, your directness firmly establishes the one-to-one relationship of the circular response. You stimulate the listener; he responds to you by meeting you eye-to-eye. The line of communication for your ideas is a real one. Third, since the circular response is facilitated, your listener is more prone to respond. He knows that what you say is meant for him. Fourth and most important, it provides you with immediate insight as to whether or not the listener is attending and responding. If he isn't, you can immediately adapt your material, change your style, and concentrate your remarks on him until he does respond. And finally, maintaining visual contact forces you to be concerned about the listeners. You have to get outside yourself. You have to communicate. It is not possible for you to be preoccupied with your own thoughts and still maintain visual contact with the listener.

Problems of Poor Contact

Examine the results of weak visual contact or none at all. This speaker looks out the window, examines his notes, studies the floor, or stares over the heads of his listeners. What is the result? First, the listener becomes a *spectator* rather than a *participator*. Such a spectator has no contact with the speaker. He might just as well be listening to a radio loudspeaker. He loses the sense of the speech's being directed to him. He establishes no sense of communication with the speaker, and he can tune the speaker out just as simply as if he were a radio. The listener in this situation does not feel that the speaker really cares whether he listens or not. As a result the listener usually doesn't listen, and he lapses into doodling and preoccupation with his own thoughts.

Weak visual contact is in itself distracting. When the speaker looks out the window the listener is motivated to do likewise. He wonders, "What's so interesting out there?" When the speaker talks to his notes, the listener wants to see them.

Completely apart from our other arguments for having strong visual contact, there is perhaps the greatest reason of all—directness. Directness is one of the clues to personality. Think of the man who is unable or unwilling to look you in the eye when he talks. What do you say about him? If you are like millions of other Americans, you think of him as "shifty"—that there must be something wrong with him.

Visual contact compels the listener's attention. If contact is maintained, doodling, ruminating and napping will never begin. You are talking to him. He knows it. As a result he bestirs himself to listen.

MAKE YOUR POSTURE COUNT

Your posture or carriage can count for you or against you. Most of you unfortunately have terrible posture or there would be little need for this particular section. Good posture gives the listener the impression of dynamics and force, of purpose and directness.

Look around you the next time you are in a classroom. Note the twisted, slumped, "knees-on-the-chin" postures of your friends. The same is true of the office, though less so because your co-workers are more interested in creating a good impression. Watch the crowd on the street corner. Note the down on one hip, slouched, leaning, slovenly postures. What impression do you get? You assume that the character and attitude of the person is characterized by the way he stands and sits, and rightly so.

The trouble with bad posture is that it becomes a habit. Then when you are asked to speak you carry the same bad habit over to the speaking situation. No speaker who slouches, who leans, who lounges can give the impressions which are necessary to good speech. Even more important, it is impossible to be enthusiastic and energetic when you are seated or standing in a completely relaxed and indolent manner.

Characteristics of Good Posture

What are the characteristics of good posture? They are very simple. Stand tall. Not as though you had a ramrod driven down your spine; such a posture will give the impression of stiffness and over-bearance. Just stand tall—stand so that your bones are stacked comfortably with each one resting on the one below. Take a firm stance— not with your feet wide apart as though you are fulfilling the military command "At ease"; not with your feet pinched together so that you don't have a firm base; but comfortably, with your feet a few inches apart. If there is anything else to be said about posture, it might be this. Stand in such a way that your bearing neither attracts nor distracts attention.

MOVE FORCEFULLY AND WITH PURPOSE

Movement may be defined as the process of getting from one place to another on the platform as opposed to gesture which is the movement of some part of the body.

Remember movement holds attention. Thus it can attract your listener to your ideas or distract him from your ideas. Misplaced movement distracts. Examples of bad movement are endless. Watch speakers in action. There is the "pacer," who ambles diligently back and forth like a prisoner in a six-foot cell. He is releasing excess energy, but his movement is not related in any way to the expression of his ideas. Before long you begin counting the number of steps to the left and the number to the right, or you calculate the number of trips he will take per minute. This movement is distracting from the speech. Then there is the "rocker." He sways back and forth, back and forth, until you either begin to sway with him or get slightly seasick watching him. Don't forget the "pawer," the man who endlessly paws the ground like a bull ready to charge, or the "bouncer," who rolls his weight up on his toes, up and down, forward and back, up and down, forward and back.

The rules of good movement are almost as simple as the rules for good posture. Move only when there is a reason to move. Stand still unless your movement can contribute something to your speech. Now don't take this as the easy way out and try to defend the idea that you don't need to move. You do.

Movement for Transition.

Movement can show *transitions* in thought. You can indicate to the listener when you have concluded one group of ideas and are beginning the next. After the idea has been completed, move, pause, stop, begin the new idea. The listener can actually see the transition. He knows you have finished with one section and are beginning another. Most movement for transition will be lateral, that is from one side of the speaker's platform to another. The movement doesn't have to be great. Actually, if you desire, the idea of a transition can be communicated by nothing more than a single step.

Move for Emphasis.

Movement has an emphatic quality. It can give force to your ideas. Let's take a simple example of how you move naturally when you are stressing a point with ever greater force. You are standing on the street talking with a friend. You become more enthusiastic about your ideas; what do you do? You move toward him; you move in. You become more excited and more enthusiastic; you move in some more. Finally, you become angry because he doesn't respond as you wish him to. You move flush against him or even in the heat of the argument grab him by the shirt front and almost physically ram your idea down his throat. Obviously you can't use such measures in a public speech, but the principles are the same. You emphasize the important ideas by moving forward. You energetically set your body in the position of attack. You physically drive your ideas home. After you have concluded the point, you move back showing the transition in your ideas.

Note in these illustrations how your body has become part of the whole speech process. Your movement and your posture reflect exactly what you mean. They show the enthusiasm and energy of your ideas. They become a part of your expression of the idea.

Free Yourself from the Speaker's Stand.

Many times you will be provided a speaking stand. It is there to hold any notes or papers you may wish to use. It is not to hide behind. One of the worst ways to meet the speaking situation is to withdraw. Even withdrawal behind the speaker's stand is a sign of retreat. Don't cling to it as though it were a life preserver. Don't lean on it as though it were your only visible means of support. It is there to help not hinder your speech. Feel free to step out from behind it. Get out in plain view of your listeners where your movement can do the most good.

In summary, movement catches attention. Movement must have a purpose. Movement can be used for transition or emphasis. Movement must be forceful, enthusiastic, and direct.

USE GESTURE, THE LANGUAGE OF SIGNS

Gestures may be defined as *the movement of any part of the body.* You can gesture with your head, your shoulders, your trunk, your face, as well as with your hands. Sign language preceded speech. It still is the basis of communication between strangers who speak different languages; just as it is a fundamental aid to communication from any speaker to his listener.

Good Gestures Communicate

What can gestures do for you? They can catch attention and hold interest. They can help you describe and illustrate. They can emphasize your ideas. They can show the mood of your speech. They can encourage responsiveness in your listeners.

Consider the simplest speech to inform, telling a listener how to get someplace. Do you believe that it can be as meaningful and clear without gestures as with? Obviously not. With gestures the listener can see the turns as well as hear about them. Suppose you were going to demonstrate an extremely simple process, such as how to thread a needle, pass a football, or hold a tennis racket. Can it be done well without gestures? No. Suppose you are trying to persuade an obstinate friend that he should accept your point of view. Can you put your point across forcefully without emphasizing your arguments and appeals with forceful gestures? I doubt it. Gestures tell your listener that you mean what you say. They can describe, emphasize, and suggest.

Descriptive gestures are a natural part of the speech to demonstrate or instruct. Your hands can show the shapes of objects, directions of movement, levels of action. They can pantomime what you are saying.

Emphatic gestures for the most part follow the normal patterns of sign language. They are the gestures of pointing, counting, giving, receiving, accepting, rejecting. These gestures do not need to be defined. You use them every day of your life. Use them and their variants well, and you can add visual emphasis to your vocal emphasis.

Suggestive gestures can suggest the mood and quality of what you are saying. They have a rhythm, a force, a speed, and a duration. All of these elements act as signals to your listener as to what you think and how you feel. Suggest the placid calm of a lake at sunset; describe the painful dragging of exhausted troops. Each needs gesture, but the gestures will differ sharply in their quality and their meaning.

What Makes a Good Gesture?

"I can't gesture. My hands feel like huge hams hanging on the end of strings. Just let me hide them and I'll be all right." Here is one more example of running away. This time instead of hiding your entire body you think you will be happy if you can just hide part of it. Think of it this way. Your hands take care of themselves twenty-four hours each day. You pay them no heed. Why should you be suddenly concerned? Leave them alone; they'll do the job for you.

A. Hands in the pockets. If you want to do it, hands in the pockets is a perfectly natural way of standing. But don't put them there to hide them. Get them out where they can act and react. What's the matter with letting them hang at your sides? All you need to do is let go, and they will hang there all by themselves. It is the most natural position for hands. Besides, when the hands are free, they're available for spontaneous gesture.

B. Let gestures be natural. You start with your hands at your sides. If you never have the inclination to describe, to emphasize, or to suggest something in or about your speech, don't gesture. But if you are really interested in making your point, you can't help but gesture. Gestures will arise because they are needed. They will have a purpose because they are well motivated. They will be well-timed because they are aroused from within. *Don't plant gestures!* Never decide in advance how you are going to gesture. Never say, "At this point I will count on my fingers; now I will clench my fist; later I will describe the ball by shaping my hands like an orange." Gesture must be spontaneous.

C. Enlarge your natural gestures. Uneasiness inhibits action. Normally, you gesture frequently and fully in conversation, but when you rise to speak, the desire to gesture is decreased. This is a natural inhibition. Most speakers still gesture, even in this situation; but their movements become vague flutterings of their hands rather than full-fledged gestures. Reactivate your desire to gesture. Enlarge or exaggerate your small tendencies to describe, emphasize, and suggest. Soon you will be gesturing freely.

D. Feel free to gesture abundantly. Sometimes you hesitate to use your hands freely because you are afraid someone might notice them and think you foolish. Just the reverse is true. It is the unnatural, stiff lack of action which will be noted. Forceful gesturing provides a new way to use up excess energy. It will help you direct your attention where it belongs—to the listener.

WATCH OUT FOR ANNOYING MANNERISMS

Nothing can be as maddening to the listener as the annoying mannerism. You all know the speaker who pulls his ear, adjusts his glasses, jingles the change in his pockets, cracks his knuckles, twists his hair, toys with his notes or a pencil. These are idiosyncrasies or nervous habits. We all have them. In the speaking situation they must be controlled.

Nervous mannerisms attract attention because they involve movement and sound. They stimulate the listener and distract from the subject. In many instances you are not even aware that you have the mannerism. Have your friends or your instructor check you when you speak next time. If you do have such a mannerism, work hard at getting rid of it.

The overuse of a single gesture can become as annoying as a nervous habit. I know an instructor whose only gesture is to cup his hands to form a circle. He makes big circles and little circles. Everytime he gestures it is a circle. It can drive the listener crazy. I was so distracted that I began to count the number of circles per lecture. During one rather special hour, he made over two hundred circles—I dropped the course. Obviously this, though completely true, is an extreme illustration. The point is obvious. Make sure that you use a variety of gestures.

——Apply the Principles

Good bodily action may be summed up in a few simple words. Free your body to reflect the mood and meaning of your message. Bodily activity isn't something which is added to spice up the presentation. It is an integral part of the speaker and his speech. You can speak without bodily activity, just as an engine can still run at ten per cent efficiency; but it is a wasteful process. You have the machine and can control it; bring your delivery up to peak efficiency.

Observation

(1) Watch an animated conversation on the street corner or in your living room. What are the characteristic postures, movements, and gestures? Is the dynamics of each person's personality reflected in his action? How?

(2) List the kinds of gestures that are used in the above conversation. Which are descriptive? Emphatic? Suggestive? About how frequently do gestures arise? Are there moments with no gesture while a person is speaking? Note how the tensions of the person show up in his posture. Can you see the difference between good and bad posture?

Practice

(1) Describe a truly exciting event to your friends. Deliberately try to do it without any movement or gesture. What happens? Why do you feel hampered, restricted, tied down?

(2) Demonstrate for your listeners the use of a product, the operation of a simple gadget, or some simple process or operation. In each case select a subject where the actual product or gadget can be employed. For example, how to work a new can opener. The can opener could be actually demonstrated. Deliver the speech twice, once with gesture only once with the actual demonstration. What are the differences? Which is easier? Why? Which is clearer? Why?

(3) Develop a persuasive speech on a subject you feel strongly about. Can you feel the need for bodily action? If you can't, something is wrong with your attitude toward the subject or the listener.

FORMULA J

$$BVFD = \frac{BA}{PFDGI}$$

(*BVFD*) *Be Visually Forceful and Direct* = Putting
(*PFDGI*) *Purpose, Force, Directness, Genuineness and Interpretation* into your (*BA*) *Bodily Activity.*

Now, apply the formula!

Have your listeners indicate what they *see* in your next speaking situation by using the scale below. Bodily action is the most neglected phase of the speaking situation. Do not treat it lightly.

Scale for Visual Concerns *From the Specific to the General*			
1–2 Unsatisfactory	*3 Neutral*		*4–5 Satisfactory*
Concerns		Score	Comments
VISUAL SPECIFICS	Approach to platform	——	
	Grooming	——	
	Carriage-Posture	——	
	Facial communication	——	
	Gestures	——	
	Movement	——	
	Interest in listeners	——	
	Interest in subject	——	
	Leaving platform	——	
CONTRIBUTIONS	Aids vocal expression	——	
	Emphasizes ideas	——	
	Relieves tension	——	
DESCRIPTION OF BODILY ACTIVITY	Purposeful	——	
	Forceful	——	
	Direct	——	
	Genuine	——	
	Interpretive	——	

be vocally
distinct and pleasant

TWENTY YEARS of radio has proved the significance of the human voice. Literally hundreds of personalities are known to us only by their voices. Their voices tell us what they are. Similarly the voice of the speaker tells us what he is.

Reread the section in the preceding chapter which answers the question, "What does the listener see?" All of the factors which the listener sees are also factors which he hears. He *hears* what you are; that is, he makes judgments concerning your personality. He *hears* your interest in him; he is able to judge your attitude toward him by the qualities he finds in your voice. He *hears* your interest in your subject; your enthusiasm or lack of it communicates itself through your voice.

YOUR VOICE SUGGESTS YOUR PERSONALITY

Listen to the voices on a radio broadcast. Radio is chosen only because you are given practically no other clues to judge a person by other than his voice. Think of the radio drama. What are the clues that you get to the kind of person who is talking?

First, you judge their characters by the general quality of their voices. The coarse, rough tenor tells us that the speaker is uncouth, uneducated, unpolished. The strident, whiny nasal twang suggests a person who is unpleasant and self-centered. The full round hearty pleasant voice might imply a person with these same characteristics. A high-pitched, hesitant, flat tone suggests a person who is unsure, afraid, and lacking in poise and maturity. These are just radio actors? No, it is more than that. These are pictures or images which we carry in our heads. They are called stereotypes, and we live by them. We have a stereotype of the uncouth man, of the polished man, of the old man, of the sweet young thing, and so on. These stereotypes carry over into our everyday living. We apply them to the people we meet. Listen to the voices of your friends. You may be surprised to find that they reflect rather exactly what you think they are. We assign meaning to vocal quality.

We judge by more than quality or tone alone. We also make a decision on the basis of the forcefulness of the voice and the speed with which the speaker talks. Think of the man who talks in fits and starts, who clips his words, who speaks in staccato phrases rather than in sentences. Think of the man who drawls his speech, who drags out his words, who "ahs" and "ers" and "and a's" his every sentence. These elements also give us clues to his personality and provide a basis for judging him.

We also judge a man by the distinctness with which he speaks. The incoherent mumbler, the man who drops out sounds, the man who mispronounces, and the man who murders the king's English provide us with a basis for judgment. In contrast, the person who speaks clearly, distinctly, pronounces correctly, and uses good grammar gives us a very different impression. Or to go still further, the man who is overly precise, who delights in hearing his own voice, who speaks with an affected style and diction also provides us with the clues necessary to determine his personality.

Two job applicants were interviewed by the personnel agent for a major corporation for a position classified as Junior Executive. Jones had approximately a "B" average in his work. Brown had almost a straight "A" average. Jones expressed himself well. Brown had slovenly speech. Which one got the job? Jones. When asked why, the personnel agent has this to say, "This job calls for an executive. Our executives must be able to deal with and impress other people. They must sound like executives. Brown may have more brains, but he is not the executive type." It all fits in with the senior Henry Ford's famous statement, "I can buy brawn at forty cents an hour. I can buy brains at a dollar an hour. But personality, that's the most expensive material there is." Change the wage scale to fit our modern times if you will, but remember the thought.

HOW IS VOICE PRODUCED?

Before you can learn to control your voice to get the results that you want, it is helpful to know something about what voice is and how it is produced.

The speaking mechanism can be divided into four parts; each division makes a distinct contribution to the production of voice and speech. The divisions are (1) respiration which provides a moving column of air, (2) phonation which supplies the vibrations necessary to the production of a tone, (3) resonation which supports, amplifies, and gives special characteristics to the tone, and (4) articulation which breaks up the sounds and noises of voice into intelligible speech.

Respiration

The biological function of respiration is obvious. It is the process of supplying the body with the necessary oxygen for survival. The respiration cycle has two phases: inhalation, the portion of the cycle during which air is sucked into the lungs, and exhalation, the portion of the cycle during which used air and waste material are forced out of the lungs. In other words, respiration is basically a simple pumping process.

The process is easily understood if you conceive of a bell jar which has both flexible sides and a flexible bottom. Inside the jar is a sealed system of tubes ending in a pair of balloons. The only way that air can get into the jar is through the tube at the top which is connected to the balloons. You know from elementary physics that air at a pressure of approximately 15 lbs. sq. in. surrounds the jar and fills the tubes and balloons inside the jar. In Figure 9, the jar is shown and the various parts of the respiratory system are represented in the bottom half of the mechanical man.

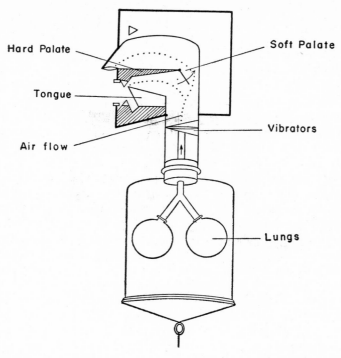

Fig. 9. The Mechanical Man. A simple mechanical schematic representation of the essential elements of the vocal process.

Working the pump is a very simple process. Pull out the sides of the jar and pull down the bottom of the jar. The space inside the jar is increased causing a decrease in pressure inside the jar. In order to equalize the pressure air rushes into the balloons. To expel the air, the sides of the jar are allowed to fall back into position and the bottom is permitted to resume its normal position. The pressure inside the jar becomes greater than that outside and the balloons are deflated.

The sides of the jar are the rib cage; the bottom of the jar is the diaphragm, the tube at the top of the jar is the trachea, or windpipe; the two tubes which lead to the balloons are the bronchial tubes; the balloons are the lungs. In inhalation or inspiration of air, you raise the rib cage by a complex muscle system and contract or straighten out the diaphragm which is also a muscle. The decrease in pressure inside the system draws in air through the trachea and the bronchial tubes into the lungs. Exhalation or expiration is a reversal of the process. In normal expiration the weight of the rib cage is sufficient to drop it back into position. The viscera, which have been pushed aside by contracting the diaphragm, push it back into position when it is relaxed. These changes create the pressure which expels the air from the lungs. In forced expiration, when you push the air out of your lungs, the chest cage is forced back into position by a different set of muscles, and the diaphragm is pushed back by contraction of the abdomen.

Respiration provides one necessary element for the production of voice—a moving column of air. Four differences between respiration for life and respiration for speech should be noted: (1) Voice production is dependent on the second phase of respiration. It uses a moving column of air on its way out of the system. We speak on expiration. (2) The normal breathing cycle is regular. The same amount of time is devoted to inspiration as to expiration. The cycle may be fast as in exertion or slow as in sleep but the two parts take the same time. In speech inspiration is quick and expiration is long. It must be long enough to produce the desired word groupings on a single breath. (3) For speech the air column must be steady enough to produce a clear and sustained tone. (4) The column of air must be controlled so that its force can be changed to meet the needs for more and less forceful utterance.

Phonation

Phonation takes place in the larynx, a boxlike formation of cartilages which encloses a pair of lips (the glottis) that acts as a valve. The primary physiological function of the valve is twofold. First, it protects the respiratory system against foreign matter. For example, it keeps food and liquids out of the windpipe. If a particle does get past the valve, an explosion known as coughing clears the pipe. Secondly, the valve can seal off the respiratory tract to provide a fixed body of air against which we can pull when we exert ourselves. You hold your breath. Try lifting while exhaling. You can't do it satisfactorily. You have to close the valve and lift against the fixed body of air. These life functions explain why you can't talk when you get something in your windpipe, and why you can't talk during moments of heavy exertion.

The glottis is used in a very different manner when sound is produced. The lips, often known as the vocal bands or cords, are brought close together, but not sealed off. The moving column of air sets them into vibration. Small puffs of air pop through the vocal lips much as air pops through a trumpeter's lips. At the risk of oversimplification think of an air siren, a spinning disc with holes in it. Direct a jet of air against the perforations and a tone is produced. Increase the speed of the disc and the pitch of the tone rises, because the frequency of the puffs has been increased. The vibration of the vocal lips is similar; however, the pitch of the tone in this case depends upon the speed of vibration, which is controlled by the length of the lips and their tension. The tension of the vocal bands is controlled by moving the cartilages of the voice box or larynx. Put your finger on your Adam's apple; this is one of the cartilages of the larynx. Sing a high note and then without stopping drop the note an octave. Notice how the cartilage moves down and back. On the high note the cartilage has stretched out the vocal bands and on the low note it has loosened them. There is more to it than this, but now you should at least have the idea.

Resonation

The resonators are a series of passages and cavities. The principle ones are the mouth, the throat, technically known as the pharynx, the upper part of the larynx, and the nasal chambers.

The life function of these cavities is obvious. The mouth, throat, and upper larynx are used to pass air and food into the system. The nasal chambers are limited to the passage of air.

In voice production the chambers act as resonators. They amplify certain parts of the sound and damp out others. They give character to the sound such as mellowness or flatness. They serve the same function as the resonating chambers of musical instruments. Without the resonating chambers, the tone produced by the vocal lips would be thin and weak. Think for a moment of a trumpeter. The sound is produced by the vibration of the trumpeter's lips. With your lips tightly compressed, try to make a high pitched raspberry sound. Note how weak and thin it is. The same is true when you add the mouth piece. But when you add the resonating chambers of the tubing and bell, the sound is amplified and given a quality.

The same is true of the voice mechanism. By changing the shape and size of the mouth and throat we are able to produce the different qualities which are known as vowel sounds. Pronounce the sound (ee) as in *feet*. Forget the lips for a moment and concentrate on the way the mouth chamber is shaped by the placement of the tongue. Now pronounce the sound (oo) as in b*oo*t. Note how the resonating chamber has been reshaped. Now pronounce the sounds (m, n, ng) as in *m*a, *n*o, and pi*ng*. These are nasal sounds which are sounded through the nasal resonating chambers. In fact, these three sounds are the only ones in English which are deliberately sounded through the nose; all others are sounded through the mouth.

Articulation

The fourth phase of speech production is articulation. Articulation may be defined as the process of breaking up the tones and noises of voice into speech sounds and joining them into an understandable grouping which we know as language.

The articulators are generally considered to be the lips, tongue, jaw, and soft palate, which are the movable parts, and the teeth, gum ridge, and roof of the mouth (hard palate), which are the fixed surfaces.

In the production of speech sounds the articulators help in the formation of the vowels by shaping the resonating chambers. The tongue, jaw, and lips all function in this manner. More important the articulators break up and join sounds to form the consonants. Without going deeply into the process, you might be interested in the major characteristics of the consonant sounds.

A. Voiced and unvoiced consonants. Some of the consonant sounds are voiced, and some are unvoiced. Compare the sound (s) in the word *s*ip with the sound (z) in the word *z*ip. The sounds (s) and (z) are formed identically. The difference is that in one case (s) just air is rushing through the groove made by the articulators, and in the other (z) the vocal lips are vibrating to make a tone. Try these other comparisans. Compare (f) as in *f*at with (v) as in *v*at. Compare (p) as in *p*at with (b) as in *b*at. Compare (t) as in *t*in with (d) as in *d*in.

Compare (k) as in *c*url with (g) as in *g*irl. In each pair the sounds are formed the same way. The difference is that they are either unvoiced or voiced.

B. *Plosives or stops.* Many of the consonant sounds are called plosives or stops. They are made by building up air pressure and then exploding it. (p) and (b) are formed by holding the lips together, and then exploding the sound. Note one is voiced the other unvoiced. The sounds (t) and (d) are exploded with the blade of the tongue against the gum ridge. The consonants (k) and (g) are exploded with the back of the tongue raised against the roof of the mouth.

C. *Fricatives.* The fricative sounds are formed by forcing either air or tone through a particularly shaped aperture. For example, (f) and (v) are formed by placing the lower lip against the upper teeth and blowing. One is unvoiced, the other voiced. Note the formation of the other fricatives: (s) and (z), (th) as in *th*in and (th) as in *th*en, (sh) as in *sh*ip and (zh) as in vi*s*ion, and finally, (h) as in *h*at, which is a voiceless sound.

D. *Affricates.* The affricates combine the qualities of the plosive and the fricative. They start with an explosion and continue with sound passing through an aperture. They are (ch) as in *ch*ur*ch* and (j) as in judge.

E. *The glides or semi-vowels* are formed with certain of the articulators in operation. They are (wh) as in *wh*y, (w) as in *w*it, (l) as in *l*ip, (r) as in *r*ut, and (y) as in *y*et. Notice the motion of the lips and tongue as these sounds are produced.

F. *The nasals.* The nasal sounds were mentioned previously. They are (m, n, ng). Note how they are formed.

Just as important as the correct formation of the sound is the manner in which you put them together. The way you *articulate* them. Now let us apply your embryonic knowledge of how speech is produced to attaining the major goals of good voice usage.

THE CHARACTERISTICS OF A VOICE

A desirable voice is (1) sufficiently forceful to be heard, (2) pleasant to listen to, (3) clear and distinct, and (4) sufficiently varied to be interesting. If you can achieve these qualities, your voice will add to the effectiveness of both you and your ideas.

Develop a Forceful Voice

A forceful voice is more than just a loud voice. Forceful speaking is more than turning up the volume. It is not yelling or talking "at the top of your voice." You wouldn't last an hour as a drill sergeant if you yelled your commands. Yelling means tension. Tension of the muscles of the larynx and throat can tear your voice to ribbons. A forceful voice depends upon correct breathing, relaxation of the vocal mechanism, complete phonation, satisfactory pitch, and full resonation.

A. Breathe correctly. The only purpose in breathing for speech is to provide a strong, sustained, controlled column of air. Little agreement exists between the experts on the question of whether abdominal or diaphragmatic breathing is any better than medial or chest breathing. Apparently the manner of breathing is not important. The timing of breath is more significant. As long as a sufficient amount of breath is inhaled and exhaled to properly support the sounds of a meaningful group of words, your breathing is correct. Breathing should contribute to a forceful voice by increasing the amount and steadiness of the column of air.

B. Relax the vocal mechanism. The great problem of most speakers who wish to turn up the volume is that they increase the tension of the throat and larynx at the same time. The result is a higher pitch and a harsh strident tone rather than more force. A full-throated tone depends on relaxation. If you wish to increase the force, relax the vocal muscles; this will keep the pitch the same or lower it. The open, relaxed tone varies much better than the tight, pinched tone.

C. Use complete phonation. Frequently voices lack force because air is being wasted. When the vocal lips are brought into vibration unvoiced air slips through. A husky or hoarse quality is the most noticeable result of poor phonation. When this occurs, you are not getting full returns in sound for your efforts. The tone is not clear and as a result doesn't carry or project well. Occasionally poor phonation is the result of injury to the vocal lips, but usually it is merely habitual misuse that causes it.

Test your phonation with a very old procedure. Light a candle and hold it in front of your mouth. Produce vowel sounds such as "ahhhhhh," "eehhhhhh" or "oohhhhhh." If you are phonating properly, the flame of the candle should barely waver. Now try words such as "pop" or "sissy." Note the action of the candle flame. This should show you the meaning of the terms plosive and fricative.

D. Choose the right pitch. Frequently the habitual pitch at which you speak is not the ideal or optimum pitch. As you know, the resonators amplify some tones and tend to damp out others. Find your optimum pitch by the following procedure. Go to a piano and find "F" above middle "C." Sing the sound "Ahhhhhh" on that note. Now go down the scale singing "ahhhhhh" for each note until you reach the point where you sense that you are forcing your voice. Now. Count up the scale three or four notes. Sound "ahhhhhh" or that note. Try the one above and the one below. Choose the note which gives the fullest most resonant tone. This is your optimum pitch. Compare it with your habitual pitch. If the two don't agree, practice speaking at your optimum pitch.

E. Open the resonators. This is really a part of relaxing the mechanism. Tension of any sort, particularly in the resonating chamber, results in poor tone and weak carrying power. Round your throat when you speak. Keep your sounds to the front; avoid swallowing them. One excellent method of relaxing the resonating chambers is yawning. A full yawn stretches out the mouth and throat and leaves them relaxed. Satisfactory resonation not only gives better force; it is an integral part of making the voice pleasing.

Develop a Pleasing Voice

A pleasant voice is a well-modulated, well-controlled voice. We dislike the voice that booms in our ears as well as the voice which we can't hear. We dislike the voice that is pitched so high that it seems shrill. We dislike the voice which has any unpleasant quality that calls attention to itself.

A. Learn to project correctly. Force, as it affects the listener, is more a matter of hearing than of voice production. You have learned how to speak with force; now learn how to modulate your force so that it fits the situation in which you are speaking. If the people with whom you talk frequently beg your pardon or ask you to speak up, it is because they cannot hear or understand. You are under-projecting your voice. It may be a problem of distinctness, but frequently it is simply a matter of your not talking loudly enough. Check your volume with your friends. They'll tell you where to tune the volume control.

In the audience situation you may be speaking too loudly (over-projecting) or too softly because you have misjudged the acoustical qualities of the room. Watch those persons at the rear of the room. If they shift and twist and lean forward, you can be certain that they are not hearing. Raise your volume. Bring your tones forward.

B. *Use your optimum pitch.* In our present society unpleasant pitch invariably means too high a pitch. We have been conditioned by the deep resonant voices on the radio and television. We admire and respond to deep voices. This doesn't mean that you should try to force your voice down into a range where it was not meant to go, but follow the procedures already laid out for finding your optimum pitch.

C. *Use good vocal quality.* Most of you have a perfectly normal and pleasant vocal quality. However, unpleasant quality or tone can be extremely distracting to your listeners. Following are some of the most typical unpleasant vocal qualities and their causes: (1) The strident, harsh, rasping tone usually comes from excessive muscle tension. (2) The husky or hoarse quality indicates that the vocal lips are not phonating properly. It can be the result of an organic defect in the structure, but it usually stems from misuse of the voice. (3) The throaty, guttural quality comes from swallowing sounds and sometimes it arises because the speaker is forcing his voice down in pitch to an undesirable level. (4) The nasal quality is flat and has a very unpleasant twang. It comes from sending sounds other than (m, n, ng) through the nasal resonators. Most frequently nasal quality is merely bad habit and can be corrected. Unfortunately one of the characteristics of certain regional dialects is a nasal twang.

Desirable quality can be obtained by maximum phonation and a relaxed vocal mechanism, particularly relaxation of the resonating chambers. A full, rich, vibrant quality suggests a forceful, hearty, pleasant personality.

Develop Distinctness and Clarity in Voice

One thing that everyone will agree upon is that there is no substitute for a distinct, clear voice. Lack of distinctness has broken down communications and cost lives during battle. It has tied up telephone lines and cost money in business. It confuses and frays the nerves of listeners everyday. It is mandatory if you are to be understood. Even if you can be understood, indistinct speech creates a bad impression of you and your abilities. Indistinctness can usually be laid at the door of either faulty articulation or mispronunciation.

A. *Articulate accurately and clearly.* Too many of us are lip lazy, jaw sluggish, and tongue tired. We just aren't willing to take the effort necessary to produce the vowels and consonants and join them together crisply. The result is muddled, mumbled, jumbled speech.

To form the vowel sounds correctly and completely, the lips, tongue, and jaw must be active. Form the vowel sound (ee) as in *feet*, then the vowel (ah) as in *father*, finally the vowel (oo) as in *boot*. Repeat these three sounds a number of times. Be sure that the "ah" and the "oo" are formed in the same forward position as was the "ee." Notice first what activity the lips perform; then repeat them again and notice the jaw; and finally try it noticing the action of the tongue. Without active use of the lips and tongue and even the jaw, the sounds can't be formed adequately. All of the vowel sounds become sort of neutral in quality without any distinguishing characteristics. If they can't be distinguished they obviously can't be understood. Repeat several sentences and lay your finger on your jaw. Is it active? If not exaggerate its use until you become accustomed to making it really work. Do the same for your tongue and lips.

In many instances sloppy articulation results in the loss of the vowel sound altogether. For example, "poem" is wrongly pronounced "pome," "diamond" becomes "dimond," "cruel" becomes "crool," "ruin" becomes "rune."

Formation of the consonant sounds requires even greater activity of the lips, tongue, and jaw. Careless articulation of the consonants always makes speech indistinct. Frequently the carelessness reaches a point where the speaker doesn't bother to form them at all. Notice the omissions when "acts" is pronounced "acs or ax," when "hundred" becomes "hunnerd," "only" becomes "ony," "didn't" becomes "dint," "lifts" becomes "lifs," "kept" becomes "kep."

Another common example of carelessness is the addition of sounds; such as "athalete" for "athlete," "fillum" instead of "film," "warsh" instead of "wash," "acrost" instead of "across," "attackted" instead of "attacked." Closely allied to adding sound is sounding consonants which should be silent. These usually occur when the spelling is misleading. For example, "often" should be pronounced "ofen."[1]

While laziness and carelessness are the causes of most problems in speaking distinctly, speed can cause trouble. The nervous or excited speaker goes so fast that it is difficult if not impossible to distinguish between the sounds which he produces. When speed is coupled with mumbling and slurring, the game is lost.

B. Take care in pronunciation. The subject of pronunciation is a confusing one. There is no correct pronunciation which can be rigidly applied everywhere. The Southerner pronounces many words differently from the Easterner. The rest of the country uses still a different set of pronunciations. The best advice that can be given is (1) conform to the standards of pronunciation used by the educated people of your own region and (2) rely on a good dictionary such as Webster, Century, or Standard.

Make the Voice Interesting

A voice which is forceful, pleasant, and distinct should by its very nature be an interesting voice, but it may not be if it lacks variety. You have all heard the monotonous reading of the quarterly report or the endless droning of your local minister. Vocal variety adds a breath of life to your speaking. It involves animation and change. The elements of voice which can be varied are *rate, force, and pitch.*

A. Develop variety in rate. Speed is relative. It can be recognized only when it is compared with slowness and vice versa. It loses its meaning when it continues over a period of time. At the start of a trip, sixty miles an hour may seem dangerously fast. After driving a while the same sixty miles an hour will begin to seem slow. When you slow down to a crawl while going through a town, a glance at the speedometer may show that you are still going at a forty mile per hour clip. It is not so much a matter of how fast to talk as how varied the rate can be. The high speed speaker becomes just as dreadfully monotonous after a bit as the low speed speaker or the average speed speaker.

Don't misunderstand. It is certainly possible to speak too fast or too slowly. Many beginning speakers speak so fast that it is impossible to

---

[1] For a more complete discussion of the problem of voice, see Louis Levy, *et. al., Voice and Speech Handbook,* Englewood Cliffs, N.J.: Prentice-Hall, Inc., 1955.

understand them and all of their material is run together into a single meaningless jumble. In contrast, some speakers speak too slowly. They drag out each word by itself. The speech groans along. The listener turns his attention to other matters.

Let's suppose that your rate averages exactly 150 words per minute. Does that mean that it is a good rate? Only if there are sharp variations in speed within the average. The rate of speaking depends upon material; it must reflect the mood and quality of the ideas. A story may be told quickly so that the buildup won't drag. The punch line probably should be slowed down to give it emphasis. Description of a sporting event may require a very fast rate; important, weighty ideas will require a slower pace. *Changes* in speed can provide emphasis and interest.

A word about *pause*. Every actor knows that pause is a potent weapon to hold interest, to emphasize a line, to set off an idea. The speaker has the same weapon. Most beginning speakers seem to have a violent fear that a pause might develop. The fear is so violent that they fill every space with "uh," "er," or "and a." Pauses act in speech as punctuation does in writing. Use them to show the breaks in thought, the changes of idea, the important point.

B. Develop variety in force. We have discussed the process of creating a forceful voice in a previous section. Now we are concerned with the uses that can be made of force or volume. The problem is identical to that of rate. The little voice that can't be heard in the back of the room must assuredly be developed and projected. At the other extreme, the loud noisy person must be toned down. But it is the *changes* in force that create interest. Contrasts in volume are necessary. As with rate, the changes must reflect the ideas which are being uttered; use force to drive home the important ideas, not the unimportant ones. The speaker who tackles his listeners with hammer and tongs soon wears them out. They are dulled by the constant use of power. Nothing has climax; nothing is subordinate. Force can be used to help the listener understand; it can be used to provide emphasis; it can be used to create mood. Note that we have said that the force should reflect the ideas. Never just turn it on like a faucet for no reason; it will sound hollow and unreal.

C. Develop variety in pitch. Don't be a "Johnny-One-Note," even if that note represents your optimum pitch. Far too many speakers are content to talk along on a single note with a downward step at the end of each sentence or thought. Words and ideas change their meaning depending upon how they are inflected. Inflex is the upward or downward slide or step in pitch. The voice actually slides up the musical scale or down it. Upward inflections normally indicate a question, doubt, unsureness. Try the sentence, "Is that right?" with an upward inflection at the end. Note that it leaves the thought up in the air. It suggests doubt and question. Now read the same sentence with a downward inflection at the end. "Is that right!" Note the change in meaning. Now it says "For heaven's sake" or "You don't say." Vary your inflection to show the meaning of what you say. Practice to get the exact meaning out of ideas.

The gradual or abrupt change in pitch within a thought or idea is called melody pattern. Most of you have your own set melody pattern which differentiates your speech from others. It is a pattern of pitch changes which you use over and over again. For example, the primary characteristic of foreign dialects is their melody pattern. Careful reflection on the meanings and particularly the mood of what you say or read will bring forth new and more varied melody patterns and make for a more interesting voice.

The voice with maximum flexibility in the use of rate, force, and pitch is an interesting voice which holds the listener's attention. It is easy to listen to; it doesn't tire the listener. More important, the voice with vocal variety gets the most out of the material. It separates the ideas; it emphasizes the important thoughts; it gives mood and quality to the speech.

——Apply the Principles

Being vocally distinct and pleasant requires thorough understanding and constant application of the principles involved. Imitation of the voice beautiful is not your goal. Strive only to be yourself at your vocal best.

(1) Record your voice or have an expert listen to your next speech. If you record, listen to the record and list your assets and your faults. In either case have an expert also make a list of your assets and faults.

(2) Find out the *causes* of your vocal problems and seek solu-

tions to them. Consult an expert. Self-improvement (without expert advice) can be dangerous.

(3) Practice, practice, practice! Remember you have been talking the same way for many years. You can't expect to change such firmly fixed habits in a day or even a week. It will take time. Be patient. The results will be worth it.

FORMULA K

BVDP = FPDI

(BVDP) Be Vocally Distinct and Pleasant = Becoming vocally *(FPDI)* Forceful, Pleasant, Distinct, and Interesting.

Now, apply the formula!

Your purpose in developing your voice is to improve your ability to communicate with a listener. Your voice is important only as it affects your listener. Below is a list of criteria which you should review for any speech you give.

Criteria for Vocal Improvement

A List of Reminders

BE VOCALLY FORCEFUL:

Breathe correctly
Relax the vocal mechanism
Use complete phonation
Choose the right pitch
Open the resonators

BE VOCALLY PLEASANT:

Project properly
Use your optimum pitch
Develop good vocal quality

BE VOCALLY DISTINCT:

Articulate accurately and clearly
Take care in pronunciation

BE VOCALLY INTERESTING:

Develop variety in rate
Develop variety in force
Develop variety in pitch

These technologists are examining the nuclear reactor built by the Battelle
Institute. What are the factors of clarity essential to this speaking situation?
(CHAPTER 7) What are the tools of interest that the speaker might include in
this speaking occasion? (CHAPTER 8) *Courtesy Battelle Memorial Institute.*

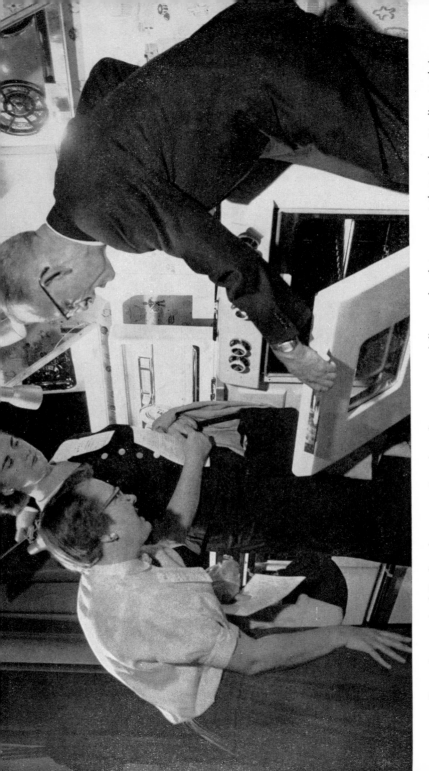

Persuasion may be defined as the process of getting others to want to believe or do what you want them to by appealing to their reason or their emotions. What types of proof is the speaker probably using? What factors of prestige may be involved? What basic drives may be involved? List some uses of suggestion which could be adapted. (CHAPTER 9) Courtesy Ohio Fuel Gas Company.

preparing the
oral technical report

Your life as a technical man is a solid string of reports. This is particularly true if you are an engineer. You make reports to conferences on engineering plans and ideas. You make reports to your employers on the results of field studies. You make reports about sales promotions, about budgets, about solutions to problems, on the results of testing materials. You make reports to lay groups who are interested in how your plans can solve their problems. You make reports to employees on the progress of the company and its work.

Many of these reports are in written form. They are submitted and that is the end of it. Some take the form of an interview in which you are asked questions; your answers constitute the report. For others you are called upon to make an oral presentation. This chapter deals with how you can best prepare and present the oral report.

KINDS OF TECHNICAL REPORTS

Reports may be classified as to their purpose. Some reports are summaries of events that have taken place, (Summary Reports). Other reports go a step further and provide new facts and information about a problem, (Fact-finding Reports). The most complex type of report analyzes, interprets, and recommends new action, (Critical Reports).

Summary Reports

The summary report is the briefest and simplest type of report. It is historical in nature for it tells about the past. You are presenting the simplest kind of summary report when you tell your friend what you did during the summer or on the date last night. Somewhat more formal summary reports are used to keep abreast of what is happening in business and industry. The shop foreman makes a weekly summary report of his unit's production. The corporation makes a summary report to the stockholders on the status of the company. The construction engineer reports on the progress of his work. The salesman reports his weekly sales.

Most summary reports are simple and brief. Frequently the report is submitted in written form with merely a brief oral summary of its contents. The purpose of the report is to boil down the known facts. The organization of the report involves little more than finding a convenient pattern for showing the facts.

Fact-Finding Reports

The fact-finding report usually includes the elements of the summary report, the known facts, and then introduces new information and evidence.

The most typical example of the information gathering report is that made by the scientist when he concludes his work in testing a material, or the engineer who has surveyed the problem, or the doctor who has examined the patient and makes his diagnosis. In each case the fact-finding report begins with a problem. Before the report can be made, the problem must be either explored or solved. It is a report on findings.

These reports can be quite complex depending upon the problem. They may be submitted in a written form but are frequently accompanied by a full oral report.

Critical Reports

The critical report may stand by itself providing the recipient or listener knows all the facts. Or it may begin with a summary of the existing facts, go on to report the new information which has been discovered, and then proceed to interpret the information and provide recommendations for future action.

In his fact-finding report the doctor gives the diagnosis; in his critical report he provides the prognosis and recommends the treatment. The engineer assembles the facts and then interprets them and recommends action. This type of report goes beyond the past and present and projects itself into the future. This is the type of report which precedes the introduction of a new process, the use of new materials, or the expansion of an operation.

The critical analysis is the most complex type of report. It is invariably submitted in written form and is accompanied by an oral presentation of at least its highlights.

Since the critical report almost always includes both of the simpler types, our discussion will center around it. If your report is a simpler one stop when you have gone as far as you need to. Please understand that the purpose here is to show how to prepare the oral presentation of your report. It may help you to write a satisfactory report, but such considerations are secondary.[1]

HOW TO PREPARE AN ORAL REPORT

The steps in preparing a technical report are very similar to those used in preparing any other type of speech, because in each situation you should follow the best procedure for developing an idea.

Determine the Specific Purpose

Your general purpose in making a report will almost always be to inform. In the critical report you may be forced to persuade your listeners that your recommendations should be accepted, but usually this comes later. The report merely informs them of your interpretation and recommendation.

Since a report is invariably made at someone's request, the definition of the specific purpose should be clear. The specific purpose is to provide a complete, thorough, and exact statement of all of the pertinent

[1] For a more complete discussion of the form, style, and preparation of the written report, see Robert Q. Brown, *Introduction to Engineering Problems,* Englewood Cliffs, N.J.: Prentice-Hall, Inc., 1948, pp. 153–177.

facts, to give a clear, concise analysis and interpretation warranted by the facts, and to provide recommendations based on the analysis.

Reports fail to fulfill the specific purpose when (1) there are omissions of pertinent facts, (2) the analysis of the facts is faulty or incomplete, or (3) the interpretations and recommendations are not warranted. A fourth reason for reports failing to satisfy the specific purpose results from a faulty analysis of the listeners.

Analyze the Listeners

In every case the report must fit the listeners. Even though the subject of the report remains unchanged, the content of the report depends upon who the listeners are. For example, suppose you are asked to report on recent developments in television circuitry. You won't prepare the same report for an audience of television repairmen as you would for the design department of a major television corporation.

The expert-lay or professional-amateur status of the listeners is particularly significant in report making. Most reports are given before technically qualified professionals. In such a report you may assume a thorough background in the subject and use all of the technical terms and jargon you desire. With the amateur listener you will have to adjust your material and take those steps necessary to understanding. (See Chapter 7.)

Remember that a technical report gives you an audience that is extremely interested in the new facts and interpretations. The transfer of the information is the primary concern; being interesting is secondary. If you can assemble and present your report so that it is completely clear, you need not worry about how interesting it is. Interest will take care of itself.

Gather the Material

The material for a report is derived primarily from two sources. First, there is the data which has already been prepared and published. Second, there is the information that is known to experts in the field. These are your best sources of information. Finally, there is the data which is discovered in field study and laboratory experimentation.

Suppose you are a geologist who has been sent to an area in search of oil. You are to study the situation and recommend the exact drilling site. You have in your hands the making or losing of hundreds of thousands of dollars. How do you go about the report? First, you gather together from reading and interviews all of the known data. You get the government geologic surveys, the reports of other companies' experiences in drilling in the area—all of the facts pertinent to your problem. Then you acquire new information by research and experimentation at the proposed site. All of these elements plus your recommendations are worked together into a report.

One of the most important aspects in gathering material for a report is the sifting of the significant and pertinent facts from those which do not contribute. Time and again reporters include information which is not needed and overlook key facts in their research. If you are reporting on a new process for making soap, there is probably no need to survey all of the known processes for making it. Yet there is every need to report on the availability of materials and the costs which would be involved in the new process.

Since accuracy of the data is of such paramount importance, you should accept only completely reliable sources. These sources should be checked and rechecked. For data which has been published go to the original document. Don't depend upon a review, résumé, or a rehash. The authors of the review may have made errors of omission or interpretation.

Organize the Oral Report

The organization of the oral report depends upon its purpose. If a detailed report has been submitted, the oral presentation may be only a summary of the important facts. If the oral report must stand by itself, the detail must be complete. In either case, the report must be organized with one question in mind. What does the listener *want* and *need* to know?

Since the accuracy is essential to sound reporting, the listener should be given not only the important elements of the data, but also the sources of the data and the method used in gathering and compiling the information. In addition he wants a clearcut summary of the essential elements and in a critical report he will want not only your recommendations but also the reasons for your conclusions.

Remember that your auditor is listening not reading. He must get all of the essential facts at one time. Avoid including so much detail in your report that it confuses rather than clarifies. Make heavy use of summaries which will pull the ideas together.

The oral report is a speech to inform. Thus its organization may follow the procedures suggested in Chapter 6 for dividing materials so that they will be clear.

The organization of your recommendations and interpretations in the critical report requires special consideration. Your evaluation must be based on some set of standards or criteria. If you are recommending a plan of action, such as drilling an oil well, your standards for comparison will be the factors involved in bringing in a producing well; for example, the depth of drilling, the difficulty in drilling, and so forth. Having set up the standards, you may then match your data against the standards and assess the chances of success or failure of this particular drilling project.

Interpretation and criticism of data may also take other forms. You may point out the limitations of the data and recommend that further study be made. You may compare the data with already known and accepted facts, interpret this relationship, and analyze the implications.

Don't overlook the possibility of negative findings. Remember the purpose of the report is to find the truth. You have no axe to grind. The conclusion that the analysis didn't show a relationship may be just as significant if not more significant than finding that a relationship does exist.

Outline the Oral Report

The form in which your report might be organized is suggested below. This is followed by a sample outline. Notice how the sample follows the requirements of the form. The outline treats the organization of a comparatively complex report. It suggests the inclusion of all of the elements necessary in the fact-finding critical report. Remember clarity is the primary consideration. Therefore, the function of the introduction changes from catching attention and creating good will to a review of the reason for the report and the sources and methods of gathering the data.

The conclusion has the sole function of drawing the pertinent ideas together. You need not worry about the mood of the audience or finishing on an ending note.

Suggested Outline Form

INTRODUCTION

I. Reason for the report
   A. Who asked for it?
   B. Why?
II. Purpose of the report
   A. Define as summary, fact-finding, or critical
   B. Give your purpose sentence
III. Sources of the data for the report
IV. Procedure in gathering the data

BODY

I. Restatement of the purpose sentence

FACT FINDING

II. Initial summary of the main divisions of the data
   A. First heading
   B. Second heading, etc.
     (The data should be divided using one of the methods shown in Chapter 6. The main headings should be supported by subheadings and their supporting data.)
III. Final summary of the pertinent data

ANALYSIS & EVALUATION

IV. Initial summary of the standards to be applied to the data
V. Application of the standards to the data
   A. First heading
   B. Second heading, etc.
     (The organization of this section is identical to that suggested above in Section II, A, B.)
VI. Final summary of the application of the data to the standards

CONCLUSIONS

I. Summary of the results
II. Interpretation of the results
III. Conclusions and recommendations for action or further study

Sample Outline and Visual Aids[2]

INTRODUCTION

(Background Information = Summary Report)

I. The employees of Company "X" are very dissatisfied with their present wage payment incentive system.
   A. Leaders of management and labor are interested in determining the reasons for the employee dissatisfaction.
   B. Continued unrest on the part of labor may lead to a damaging strike.

II. This report will analyze the present incentive system in an attempt to determine its merit.
   A. Facts relative to the operation of the incentive will be gathered.
   B. It is my intention to investigate these facts thoroughly and determine whether the incentive system actually does work mutually in the interest of the employees and the company or whether it benefits unduly one party at the expense of the other.

III. Wage payment data and the union contracts will provide most of the information necessary for analysis.

IV. The two incentive plans involved under the company incentive system will be analyzed.
   A. The purpose of the two incentive plans will be investigated.
   B. The qualities of these plans will be checked against those qualities which normally describe effective incentive systems.

BODY

(Plus Research and Results = Fact-Finding Report)

I. It is my intention to determine whether the incentive system of Company "X" actually does work mutually in the interest of the employees and the company or whether it benefits unduly one party at the expense of the other.

II. The incentive system of Company "X" involves two plans, one referred to as the basic plan and the other as the one-fifth plan.
   A. The basic plan is used on jobs of a permanent nature.

---

[2] Prepared by Donald G. Shively, fifth-year Industrial Engineering major, The Ohio State University, Columbus, Ohio, August, 1956. (This outline represents only one phase of study concerning the problem.)

1. Through job analysis and time study, performance standards are set for each job.
2. Payment of the employee varies depending upon his production with relation to the performance standard.
   a. With no restrictions during working cycle, it is possible for skilled workers working at the expected incentive pace to produce at about 133% performance.
   b. A process allowance is given the worker for performance under 133%.
      (1) This allowance increases as performance decreases from 133%.
      (2) The principle here being the lower the performance the more unavoidable delays encountered.
      (3) The actual allowance is one-half the difference between the actual performance and the expected 133%.
3. All employees are payed a base rate per hour for their work regardless of production.
4. Extra pay above base rate is determined by summing per cent performance above standard and the process allowance and multiplying that per cent times the base pay earned for the work period.

B. The one-fifth plan is set up to apply to jobs that are temporary.
   1. Standard performance is roughly estimated using very little job analysis or time study, as the time and expense required in using these procedures would not be economical for short run jobs.
   2. Payment of employees varies depending upon the workers' production with relation to this standard.
      a. All employees are paid a base rate per hour for their work regardless of production.
      b. Extra pay above base rate is determined by multiplying one-fifth times the number of standard hours produced for the job.
         (1) Standard hours are the number of hours required to produce 100 units.
         (2) Standard hours are figured for each day's production.
   3. Total pay is determined by summing the bonus time which is converted into money with the base rate.

III. There are several basic differences in these two plans as far as wage payment is concerned.
   A. With the basic plan the financial reward increases on a one to one basis for all production above 100% (standard).
   B. With the one-fifth plan the financial reward increases at a diminishing rate as production increases from 0%.

IV. There are several basic principles which should apply for good effective incentive systems.
   A. Bonus earned should be related to effort expended.
   B. Methods for the determination of standards and pay rates should be as consistent as possible.
   C. Record keeping and bonus determination should be reasonably easy.
   D. It should be easy to administer and prove agreeable with the people paid under it.
   E. Payment of the bonus should be reasonably close to the time when the effort was expended.

V. The two incentive systems used by Company "X" vary in the degree to which they conform to the principles of effective incentive systems.
   A. The basic plan seems to satisfy all of the principles quite well.
   B. The one-fifth plan seems to violate several of the principles to a large degree.
      1. The bonus rate decreases as production increases.
      2. Methods for determination of standards are not consistent as they do not involve the use of job analysis and time study.
      3. The employees paid under it seem to be dissatisfied.

CONCLUSIONS

(Plus Evaluation and Recommendations = Critical Report)
I. From the foregoing analysis it would seem that the basic incentive plan is quite adequate while the one-fifth plan leaves something to be desired.

II. It should be remembered that each plan is used under different circumstances.
   A. The basic plan is used for jobs of a permanent nature.
      1. It is economical under this situation to apply job analysis and time study.
      2. Good consistent standards can be determined.
   B. The one-fifth plan is used for jobs of a temporary nature.
      1. It is not economical under this situation to apply job analysis and time study.
         a. Jobs are continually changing in content.
         b. Expense of analysis and time study for a job after each change would be prohibitive.
      2. It is inevitable to have jobs of this type in any production situation.
   C. The one-fifth plan protects the worker from standards that are set too high and the company from standards that are set too low.

III. Two ideas remain.
   A. If the company is making an honest effort to minimize situations which involve the one-fifth plan, they are justified in applying the plan to the temporary job.
   B. A study should be made of the temporary job situation to clear the issue for both labor and management.

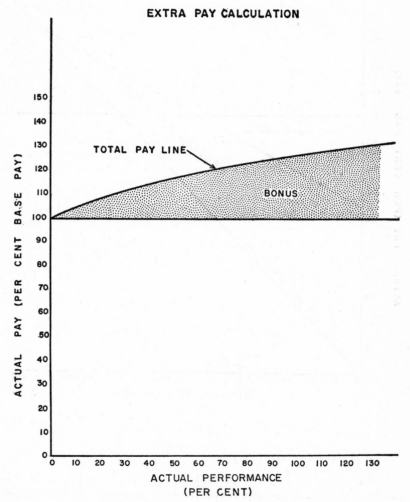

Fig. 10. Financial Reward Under the One-Fifth Plan.

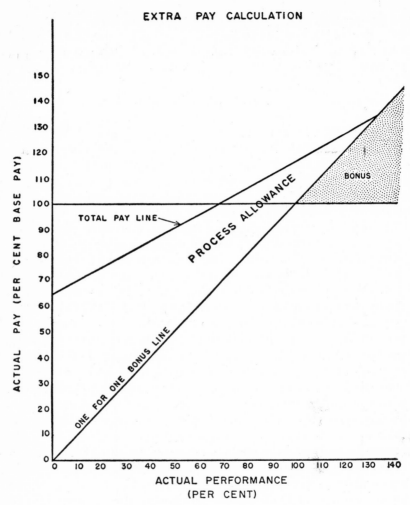

Fig. 11. Financial Reward Under the Basic Plan.

Visual Aids in the Oral Report

Use visual aids to help crystallize your ideas for the listeners. Maps, charts, diagrams, and graphs are particularly applicable to the technical report. In preparing a graph or chart, be certain that the ideas have been boiled down into their simplest and most representative form. Remember that the purpose is clarity. Eliminate all unnecessary details. Reread the material on preparing and presenting visual aids in Chapter 7. See the visual aids (Figures 10 and 11) attached to the sample report.

HOW TO PRESENT THE ORAL REPORT

The way you present an oral report depends upon a number of factors. Does your report appear in written form? Will your listeners have access to the report so that they can study it? Have they already seen it? How much time is available for your report? How informed and experienced are your listeners? Should your report be a completely oral presentation? Should you read portions of it? Should it all be read? These questions should make the alternatives clear. They are (1) the oral summary of a written report, (2) a complete oral report, (3) reading aloud parts of a written report with extemporaneous inserts, and (4) reading aloud the entire written report.

A. The oral summary of the written report. The length and complexity of the oral summary of a written report depends on the length of time available and the purpose of the summary. Frequently too much is included in the summary. All the listeners want is a brief summary which will give the gist of the report to all of the members of the group. In this instance boil down the report to the bare minimum. Excessive detail merely annoys your audience. Separate out what you know are the main points and list them with as little amplification as possible. If the listeners have already seen the report, the summary can be even briefer. Don't waste time or ideas. Get to the core of the problem. Use visual aids to help do the job.

B. The completely oral report. The complete oral report is a speech very similar to any other speech to inform. The outline provided under "Outline the Oral Report" is typical of its organization. The length of the report in this instance depends upon the complexity of the material. Presumably enough time will be provided. The chief differences between the oral report and the usual speech to inform have already been noted. You need not concern yourself primarily with the problems of interest if you can rightly assume that your audience is already interested. However, with the lay audience your report may have to include all of the interest elements of the speech to inform.

Be as technical as your listener's experience will permit. Use visual ideas to help clarify your ideas. Avoid excessive detail; you may go beyond the interest of your audience in the subject.

C. The half-and-half presentation. Frequently the entire report is too long and complex to be read, but portions of it should be read in order to preserve accuracy. The presentation of committee reports often presents this problem. You know that the listeners are not interested in hearing all of the steps the committee went through. That detail appears in the written report. Yet the framing of the specific action suggested represents a group effort and has been carefully worded. This portion must be read. The half and half report is obviously a split technique. Those sections which are reported orally should be treated in the same manner as the oral summary. Sometimes the written report which is being read has complexities or confusions that can be cleared up by leaving the manuscript and defining or amplifying the ideas. In this case the speaker may use the tools of clarity in their usual way. The greatest difficulty in the "half-and-half" report lies in the transitions. Try to phrase the transitions from reading to speaking in a manner which maintains the continuity of the report.

D. Reading the written report. Occasionally you may be forced by circumstances to read all of your report. Don't do it unless you actually have to. The disadvantages of reading it far outweigh the advantages in most situations. The only advantage is accuracy. Sometimes this will be the paramount factor; if so, then read it.

The chief disadvantage of reading the written report is the difference between written and oral style. The style of written language is more abstract than the style of oral language; written style is more complex, more general, and less direct; it is phrased for the general rather than the specific audience. In short, good essays seldom make good speeches; and good speeches seldom make good essays.

If you have no choice, read it and read it well.

HOW TO READ A MANUSCRIPT

The problems of learning to read aloud are the same whether you are reading a technical report or the greatest literature. You must transfer the meanings of the printed or typewritten page into living speech which communicates ideas to the listener. The problems involved in reading aloud are of two types—vocal problems and visual problems.

Vocal Problems in Reading Aloud

All of the words on the printed or typewritten page look alike. They have about the same amount of ink and look as though they are all equally important. The printed page is a magnificent example of monotony. As a result there is a great tendency to give equal value to each of the words. In addition, the complex structure of written style with its commas, colons, periods, semicolons, quotation marks, parentheses, and dashes tends to be confusing. These two factors coupled with the fact that most of you have had little or no experience or practice in reading aloud means that you probably read badly. The steps in learning to read aloud well are simple. Practicing them takes time.

A. Determine the exact meaning. In silent reading you can go back when you don't understand a sentence. Sometimes you may read a poor sentence several times to get its meaning. Neither you nor the listener can afford to go back when you are reading aloud. The meaning must be clear the first and only time. You must highlight the essential elements of the passage for your listener.

B. Find the stressed words and the unstressed ones. Nouns, adjectives, verbs, and adverbs are usually idea words that should be stressed, that is, given emphasis. Articles and prepositions are usually unstressed. Look at the heading above. The idea words are: *Find . . . stressed words . . . unstressed ones.* These words must be lifted out and given meaning.

C. Learn to phrase correctly. Phrasing in oral reading involves putting closely associated word clusters together. In its simplest sense it is the putting together of the elements of an idea. With modern day open punctuation you will find few commas to guide you. In preparing your copy to be read, add commas, dashes, and so forth to serve as signposts leading you to proper phrasing. Note how the first sentence in this paragraph should be phrased.

Phrasing in *oral reading*——*involves*——putting the *closely associated word clusters*——*together.* The dashes indicate the pauses between phrases in the idea. The italicized words are the idea words which receive stress. Note that there is no punctuation in the sentence to guide you. You must isolate the meaning and project it to your listener.

D. *Watch your rate of reading*. Never hurry oral reading. The complexities of the style are such that too fast a rate destroys comprehension. The rate of extemporaneous speaking is usually faster than the rate of oral reading. A good oral reading rate is approximately 125 words per minute. Check yourself. If you are going faster than this, you may be losing your listeners either because they can't understand or because you are running ideas together in a continuous monotonous stream.

Remember! The four steps listed above must be evident as you read aloud. Too frequently the four steps are rigidly followed during the preparation period, only to be forgotten during the actual reading. You must have the exact meaning in mind as you read aloud. You must stress the right words as you read aloud. You must phrase correctly as you read aloud. You must watch your rate of reading as you read aloud.

Visual Problems in Reading Aloud

Visual contact is of prime importance to communication. But you say, "How can I look at my audience and the page at the same time?" This contradiction is the greatest visual problem in oral reading. If you don't look at your listener, he becomes a mere spectator rather than a participator. If you do look at him, you lose your place. Practice alternating your eyes from the page to the listener. Don't just peek at the listener. Let your eyes run ahead a sentence or so; mark the point on the page with your finger; look up at the audience and talk with them!

You have written the report. You know and understand every element of it. Now your job is breathe life into it. Obviously your oral reading must clarify and vitalize, or there is no need to read aloud that which can be read silently. Learn the exact meanings, determine the stressed words, phrase the ideas correctly, and speak slowly enough for your listeners to comprehend. Rehearse your material completely enough so that you need only an occasional glance at your paper. Direct your "free" time to communicating your report to your listeners—eye-to-eye.

——Apply the Principles

Preparing the oral technical report will be a regular part of your job responsibilities. Practice in organizing and outlining your reports is basic to the success of this responsibility. The final test of your success rests with your ability to orally communicate your report. Remember that the best organizing and outlining can appear inadequate when the oral delivery of it is not effective.

(1) Listen to speeches read from manuscript. What are the common faults? What are the causes of these faults?

(2) Practice reading aloud portions of speeches from *Vital Speeches* or some other source. First, study the manuscript thoroughly. Second, practice reading aloud. Remember! Your purpose is to gain a favorable response from your listener.

(3) Write a critical report based on a project you have recently completed. Read your report to a group of listeners. Even though you have written the report and obviously understand it, you must now read it aloud in such a way that your listeners also gain understanding.

(4) Become familiar enough with your manuscript to insure frequent and sustained contact with your listeners. Think and understand the ideas you read as you read them.

(5) Read, read, read. Effective oral reading is not easy. On the other hand, if it were easy, it wouldn't be a challenge.

FORMULA L

POTR = EP + EC

(*POTR*) *Preparing the Oral Technical Report* = (*EP*) *Effective Preparation* plus (*EC*) *Effective Communication*. (Effective preparation includes determining the specific purpose, analyzing the listener, gathering the material, organizing the report, outlining the organization, and preparing visual aids if pertinent. Effective communication involves those principles previously mentioned in this book. In the case of oral reading emphasis is placed on determining exact meaning, meaningful stress, phrasing, and rate.)

Now, apply the formula!

Prepare a critical report to be read orally to a specific audience. Have a group of your listeners react to the preparation of your report by using the scale at the end of Chapter 6. Have another group of your listeners react to the communication effectiveness of your oral reading by using the scale below.

Technical Report Oral Reading Scale		
1–2 Weak *3 Average* *4–5 Strong*		
Criteria	Score	Comments
MEANING Reader gave evidence of understanding material. He vitalized the material.		
STRESS Reader's emphasis made material more meaningful. He called attention to the important parts.		
PHRASING Reader grouped words to promote understanding. He clarified the material.		

Technical Report Oral Reading Scale (*cont.*)

1–2 Weak   *3 Average*   *4–5 Strong*

Criteria	Score	Comments
DIRECTNESS Reader established eye-to-eye contact with listener. He was sufficiently familiar with the manuscript.		
RATE Reader allowed time for listener to grasp and understand material. He listened and visualized as he read.		
General Effectiveness		
Total *Average*		

holding
the interview

THE SCENE IS an outer office. The secretary listens for a moment to the intercom and turns to one of the young men seated across the room, "Mr. Jones? Mr. Arthur will see you now. The third door to the left." Another interview is about to begin. Mr. Jones may be a salesman, an applicant for a job, a student, or an employee. Mr. Arthur may be a purchasing agent, a personnel director, a plant manager, the head of an instructional department, or the president of a corporation. Their names and their positions are not important.

The important thing is that a turning point has been reached. An idea is to be presented and accepted or rejected; a job is to be filled or left open; a product is to be sold or not sold; a grade is to be changed or not changed. Most traffic in ideas, jobs, or products occurs not in the lecture hall but in the office, the conference room, or even the restaurant or on the golf course. Most important transactions in ideas do not involve dozens or hundreds of people. Usually they involve two or three or at the outside eight to ten. The interview is one of the everyday practical situations in which the technical man does his speaking. It is worthy of careful examination. Your immediate future hangs in the balance. *What* you say and *how* you say it are crucial factors in determining the success or failure of the interview.

INTERVIEW VERSUS CONVERSATION

One of the best ways to define the interview is to differentiate it from the conversation. At first glance they appear to be alike but closer scrutiny shows some important differences.

Conversations frequently just happen. They are called time-taking-talk. This does not mean that they can't have a purpose, but it does imply that they are a social pastime. They represent a free exchange of ideas.

In contrast, the interview is arranged. It almost never just happens. Unlike the conversation the interview always has a specific purpose. The interview is almost always persuasive in nature and the development of the ideas is carefully controlled. Without the persuasive factor the interview becomes a conversation with a free exchange of ideas or an informative report (see Chapter 12).

Probably the greatest difference between the interview and the conversation is the difference in status of the participants. In the interview the participants are rarely on a completely equal footing. The interviewer usually has a status above the interviewee. As a result of this difference in status, the interview is usually controlled by one party—the interviewer. He permits the interview, arranges it, and terminates it. This is in marked contrast to the conversation with its elements of equality.

A final difference between the conversation and the interview is the difference in the wants or desires of the participants. Both parties want something; but their wants are never identical. The purchasing agent wants a better product; the salesman wants to sell his product. The personnel manager wants to fill a job; the applicant wants the job himself. The instructor wants his grades to be fair judgments of accomplishment; the student wants his grade raised. The plant manager wants greater efficiency in production; the planning engineer wants his idea accepted.

This difference in wants explains the function of the interview. The interview brings together the different wants of the interviewer and the interviewee. If both parties get the results they desire, the interview is successful. The chart below summarizes the differences between the conversation and the interview.

Difference Between Conversation
and Interview

	CONVERSATION	INTERVIEW
1. The participants are	friends, co-workers	interviewer, interviewee
2. The meeting	just occurs	is arranged
3. The ideas are	freely exchanged	controlled
4. The purpose is	varied	usually persuasive
5. The status of participants is	equal	interviewer in control

Since these differences exist, most interviewees would like to accomplish the purpose of an interview within the framework of the conversational situation. The salesman invites his prospective client out to dinner. The dinner engagement is a social or conversational situation. The participants are on equal footing and can freely exchange ideas. The salesman tries to maintain the informality, the good fellowship of the conversation and still do his selling. He cloaks the business of the interview in the conversation. Note that he even tries to reverse the control in the situation. He is footing the bill; he is the host; he is the leader. In addition, of course, he hopes that his kindness, the good dinner, and the vintage wines will be appreciated. If he is successful, he sells his product without having to face the interview.

KINDS OF INTERVIEWS

Interviews are of three general types. While they may overlap, they have sufficiently different characteristics to warrant differentiation. They are (1) the application interview, (2) the sales interview, (3) the professional interview. They deal with the basic commodities with which we all work—persons, products, and ideas.

The Job Application Interview

Sooner or later everyone applies for a job. These interviews represent turning points in your life. Success or failure here probably has a more lasting effect than in any other speech situation.

The job application interview is usually the most formal of the various kinds of interviews. It is a full dress appearance. Usually the interview is preceded by a formal application which includes a résumé of your previous experience, perhaps a transcript of your school work if it is your first job, and recommendations.

The interview includes an interviewer who is an employee of the company and you, who are not. The interviewer is usually a person skilled in the process of hiring personnel. He has been through hundreds of these interviews. His job is to assess you both as an individual and as a prospective employee of the company. He wants the best man.

You on the other hand have probably had few job application interviews. But you do know your product—yourself—better than anyone else in the world. Your success is based upon your ability to show the interviewer that you are the man he wants.

The Sales Interview

The sales interview is similar to the job application interview except that a product rather than a person is the commodity involved. In a large corporation the interview is usually comparatively formal. Purchasing agents are swamped with salesmen and have to limit the time and the number of salesmen they can see each day. In the sales interview the interviewer is looking for the best product at the lowest price. The interviewee on the other hand is concerned with proving that his product can do the best job at a reasonable price. The success of the sales interview is based upon an agreement being reached on the need for and the price of the product.

The Professional Interview

The professional interview, sometimes called the "idea" interview, differs in several respects from each of the other types. First, the interview is usually between employees of the same institution or company, though a difference in status still exists. For example, the young accountant is interviewed by the head of the accounting department, or the shop foreman is called in by his supervisor.

Second, the interview is concerned solely with ideas. They are the commodity which is sold rather than people or products. Third, it is usually much more informal than either the job application or sales interview. And fourth, it is sometimes not persuasive in nature. Finally, the desires of the interviewer and the interviewee are frequently more closely aligned. This stems from the fact that both men are members of the same organization. The interviewer is interested in new and better ways of doing the work. The interviewee is interested in the same goal.

This type of interview will arise dozens of times in your professional careers. The professional interview will provide you not only with opportunities to sell ideas but also with chances to sell yourself.

PREPARATION FOR THE INTERVIEW

Early in your professional life you will usually be the one who is interviewed, but later on you will do the interviewing. Whether you are the interviewee or the interviewer, it is important to know about both sides of the street. In other words, if you are to be a good interviewer, you must know your own job and know the interviewee's problems of preparation and presentation. At the same time to be a superior interviewee you must understand the problems of the interviewer. In the following paragraphs the problems of both the interviewer and the interviewee are discussed. Regardless of what your particular job may be, study them both carefully.

The Interviewer Prepares

The job of interviewing is an extremely important one. Make sure that you fulfill your obligations and that the results in men, products, or ideas will be worth it. The following steps should lead the way to the successful interview.

A. Make careful arrangements. You plan the interview, so do it with care. Select an appropriate time. Allow enough time to find out what you need to know. Some interviews can be terminated quickly when you see that there is little chance of reaching a satisfactory conclusion. Others will take time. If you allow too little, you may overlook possibilities which are important to you.

Try to make the physical arrangements as comfortable as possible for all concerned. Extend the common courtesies; you are in a sense the host.

B. Determine the purpose of the interview. You must judge the applicant, the product, or the idea which is presented for your consideration in a very short period of time. Don't let the interview get off the track. Pleasant conversation is enjoyable but it won't solve your problems. Decide in advance exactly what you need to know about the interviewee or his product.

C. Explore the background of the interview. Never enter the interview situation unprepared. You will lose too much time covering ground that can easily be covered in advance, or you will conclude the interview and suddenly realize that areas which are important have not been covered.

When preparing for the job application interview, read the applicant's letter. Acquaint yourself with his background and qualifications. Determine the aspects of his background and experience which need further exploration. For the idea interview try to get hold of the facts beforehand. Determine the strengths and weaknesses of the plan. In other words, provide the basis for the searching analysis which the plan deserves.

D. Organize the ground to be covered. Set up an outline of the things you wish to know. Have a battery of questions ready beforehand. Work out a check sheet which covers all of the essential elements. In the job interview decide what qualifications you are seeking and list them so that at the end of the interview you will have a clearcut judgment upon each of the qualifications.

The Interviewee Prepares

The preparation of the job applicant, the salesman, and the man with a plan or idea will undoubtedly be more extensive and more intensive than that of the interviewer. The interviewer has greater command of the situation and greater experience. Generally, the interviewee develops a single presentation which he hopes can be adapted to numerous situations.

A. Make careful arrangements. The arrangements are considerably different for the three types of interviews. As a job applicant you must make the initial contact. You may answer a want-ad or go to an employment agency. As a graduating engineer you send a letter or make direct contact with a personnel agent who is coming to the campus. In each case, getting the interview is based upon your ability to write a first class letter of application. Frequently there are as many as 150 applicants for a single job. Obviously not all of those writing letters will be interviewed. Your letter must be good enough to command an interview for you. Study one or more of the good books on the subject of business-letter writing. One particularly good analysis of the application interview can be found in Huston, Sandberg, and Mills, *Effective Speaking in Business*.[1]

The arrangements for the sales interview are considerably simpler. Most large companies have purchasing departments which reserve time for salesmen. You apply directly to the purchasing agent or his secretary. With the small business the arrangements are much more casual. You drop into the store or office and wait until the proprietor is free. Never force yourself into the midst of a sales transaction. You will lose the owner's good will, and your interview will fail before it starts.

Arranging the professional idea interview is simple. The boss's door is always open to good suggestions. Arrangements may be made through his secretary. The problem here is one of timing. Your idea is burning inside you. You make a date to see the boss and rush in—unprepared. Your idea must be supported; your plan must be carefully worked out.

B. Find out about the interviewer. "Know your listener" has been the keynote of our entire approach to speaking. The interview is as much a communication process as any other type of speech. The interviewer is a listener with needs, wants, desires, and a job to do. He is persuaded by the same techniques and devices as any other listener. Learn what you can about him in advance. Don't depend upon your ability to size him up during the interview.

The job application interview offers the greatest difficulties in analyzing your listener. You have little or no contact with him prior to the interview itself. However, you can find out about his company. You can learn its practices and its goals. What is the basic organization? Training program? Policy? Such knowledge serves three purposes. First, it helps you decide whether or not it is the kind of company you would like to work for. Second, it gives you clues to the interviewer whom you are to meet since he is a loyal member of the

---

[1] Alfred D. Huston, Robert A. Sandberg, Jack Mills, *Effective Speaking in Business*, Englewood Cliffs, N.J.: Prentice-Hall, Inc., 1955, pp. 159–190.

company. And finally, it helps you show the interviewer during the interview that you have been sufficiently interested in the company to find out about it.

The task of analyzing the listener in the sales interview is much easier. Your fellow salesmen can help you. Inquiries and conversations with other business men can provide you with leads.

In the professional idea interview there is no excuse for not knowing every aspect of your listener's attitudes and behavior. Since you both work for the same company and undoubtedly have everyday dealings, your knowledge should be complete.

C. Determine the purpose of the interview. Know what you are going after. To be "willing to work," to "want a job—any job," is not enough. The day of the specialist is here. You are not qualified for every job. Your training and experience fits you for only certain types of work. Remember that it is just as important that the job fit you as it is that you fit the job. Therefore apply for a definite type of job. The qualified applicant who knows what he wants is always in demand.

The general purpose of the sales interview is obvious. You want to sell your product. The specific purpose of the sales interview is more complicated and may need a great deal of thought and study. You want to sell your product to a specific company for a specific use. Suppose you are selling oil. You must determine in advance exactly what kinds, what grades, and so forth you can sell to a particular company.

The possible purposes of the idea interview are similar to those of any speech. You may merely want to interest your listener in your plan; you may want him to take your plan under consideration; you may want him to act on your idea. The specific purpose depends upon the circumstances and upon the superior to whom it is presented. Your boss may have the power to act and he may not. You may be better off by encouraging him to join forces with you to present the idea to a higher echelon. These possibilities must be analyzed and a course of action set before the interview.

D. Gather your supporting materials beforehand. The good salesman knows his product. He can prove its worth. He can compare it with competitive products. He can illustrate its economy. Each of these supporting materials is adapted to the specific sales situation of the moment. The job applicant gathers the materials which show his background, his education, his work experience, and his recommendations. He prepares a résumé or data sheet which includes all of the necessary details in a clear and interesting form. In addition he does a job analysis on the type of job he is seeking. Dozens of guidance manuals can be found in your library which lay out the general specifications for various types of jobs. Many large companies also turn out brochures which suggest job opportunities. They detail the special educational requirements, need for experience, special aptitudes, special duties and personality traits essential to success in the job. The applicant then matches his attributes with the general requirements of the job. With this material in hand he is well prepared for the interview.

The most complete and certain preparation can be made in the idea interview because you have access to all of the information that you need about the operation of the company or department in which you work. Preparation of your own plan can also be complete. Your data should answer such questions as: What is the reason for the plan? What can it accomplish? How is it better than the present procedure? What will be its costs? How complicated will it be to put into operation. There is no substitute for preparation if you are to expect success.

E. Organize your ideas in advance. The interview is the ideal test of the good bread-and-butter speaker. You are forced to think on your feet, adapt to your listener, and speak forcefully. Probably nothing is more disasterous than the "canned speech." It breaks all of the rules of good bread-and-butter speaking. (See Chapter 1). On the other hand, you dare not approach the interview without a clearcut decision as to the ideas you wish to present and the order of their importance. You may be asked to give what amounts to a speech in which case you should be prepared to do so. More frequently you will be asked a series of questions. You must be prepared to introduce your points in the particular manner or sequence that is requested. Avoid rigidity in your thinking.

A special word about the job application interview. You will need to organize two sets of data: first, the information about yourself, the experience and capabilities which you wish to demonstrate during the interview; and second, the information about the job which you want to carry away from the interview. Both are essential.

THE INTERVIEWER AND THE INTERVIEWEE

The successful interview is in reality a conversation with a purpose. The exchange of ideas is carefully controlled and developed in a manner which permits both the interviewer and the interviewee to reach his goal. Sincere, direct, simple yet forceful expression is the speech foundation upon which the successful interview is built. Careful, attentive, critical listening insures good communication.

The Responsibilities of the Interviewer

The interviewer who fulfills his responsibilities to both the interviewee and himself can expect success in the job of interviewing.

A. Put the interviewee at ease. The interviewee is bound to be nervous and excited. Do your best to make him comfortable and easy. Act as a pleasant host. Your consideration can encourage him to do his best. Invite him into your office. Ask him to be seated. Open the interview with pleasant remarks which relieve the tension. You want to see the interviewee at his best.

B. Encourage the interviewee to express himself. Three alternatives are open to you. You may do all the talking. You may force the interviewee to do the talking. Or you may set up a mutual exchange of ideas.

Avoid talking too much yourself. This is a pitfall into which many interviewers fall. They become so wound up in their own thoughts that the interviewee finds it difficult to express himself. At the finish of this kind of interview, the interviewer suddenly finds that he hasn't found out what he needs to know.

Make the interviewee do most of the talking. Give him a subject that is broad and general and have him talk for ten or fifteen minutes straight—for example "What do you feel is chemical engineering's place in a modern society?" You will find out a great deal about him immediately. If he doesn't know what he is talking about, he will soon begin to sputter and finally sink. If he is a good bread-and-butter speaker who can think straight, think on his feet, and talk clearly and forcefully to a point, that too will become apparent.

The third method is composed of many questions with short answers. Ask penetrating questions. Ask questions which reveal his

knowledge and background. Ask questions which reveal his energy
and enthusiasm. Ask questions which reveal his attitudes toward the
job, toward the company, toward life itself.

C. Direct the interview into the channels you desire. You are the
leader; therefore it is up to you to control the interview. The questions you ask direct the interviewee's thinking. You are in position
to press for clarification of ideas. Follow the progress of the interview
on a check list of the things you want to know.

Remember your goals in the interview. You are in the process of
finding a new worker, a new product, a new idea. Spend your time
testing your initial judgment. This is the opportunity to discover all
of the pertinent facts. Make use of it.

D. Conclude the interview gracefully. One of the most difficult
jobs for the man being interviewed is knowing when and how to
stop. Termination of the interview is your responsibility. When you
have the information you need and are satisfied that the interviewee
has been given the information he needs, thank him for coming and
rise. This should provide him with the needed sign. If he is sensitive,
he will also rise. Walk with him to the door and usher him out. If
he is insensitive and shows no inclination to go, you may pleasantly
ask him to leave so that you may turn to your next task. In such a
case you will have found out one more thing about him.

The Responsibilities of the Interviewee

The success of your interview frequently depends as much upon
how you conduct yourself as upon the ideas you express. Observe
the following suggestions for being a good interviewee.

A. Don't sell yourself short. Remember that the interview is a two-
way street. Both you and the interviewer want something. Don't
succumb to the tendency to become subservient. Stand up and be
heard. After all, you *are* the man for his job; you have the product
which will *serve* him; you have the idea which means *progress*. Don't
let the difference in status stand in the way of your accomplishing
your purpose.

On the other hand, don't go to the opposite extreme. The loud
mouthed, aggressive, hail-fellow-well-met attitude will get you nowhere. Try to maintain a pleasant balance between overly subservient
and overly aggressive attitudes.

B. *Recognize and adapt to the circumstances.* You have been invited to your host's office. You are using his time. Act as though you respect his extending you these courtesies. He is the leader. He sets the rules of the game. Abide by them.

C. *Observe the common courtesies.* Let the interviewer take the lead. Wait patiently and quietly until he gives the cue to respond, and then respond forcefully and well. Don't try to be funny. Nothing is as painful as the pathetic attempt on the part of the man being interviewed to relieve the tensions with halfhearted humor. Don't sit until you are invited to do so. Smoke only if a cigarette is offered. Avoid the common annoyances such as gum chewing and doodling. Remember that you are a guest. Act like one.

D. *Stay on the subject.* Remember that the reason for the interview determines the subject. Stick with it. If the interviewer apparently leads you astray, respond with him but don't prolong the tangent. Let him do the leading. If he doesn't show you a course to follow, then you should set up a clearly organized course of your own which is directed to the point of the interview.

E. *Don't apologize.* The apologetic attitude is always remembered with distaste. Encourage the interviewer to accept you as you are. If you feel apologetic, it means you are not prepared. Don't be afraid to say "I don't know." No one knows everything. Obviously you can't afford to say "I don't know" too often, but don't try to bluff. The chances are that the interviewer knows more about the subject than you may think. The bluffer digs his own grave sentence by sentence.

F. *Listen attentively.* It is easy in the interview to become so preoccupied with your own thoughts and wishes that you don't listen attentively. Failure to listen can cause you trouble. Listen with great care to the questions asked. Frequently they may be double barreled, that is, embrace two different subjects at once. Careful listening will enable you to break the question down and answer both its parts. Sometimes the questions will be confusing. If you have listened carefully, you will know that the question needs clarification and can afford to ask for a restatement of it. If you haven't listened carefully, you won't know how to ask for clarification. Sometimes the question will be so general as to be incomplete; for example, "Tell me about yourself." Don't just plunge in with "I was born on March 20, 1925, in Chicago, Illinois." It is very doubtful that the interviewer wants

Your life as a technical man is a solid string of reports. Discuss the various ways of presenting the oral report. What are the problems involved in reading a manuscript? What reading techniques are apparent in the picture? (CHAPTER 12) *Courtesy Battelle Memorial Institute.*

The interview is one of the everyday practical situations in which the technical man does his speaking. In reality it is a conversation with a purpose. Which of the responsibilities of the interviewer and the interviewee are apparent in the picture? (CHAPTER 13) *Courtesy Ohio Fuel Gas Company.*

The democratic way to solve a problem is to submit it for discussion and solution by the people involved. The conference is one of the keystones of the democratic process. What characteristics of a conference are apparent in the picture? What evidence of preparation is apparent? What chances of success do you feel this conference has? (CHAPTER 14) *Courtesy Battelle Memorial Institute.*

a complete autobiography. Turn the question back to him with a request for clarity; for example, "Do you want to know about my training and experience?" If you can recognize that listening is just as important as talking, your interview will stand a greater chance for success.

G. *Adapt to the pattern suggested by the interviewer.* You may feel that the material of the interview should be developed one way. The interviewer chooses another. Then what? Follow the interviewer's pattern. Your material should be well enough in hand so that you can freely change it about. This is the test of good bread-and-butter speaking. Think constantly in terms of what the interviewer wants. This is the best way to get what you want.

H. *Be prepared to face pressure.* Frequently the interviewer may be interested in finding out how you respond to pressure. For example, when you are ushered into his office, he may leave you standing for a minute or so while he completes work on his desk. This may be simply a test of your poise. Stand comfortably and quietly and wait. Sometimes after answering a question the interviewer may let a long unaccountable pause open up. Don't be embarrassed, just sit quietly and wait. Some interviewers fire questions like a prosecuting attorney. Take your time. Think out your answers. Answer simply and directly. In other words, regardless of what comes, don't become flustered. The interviewer is probably testing you and will respect your ability to remain calm and collected.

I. *Dress to fit the occasion.* The interview is no different from any other speech occasion. Neither overdress nor underdress. You don't want to be remembered for the unpressed suit or the hand painted Christmas tie. Dress so that your best taste and judgment is shown. Dress so that your dress won't be noted except as a background for your naturally crisp neat appearance.

J. *Speak simply, directly, forcefully.* A large part of the impression you create comes from the way you speak. Remember the keys to the correct speaking attitude (see Chapter 3) and to personal prestige (see Chapter 9). Be friendly and direct. Look your listener in the eye when you talk to him. Sit tall, strong, and comfortably.

Be forceful, but not aggressive. Never put the interviewer on the defensive. He will resent it and act accordingly. Watch your grammar. It is a clue to your personality and your education. The stories about the success of the rough-cut diamond are frequently overrated.

K. Learn how to say "goodbye". Saying goodbye is extremely simple if you will watch for the cue to terminate the interview. The interviewer will let you know when to stop. Watch for the indication and be smart enough to respond to it quickly! When the interviewer says, "Thank you, Mr. Jones, for . . .", you should accept the cue immediately and rise. If the interviewer rises first, the cue is reinforced; you should rise with him. After he has concluded his sentence thanking you, respond in kind and thank him for the courtesy of seeing you. Don't omit the closing!

L. Use a firm closing. You cannot let the interview end without having certain things straight. You must find out when the interviewer will let you know his decision. Do you get the job? Will he buy your product? Will he accept your plan? The interviewer may not want to give you the answer to your final question at the close of the interview. If you aren't careful, you will be out in the hall knowing nothing of where you stand.

After thanking the interviewer for his time and courtesy, ask him when you may expect his decision. If he is still evasive, ask him if you may contact him or write to him at a future date. In other words make sure that when you do land in the hall, you have some kind of assurance that you will be notified when the decision is made.

The importance of the successful interview cannot be overrated. It is always a primary contact with someone who can help you solve your problems. You can't afford to muff it. Practice interviewing with your friends or with your instructors. Students who have had the opportunity to try it out in practice situations are always thankful for the experience when they meet the real test.

—*Apply the Principles*

The interview may be your most crucial step to satisfactory employment. The success of this step is based almost entirely on your ideas and your ability to effectively communicate them. Be prepared!

(1) Role-play the interview situation. In other words, assume the role of an interviewee and have a friend assume the role of an interviewer. Assume a specific company and a specific

job within that company. Hold an interview exactly as you assume it would happen. Prepare for the role-playing interview with the same thoroughness you would give to an actual interview.

(2) Change roles. Now you be the interviewer and have your friend be the interviewee. Try to get the feelings that the man on the other side of the desk experiences in the interview situation. If you can put yourself in his place, you will be better prepared to successfully communicate with him. Role-playing not only prepares you for the interview situation, it gives you insight into the problems of the interviewer and the interviewee.

(3) Review the sections dealing with preparation for the interview, the responsibilities of the interviewer, and the responsibilities of the interviewee. Analyze your role-playing attempts in terms of this review. What did you do that was wrong? What aspects could be improved? What impressions do you think you would have made? What might the results of the interview have been?

(4) At this point you should be better prepared for your next real interview. Always prepare thoroughly. Proceed with confidence. Good luck!

FORMULA M

$$HI = IP + \frac{I_{er}}{REDC} + \frac{I_{ee}}{SALC}$$

(*HI*) *Holding the Interview* = Thorough (*IP*) *Interview Preparation* plus an (*I$_{er}$*) *Interviewer* who can communicate in such a way that he (*REDC*) *Relaxes, Encourages, Directs,* and *Concludes* effectively plus an (*I$_{ee}$*) *Interviewee* who can communicate in such a way that he (*SALC*) *Sells, Adapts, Listens,* and *Concludes* effectively.

Now, apply the formula!

Below is a check list of reminders for the interview situation. Study it and follow it for each interview.

Interviewer-Interviewee Check List

Some Reminders

KIND OF INTERVIEW:

Job Application Interview
Sales Interview
Professional Interview

PREPARATION:

The Interviewer:

1. Select appropriate time
2. Allow time for preparation
3. Make physical arrangements
4. Extend the common courtesies
5. Determine purpose of interview
6. Determine information desired
7. Acquaint yourself with background information
8. Prepare check list covering essential elements
9. Prepare a battery of questions

The Interviewee:

1. Make initial contact effective
2. Find out about the interviewer
3. Determine the purpose of interview
4. Gather necessary supporting materials
5. Organize your ideas

---

6. Extemporize your ideas
7. Organize most pertinent personal data
8. Determine job information you wish to know

THE INTERVIEW:

The Interviewer:

1. Put interviewee at ease
2. Encourage interviewee to express himself
3. Direct interview into desired channels
4. Conclude the interview gracefully

The Interviewee:

1. Don't sell yourself short
2. Recognize and adapt to the circumstances
3. Observe common courtesies
4. Stay on the subject
5. Don't apologize
6. Listen attentively
7. Adapt to pattern suggested by interviewer
8. Be prepared to face pressure
9. Dress to fit the occasion
10. Speak simply, directly, purposefully
11. Conclude interview effectively

conference
speaking

THE SIMPLEST FORM of the conference is the "bull session." You get together with your friends to hash out a problem or exchange ideas. The most complex form of the conference is the international meeting. The heads of nations sit down together to iron out problems which mean life or death, war or peace. In between these two extremes are the thousands of conferences which make up life in a democratic society. The totalitarian way to solve a problem is by command or decree; the democratic way to solve a problem is to submit it to the people involved for discussion and solution. The conference is one of the keystones of the democratic process.

WHAT IS A CONFERENCE?

A conference is more than a conversation, different from an interview, and unlike a business meeting. It has a set of characteristics which are peculiar to it.

A. The conference is an investigation. It is the careful study of a problem. The conference explores the background of the problem, analyzes the problem in detail, investigates each of the possible solutions, and determines what is believed to be the best solution.

B. *The conference depends upon cooperation.* The conference is a cooperative investigation. It involves people working together for a single common goal—the truth or the best solution to a problem. There is no place in the conference for the uncooperative individual.

C. *The conference depends upon reflective thinking.* The debater and the persuader have made up their minds in advance. They aim to persuade you that their point of view is right. This is intentional thinking; the mind is closed. Reflective thinking is the reverse of intentional thinking. It employs the scientific method to reach the solution to a problem. The decision has not been made in advance, and the mind is open. Facts are sifted and winnowed. The search is for the truth. Reflective thinking is the basis of the conference.

D. *The conference depends upon the free exchange of ideas.* The conference is a collection of individuals thinking reflectively together. Each brings the weight of his own experience and ability to bear on the problem. The conference involves group analysis, group thought, group communication. It should be characterized by a meeting of the minds. There must be complete freedom for the exchange of ideas.

E. *The conference requires equal status for the participants.* The interview brings persons of different levels or status together. One man is above, another below. In the conference every effort is made to insure complete equality. Even the conference leader has no vested authority. He is not a boss; he does not run the meeting; he is merely a guide and a moderator of the group's thinking.

F. *The conference group must be limited in size.* Conference groups are ideally composed of from three to fifteen members. When the group gets larger than ten to a dozen members, the possibility of cooperative thinking with a free exchange of ideas begins to diminish quickly. Some members hesitate to speak. Other stronger personalities begin to control the meeting. A formality tends to develop. Any of these qualities will limit the effectiveness of the conference as a cooperative investigation.

G. *The conference is arranged for a purpose.* Conferences don't just happen. They are arranged. They result from a need. They are arranged with the definite purpose of solving a problem.

In summary, the conference may be defined as a process which brings together a group of qualified people for the purpose of thinking together toward the solution of a common problem.

THE ADVANTAGES OF THE CONFERENCE METHOD

The conference method helps in two ways: (1) it serves as the ideal way to solve problems and (2) it provides experiences for the participator which help him to become a more efficient and effective worker.

A. The conference pools the knowledge and experience of the group. Assuming qualified participants, that is, participants who can contribute knowledge and experience toward solving the problem, the conference makes use of what the group already knows. Suppose you were to discuss the problem of economic aid to Indo-China. Think of the vast resources available if the participants were an historian, an economist, a sociologist, a political scientist, and a military expert. In addition, since no individual has a corner on all the knowledge, each man may learn from the others. There is an old saying that if we exchange dollar bills, each of us will have a one dollar bill, but if we exchange ideas, each of us will have two ideas.

B. The conference helps clear up misunderstandings. Many disagreements develop because of a lack of understanding. The free exchange of ideas in the conference provides opportunities to understand and question the other fellow's point of view. In addition, it helps change attitudes. Many of us have fixed opinions on many subjects, particularly those about which we have a small store of knowledge. Question and analysis and understanding can change those attitudes.

C. The conference helps develop analytical ability. Since the conference method is based upon the search for truth or for the best solution to a problem, all ideas are submitted to analysis and a questioning attitude. Each participant has a chance to analyze and evaluate the ideas of others. Perhaps more important, he can see his own ideas analyzed before his eyes.

D. The conference encourages straight thinking. The dynamic conference is an "on the toes" situation. It requires real thought and energy. The analytical attitude which pervades puts the pressure on you to think straight.

E. The conference defines areas of agreement and disagreement. Conferences are not merely a getting together to agree. They frequently expose basic disagreements. The examination of the areas of agreement and disagreement provides the soundest basis for decision. Disagreements are examined in the light of day with logical rather than emotional reasoning. The result is a reasoned result even though frank disagreements still exist.

F. *The conference encourages good bread-and-butter speaking.* The ability to think straight, to adapt to others, to organize your ideas, and to express them simply and forcefully are needed in the conference. Though the conference is not a place to aggrandize your own personality, it does provide the opportunity to show your ability through the contribution you can make.

G. *The conference provides a group solution to a problem.* As mentioned above, the group decision is basic to democratic life. It might also be added that the decision of a well-qualified group has a greater chance of being right, simply because it brings a number of minds to bear on a particular problem.

WEAKNESSES IN THE CONFERENCE METHOD

A. *The conference is slow.* Probably the greatest disadvantage of the conference is that it takes a good deal of time. It is much easier to make a decision, right or wrong, and put it into force. The platoon sergeant on the battle field doesn't have time in the midst of an enemy barrage to sit down with his men and analyze the problem. He must make a decision. If the platoon succeeds he is a hero; if it is wiped out, *c'est la guerre.* Happily, most major decisions do not have to be made with such speed; there is time to search out the best method.

B. *The conference is costly.* Since the conference is slow, it is at the same time costly. Assume a modestly paid group of executives, say twelve men worth $6.00 an hour each. A one hour conference costs $72.00. An eight hour conference costs $576.00, not counting the overhead or the work left undone in the various departments. The reason for mentioning the cost is to stress the importance of a clear-cut purpose and the need to stick with the subject under discussion.

C. *Some conferences pool ignorance.* The "pooling of ignorance" is not a fault inherent in the conference method, but nonetheless it frequently occurs. The conference cannot hope to be successful unless the conferees are qualified by knowledge, experience, and hard work to contribute to the solution of the problem. Each participant must be able to add something to the general knowledge, or the conference will be a bust. Imagine trying to solve the problem of how best to lay out the Saint Lawrence Waterway with a conference made up of a group of tugboat captains. The results might be an entertaining "bull session," but it would not be a successful problem solving conference.

D. *Some conferences break down because of closed minds.* Again this is not a weakness of the method, but often a corollary to it. The conference has been defined as a cooperative investigation. Without cooperation and reflective thinking the conference can not be expected to succeed. The man with a closed mind who has decided in advance that what he believes is the only solution and who backs up his decision with emotional and personal arguments, can destroy the conference. The most perfect examples of this situation can be seen in many of the international conferences. They are split before they start. Time is spent jockeying for position. Each group's purpose is to propagandize its own point of view. These are conferences in name only.

The advantages of the conference outweigh its potential weaknesses. Whether it be a social committee meeting, a plant planning conference, a general policy conference, or an industrial training conference, it is the best group problem solving method yet devised by man.

KINDS OF THINKING

There are essentially three kinds of thinking: (1) random thinking, (2) intentional thinking, and (3) reflective thinking. Neither random nor intentional thinking has any place in the conference.

Random Thinking

Random thinking is characterized by its lack of purpose. In its most extreme form it is day dreaming. We allow our thoughts to drift aimlessly as they will. Random thinking is found in most informal social conversations. One idea is casually considered for a while, then the conversation drifts to another subject, and then another. Random thinking lacks the power of analysis. It does not involve concentration. Frequently it is a thinking process that moves in circles rather than a straight line. It may be lots of fun, but it isn't very useful in the conference.

Intentional Thinking

Intentional thinking is fixed or prejudiced thinking. It is never random. It is fixed in a straight line. It has but one purpose—to support a decision which has already been made. As mentioned before, the persuader uses intentional thinking. He says, "My product (or idea) is the best product (or idea), and I shall prove it to you." All of his thought goes to fulfilling his declared intention—the proof of the point. It is prejudiced. Any contradictory idea is immediately rejected merely because it is contradictory. The worth of the contradiction is never evaluated. It disagrees with my point of view; therefore it is wrong. Intentional thinking thrives in the atmosphere of the "either—or," "one-or-the-other," "black-or-white." Intentional thinking is emotionalized thinking. It is the support of a point of view because we "want to" or "feel like it." It doesn't depend upon logical analysis and decision. Obviously it has no place in those stages of a conference which are concerned with the search for the truth or the unbiased logical solution of a problem.

Reflective Thinking

Reflective thinking is an intellectual rather than an emotional process. It is straight thinking which analyzes and evaluates all aspects and phases of the problem. It is thinking which eliminates prejudice and bias. It is thinking which searches out the facts. It is the scientific method of approaching a problem. It is the heart of the successful discussion.

REFLECTIVE THINKING: THE KEY TO
CONFERENCE SUCCESS

John Dewey, one of America's foremost educators, is responsible for laying out the steps of reflective thinking.[1] There are five steps

---

[1] John Dewey, *How We Think*, Boston: D. C. Heath and Company, 1944, p. 15.

in the reflective thinking process: (1) awareness of the problem, (2) analysis of the problem, (3) determining the tentative solutions, (4) examination of the solutions, (5) choosing one solution and trying it out. Frequently a sixth step is added—the verification of the solution. If the solution which has been chosen doesn't work, the thinker must return to the fourth step and examine the other possible solutions in the light of his new knowledge and try again.

Reflective Thinking and the Scientific Problem.

All problems in the sciences are approached through the steps of reflective thinking. Let's illustrate. Suppose you have a gravel pit from which you scoop the sand and gravel from under water. You find that the belt which drives the scoops constantly stretches and slips. *Step #1:* You are aware of a problem: how to keep the belt from stretching and slipping. *Step #2:* You analyse the problem. You find the causes of the problem. What factors makes the belt stretch? Why does it slip? *Step #3:* What are the possible solutions? You could use a suction system rather than a scoop system. You could change the kind of belt. You could redesign the drive mechanism. And so forth. *Step #4:* You examine the advantages and disadvantages of each of the possible solutions. One may be too costly; another may be impractical; a third may seem to be the answer. *Step #5:* You choose the third solution and try it out. *Step #6:* The new belt still stretches and slips; you must go back to *Step #4* and, using what you have just learned, choose another solution.

Think of the discovery of Insulin. *Step #1:* Patients were dying of diabetes. Medical science was aware of the problem. *Step #2:* Analysis. What were the causes of death from diabetes? *Step #3:* Possible solutions. Hundreds of scienctific teams worked on new ways to combat the disease. *Step #4:* Each new possible solution was evaluated pro and con. *Step #5:* A solution was selected and put into operation on a test basis. *Step #6:* Dozens if not hundreds of times the solutions failed. Each time the knowledge learned aided in developing new solutions to the problem. Finally, Insulin was developed. It was tried, and it worked. The problem of death from diabetes was solved.

Reflective Thinking and the Social Problem

The same scientific method of reflective thinking can be applied to most social problems. *Step #1:* Awareness. Management is concerned about the poor morale of the men in the plant. A committee is formed to solve the problem. *Step #2:* Analysis. The committee tries to find out all the facts. It analyzes the grievances expressed by the men—the working conditions, the pressures to produce, the production system, and so forth. *Step #3:* Tentative solutions. The committee can recommend firing the ring leaders, raising wages, slowing down the production schedule, reducing the number of working hours, improving the working conditions, and so forth. *Step #4:* Examining the solutions. The committee weighs the advantages and disadvantages of each solution. *Step #5:* Selecting a solution and trying it out. The committee recommends a new lighting system for the plant. The lighting system is installed, and the complaints decrease. The problem has been solved.

Take a personal problem. You are a student and you can't decide what field to major in. *Step #1:* You are aware of the problem and know you soon must make a decision. *Step #2:* You analyze all of your interests. You decide what you want out of life. You take aptitude tests. You ask advice. *Step #3:* You narrow your choice down to a few conceivable directions. You decide that you could major in physics or chemistry. *Step #4:* You examine the consequences of choosing one or the other. In other words, you analyze the pros and cons. *Step #5:* You decide on chemistry and begin the major. *Step #6:* You find during the very first courses that you aren't interested and have made a mistake. You then go back with this knowledge and try to select another solution. Maybe it will be physics, but perhaps your experience in chemistry has shown you that the sciences are not for you. You make another decision and try again.

Reflective Thinking and the Conference Discussion Outline.

The steps of reflective thinking form the basis of the discussion outline. The importance of an outline for the conference cannot be overemphasized. First, it keeps the discussion on the track. Second, it helps make conferring an orderly process. Third, it provides a basis for summarizing the materials which have been covered. Fourth, it demands that first things be treated first. Finally, it shows the right way to approach a problem. A sample generalized outline appears below. The parts are phrased as questions which need discussion.

Outline for a Problem Solving Conference

I. Awareness of the Problem

    A. Why has this conference been called together?
    B. What is the problem?
        1. It it of a workable size?
        2. Are there terms that need defining?
    C. How does the problem affect the members of the group?
    D. Who else is affected by the problem?
    E. What will happen if the problem isn't solved?
        1. Will it get worse?
        2. Will it solve itself?
    F. Does the problem need to be discussed now?
    G. Does the problem have to be solved now?

II. Analyzing the Problem

    A. What kind of a problem is it?
        1. Is it an economic problem?
        2. Is it a social problem?
        3. Is it a political problem?
    B. What is the historical background of the problem?
        1. Has it arisen before?
        2. Has it been solved? How?
    C. What are the alleged causes of the problem?
        1. Can the causes be clearly defined and listed?
        2. Can the causes be analyzed?

III. Determining the Possible Solutions

    A. What criteria must the solutions have?
        1. What qualities will make a solution worth considering?
        2. What must the solution be able to accomplish?
    B. What are the possible solutions to the problem?
        1. Solution A.
        2. Solution B, etc.

IV. Examination of the Tentative Solutions

    A. What are the advantages and disadvantages of Solution A?
        1. How does it fit the criteria for a good solution?
        2. What does it accomplish?
        3. What are its weaknesses?
    B. What are the advantages and disadvantages of Solution B, C, etc.?

V. Choosing a Single Solution and Putting It into Effect
  A. Which solution is most desirable?
  B. Can its use be justified for this problem?
  C. Does this solution have shortcomings?
    1. Can the solution be improved?
    2. How can it be perfected?
  D. How can it best be put into effect?
    1. What steps are necessary to put it into effect?
    2. Who is responsible for putting it into effect?
    3. What formal action is necessary?

PREPARING FOR THE CONFERENCE

The preparation for a conference is no less arduous than the preparation for a speech. It is a systematic route to reach the final goal, the solution of the problem.

Determine the Purpose and the Subject

Define the goals which you believe the conference should attain. Is it to be an advisory discussion? Should specific action result from the discussion? Is it a planning conference? Will the exchange of ideas be sufficient?

Examine the subject of the conference in detail. Is it timely and important? Must it be dealt with now? Can it be confined to a reasonable time period? Is it too broad for complete discussion? Should one or two phases of the subject be selected for this particular conference with others left to another time? Does the subject have sufficient interest? Are there several different points of view that can be explored? A conference serves no purpose if everyone is in agreement at the outset. These and similar questions must be asked and answered before a suitable conference subject can be determined.

Select the Participants

Many conferences fail because the men and women who have been invited to participate are not qualified to contribute anything to the discussion. The ideal conferee should have experience with the subject under consideration. He should be a cooperative individual. He should have an understanding of the subject. He should have a point of view. Obviously all of the participants cannot fulfill all of the qualifications; but where selection is possible, choose those participants who are best qualified. Limit the invitations to ten to twelve people if possible.

Develop the Discussion Plan

The discussion outline on page 261 is the basis of the discussion plan. But the actual procedure for getting the conference underway and adapting the subject to the discussion outline are important steps in preplanning for the conference. Decide how and why the discussion should be limited. Acquire a thorough knowledge of the subject matter yourself. Try to determine where definitions will be needed. Select the point at which summaries will be most helpful in keeping the discussion on the track. Decide how you will get the discussion started. Determine your opening remarks if you are the leader. Anticipate the situations and problems which may arise. Make sure that plenty of time is available. Try to set up a timetable which the conference can strive to adhere to.

Plan the Physical Arrangements

The conference is a face to face situation. Make certain that the physical arrangement of the chairs and table are such that each participant can see and hear every other participant. The standard arrangement is the circle, for larger groups the oval or rectangle. Make every effort to make the participant comfortable. See that there is adequate light and heat, that pencils and papers are available, and so forth. Above all, remember to invite the conferees. Give them the exact time and place. Notify them sufficiently in advance so that you can expect them to fit the conference into their already busy schedules.

CONFERENCE DISCUSSION LEADERSHIP

In the introductory definition of a conference it was stated that the members of the conference including the leader were all on an equal footing. No one is the boss. No one has any special authority. It was further stated that the leader was a guide or moderator. What does this mean?

The conference discussion leader's job is threefold: (1) he encourages full participation by all of the members of the group; (2) he leads the discussion in a manner which insures its staying on the track of the scientific method; and (3) he draws together and summarizes the accomplishments of the group. In the ideal situation any member of the discussion group should be able to slide into the leader's seat; but to do so he must have certain rather definite characteristics.

The Qualities of a Good Conference Leader

The conference leader must be a straight and fast thinker. In order to command the respect of the group he must be able to think with the best of them.

The conference leader must be a good bread-and-butter speaker. He must be able to express himself easily and well. Much of his contribution will be in untangling problems of language, encouraging the contributions of others, and providing clear impartial summaries.

The conference leader must be able to analyze quickly. He must sift the wheat from the chaff of the discussion. He must note the ideas which contribute the most to the solution. He must be able to recognize tangents and guide the discussion back on the track.

The conference leader must be the personification of fairness, tactfulness, and patience. He must see that each participator gets a fair hearing. He must discourage intentional thinking on the part of the members. He must not let his personal feelings interfere with the progress of the meeting. He must be tactful in handling uncooperative attitudes. He must be patient with those who have difficulty in expressing themselves.

The conference leader must be willing to encourage discussion in others rather than talking himself. He must avoid acting as an expert or a judge. He must learn to control through cooperation.

Introducing the Conference

The leader gets the conference started. He usually introduces the conference with a greeting to the members. He tries to establish a feeling of informality and good will. In the small group he makes sure that all of the participants know each other. In many training conferences each member clearly identifies himself and his work.

He impresses on the members of the group the necessity for trading ideas and usually explains exactly what his function in the process will be.

He introduces the topic, usually vitalizing it by reference to some current incident or well known person who has been connected with it. He encourages discussion from this point forward, gradually taking less and less part himself.

Getting Full Participation

The success of a conference is in part measured by the contribution of its members. The conference leader encourages participation. This may mean controlling the stronger members and urging the reticent ones. The key to full participation lies in the art of asking questions.

There are two types of questions, the direct question, which is aimed at a specific member of the group, and the general question, sometimes called the overhead question, which is directed to the entire group. The first is used to encourage response from reticent members; the second is used to stimulate different opinions.

The best questions are those which can't be answered by a simple *Yes* or *No*. They are questions which demand a full answer. They are the *who, what, when, where, why,* and *how* questions. The leader who is a master in the art of asking questions can encourage discussion, stimulate interest, and direct the discussion with them.

Summarizing the Discussion

One of the best ways to summarize the discussion is to write on the blackboard as you go along the points that bear on the problem. This serves two purposes. It provides a framework for the discussion, and it helps the members to keep the progress of the discussion in mind.

The oral summary is another responsibility of the conference leader. He may summarize during the discussion to pull the ideas together and keep the discussion following the steps in the conference outline. Certainly summaries are needed after each of the five steps of the scientific process.

Summaries can also be used to direct the discussion that is getting out of hand. A summary of the essential points which have been made tends to cut off unnecessary overexpansion of an idea.

The leader should always summarize the ideas of the conference at its conclusion. Presumably some agreement has been reached. The summary should include the ideas involved in the agreement but should also recognize any basic disagreements which still exist.

PARTICIPATING IN THE CONFERENCE

The qualities of a good conference leader are also the qualities of the ideal conference participator. Go back and reread them. The attitudes which the participator should have and the procedures he should follow are suggested below.

Develop a Sense of Responsibility Toward the Group

Remember that effective conference discussion depends upon you. Each member must contribute from his knowledge and experience. You are dependent upon the ideas of others, and they in turn are dependent upon your ideas. Get into the group spirit. Analyze, evaluate, and express yourself.

Know the Subject

This may be stated "don't pool ignorance." If you are to be an effective member of the conference, you must be prepared. You will be told the subject of the conference well in advance. Take the time to sharpen up your own thinking and increase your background.

Participate Correctly

In the discussion no one makes any speeches. Instead, you participate. Some good rules for participation follow. One person at a time; let the other fellow finish before you begin speaking. Keep your contributions short, no longer than one minute. Participate frequently, but never demand more than your share of the time. Don't make speeches.

Use the Reflective Thinking Process

Don't allow your thinking to become random or intentional. Analyze the ideas of others. Speak only when you have something to say that will contribute to the search for the truth. Analyze new concepts and accept new ideas. Evaluate your own thinking process. Don't get into arguments. Argument means that you have closed your mind. Keep it open and free to adjust to the thought of others. Avoid the *yes or no* and the *black or white* attitudes. No problem is solved with a flat decision between two extremes. Try to find the shades of gray. Examine the maybe.

Be a Good Bread-and-Butter Speaker

Think straight; think on your feet; organize what you have to say clearly; express yourself forcefully. Your ability to be clear and concise will help the development of the conference immeasurably. It is not enough to participate; you must participate well. The conference provides you with the opportunity to show your ability to work in the cooperative situation; to show that you can think with others. Be concrete; be specific. Bring your own experience and knowledge to bear.

These are the principles which govern the problem solving conference. But this is not the only way to discuss a problem. Some of the other types of discussion are worth consideration.

OTHER TYPES OF DISCUSSION

Most conferring is done within the framework of the committee meeting or the conference. However, several other discussion procedures are better adapted to differing listener situations.

The Round Table

The round table is a special name given to conference discussion. It implies a face to face situation—around a table. There is no audience present, though a radio audience may be eavesdroppers on the conference. This is true in the Chicago Roundtable of the Air or the Northwestern Reviewing Stand, both of which are outstanding radio examples of the round-table conference. The listeners are able to hear the interplay of the conference on many vital issues of the day.

The Panel Discussion

The panel discussion is a conference before an audience. The participants are seated so that they face the listeners. The panel usually consists of from three to five persons. The panelists conduct a conference on some vital issue before an audience which is small enough to get the feeling of participation.

The Symposium

The symposium is a more formal type of discussion. It includes several prepared speeches delivered by experts on different phases of the same subject or speeches expressing different points of view. For example, a symposium on religion might include a catholic priest, a protestant minister, a jewish rabbi, and an agnostic free-thinker as speakers. There would be no actual interplay among the speakers, though each man might adapt his remarks to the preceding speakers. The audience for the symposium may run into the hundreds or thousands. The formality of the symposium tends to destroy most of the advantages derived from group thinking.

The Forum

Simply stated, the forum merely means questions or contributions from the audience. For example, the preceding forms of discussion may be combined. You may have a lecture-forum, a speech with questions from the audience. You may have a panel-forum or a symposium-forum. The "Town Meeting of the Air" is essentially a symposium-forum.

A great many other variants of the four types of discussion can be found. Each of them tries to maintain the reflective thinking process. Each represents a group-thinking approach to a problem.

——Apply the Principles

Be sure that you understand the set of characteristics which are peculiar to conference speaking and the advantages and weaknesses of the conference method. Always be mindful of the steps of reflective thinking. Practice and participate. You will be involved in conferences regularly and your contributions will continually serve as a basis for the evaluation of your worth.

(1) Prepare for a conference dealing with a technical problem of present concern. Prepare your own outline following the five steps in the reflective thinking process.

(2) Invite others to participate. Have the group review your outline and make any necessary adjustments. Set a date for the conference. Select a leader. Each individual should now prepare himself for effective participation in the discussion.

(3) Hold the conference. Be sure to adhere to the definitions of a good conference as discussed at the beginning of this chapter. Practice reflective thinking.

(4) Review the results of your conference discussion. Were the results worthwhile? What were the major weaknesses? What were the major strengths? How could the process have been better?

(5) Participate in a conference discussion as frequently as possible. Discussion is the democratic way. It needs to be understood and practiced.

FORMULA N

$$CS = UC + PC + EP$$

(CS) Conference Speaking = (UC) Understanding what
the *Conference* is plus *(PC) Preparing for the Conference*
plus *(EP) Effective Participation.*

Now, apply the formula!

Have a group of listeners attend your next conference
discussion for the purpose of evaluating *you and the group*
by using the scale below. Each listener evaluates a different participant. Each listener evaluates the same group.
The average group score for each category will be a
good indicator of the discussion effectiveness of the group.

Conference Discussion Scale			
1–2 Weak *3 Average* *4–5 Strong*			
Criteria	*Individual Contribu- tion*	*Group Contribu- tion*	*Comments*
THE PROCESS: (1) Awareness of the problem	*Score 1–5*	*Score 1–5*	
(2) Analysis of the problem			
(3) Determining tentative so- lutions			
(4) Examination of the solu- tions			
(5) Choosing a solution			

Conference Discussion Scale (*cont.*)			
1–2 Weak *3 Average* *4–5 Strong*			
Criteria	*Individual Contribution*	*Group Contribution*	*Comments*
THE MEANS: (1) Cooperation			
(2) Reflective thought			
(3) Communication			
(4) Knowledge			
(5) Discussion outline			
Totals			
Averages			

participating in
the business meeting

EVERY TECHNOLOGIST will sooner or later become a participant in some type of business meeting as a part of his job responsibility. It is to be expected that this responsibility will be accepted and treated with intelligence. These business meetings may range from the more informal meeting of an activity committee to the more formal meeting of a policy committee. In either case the basic requirements of parliamentary procedure can be an aid to orderly discussion.

You will soon discover that it is to your advantage to be an informed participant. To know accepted procedure is to know when and how to make your opinions heard. To know accepted procedure is to gain a sense of timing in airing your views. To know accepted procedure is to be recognized as a responsible member of the business meeting group. To know accepted procedure is to call attention to your own individual worth.

This chapter is concerned with those basic requirements of parliamentary procedure most needed by the technologist in his everyday business meeting experiences. The less frequent, highly formalized business meeting requires a more thorough knowledge of parliamentary procedures. In this case the technologist should consult such aids as *Robert's Rules of Order.*

273

THE AGENDA

An agenda is simply a list of things to be done. Its chief value is its contribution to orderly progress. In the business meeting the things to be done are fairly standard. A typical business meeting agenda is as follows:

1. The Call to Order
2. Calling the Roll
3. Reading the Minutes
4. Committee Reports and Announcements
5. Unfinished Business
6. New Business
7. Adjournment

The agenda is frequently worked out in greater detail, particularly in terms of unfinished and new business. In such a case it is desirable to post or hand each member of the group a copy. Prior knowledge of a detailed agenda helps to focus attention on the main issues and is an aid to efficient progress.

THE CALL TO ORDER

Every business meeting opens with a call to order. This is the responsibility of the chairman of the group. He may simply say, with or without pounding his gavel, "*The chair calls this meeting to order.*" From this point on it is the chairman's responsibility to maintain order. It is important that all participants recognize that the chair has this power.

The call to order also signals that from this point on each speaker is required to address the chairman and be recognized before proceeding. Only one speaker may be recognized at a time. Only one speaker may be heard at a time. The most successful meetings are the most orderly meetings. It is essential, therefore, that the call to order be sustained throughout the meeting.

CALLING THE ROLL

Occasionally the roll call is omitted in the more informal meeting. More often than not, however, the roll call follows the call to order. Calling the roll becomes the responsibility of the secretary.

Three functions are fulfilled in calling the role:

(1) It provides a record of attendance.
(2) It establishes the existence of a quorum (as established by the constitution or members present) or a majority.
(3) It acts as a social force recognizing those members present as well as those absent.

The secretary should call the role with alertness, briskness, and efficiency. This procedure can set the stage for an alert, brisk, efficient meeting. The dull monotony of hollow-toned sounds repeating name after name can be contagious.

READING THE MINUTES

The next order of business is reading the minutes. The minutes should represent a comprehensive, yet concise, report of the events of the last meeting. It is of the utmost importance that these events be recorded with accuracy. The minutes of a meeting are an objective report. They are not subject to the bias of the secretary.

The secretary would be well advised in *preparing* for an effective reading of the minutes. Reread the portion of Chapter 12 which concerns oral reading of a manuscript. The same principles apply here. The exact meaning must be communicated. Stress must be properly placed. Phrasing must lead to understanding. The rate of reading must allow time for the listeners to grasp what is read. The effective reading of the minutes of a meeting is a rare occurrence. But remember: rarity has its rewards.

The minutes of the last meeting are subject to correction and approval. At the conclusion of the reading, the chairman may simply ask, "Are there any corrections or additions?" If so, a member after receiving recognition from the chair says, "Mr. Chairman, I move that the minutes be changed to read . . . . . " Another person must supply a second: "Mr. Chairman, I second the motion" or simply "Second." The chair then asks if there is any discussion. Following the discussion or in the absence of any discussion a vote is taken. A majority vote carries the motion.

In the event that there are no corrections or additions, a motion may be made to the effect that the minutes of the meeting be approved as read. A second and a majority vote in favor closes this order of business.

COMMITTEE REPORTS AND ANNOUNCEMENTS

Committee reports and announcements, whether they be read aloud or given extemporaneously, should be communicated by only the most effective speakers in the group. Frequently committees engage in hours of deliberation. The report of this work deserves the most effective means of communication possible. The same is true of announcements. If it's worth saying at all, it's worth saying well.

At the conclusion of a report it is customary for the chairman to entertain a motion of acceptance or adoption of the report.

> Mr. Jones: Mr. Chairman.
> Chairman: Mr. Jones.
> Mr. Jones: I move that the report be accepted as read *or* I move that the recommendations be adopted as stated.
> Mr. Smith: Second.
> Chairman: It has been moved and seconded that . . . . . Is there any discussion?
> Discussion: . . . .
> Mr. Smith: Question.
> Mr. Chairman: The previous question has been called for. Those in favor signify by saying Aye. Opposed No.

UNFINISHED BUSINESS

Unfinished business is that business not concluded at the last meeting. It has already been reviewed in the reading of the minutes. The procedure followed in taking care of unfinished business is similar to the procedure followed in taking care of new business. It can involve motions, seconds, discussion, division of the motion, amendment of the motion, voting on the motion, postponing the motion, referring the motion to a committee.

A. Motions and seconds. The procedure for making a motion is simple. A table of parliamentary motions is found in Figure 12. Following is a sample procedure:

MOTIONS	Need a Second?	Amendable?	Debatable?	Vote Required?	May Interrupt a Speaker?
I. Principal Motion					
1. Any main question or any independent matter of business before the meeting	yes	yes	yes	maj.	no
II. Subsidiary Motions					
2. To amend	yes	yes	yes	maj.	no
3. To postpone indefinitely	yes	no	yes	maj.	no
4. To refer to a committee	yes	yes	yes	maj.	no
5. To postpone to a certain time	yes	yes	yes	maj.	no
6. Previous question	yes	no	no	⅔	no
7. To lay on (or take from) the table	yes	no	no	maj.	no
III. Incidental Motions					
8. To suspend a rule	yes	no	no	⅔	no
9. To withdraw a motion	yes	no	no	maj.	no
10. Question of consideration	no	no	no	⅔	yes
11. A point of order	no	no	no	Chair[a]	yes
12. Appeal from decision of chair	yes	no	no	maj.	yes
IV. Privileged Motions					
13. To make a matter of business a "special order" for a given time	no	no	no	⅔	yes
14. Questions of rights and privileges	no	no	no	Chair[a]	yes
15. To adjourn (unqualified)	yes	no	no	maj.	no
16. To fix time for next meeting	yes	yes	no	maj.	no

[a]Require only decision of Chair; no vote unless appealed.

Fig. 12. Table of Parliamentary Motions.[1]

---

[1] Quoted with some changes from *Gregg's Handbook of Parliamentary Law* (Boston: Ginn and Company, 1910) in J. M. O'Neill, ed., *Foundations of Speech*, Englewood Cliffs, N.J.: Prentice-Hall, Inc., 1941, p. 395.

Mr. Jones: Mr. Chairman.
Mr. Chairman: Mr. Jones.
Mr. Jones: Mr. Chairman, I move that . . . .
Mr. Smith: Second.
Mr. Chairman: The motion has been made and seconded that . . . .
Is there any discussion?

It is particularly important that Mr. Jones state his motion clearly and concisely. Remember: like all communication, the purpose of a motion is to gain a favorable response.

B. *Discussion*. It is not essential that each seconded motion be discussed. On the other hand, time should always be provided for clarification and questioning if anybody so desires. The chair *must* ask "Is there any discussion?" before calling for a vote on the motion.

The discussion of any motion may take one of three possible courses:

(1) The discussion may concern the motion as originally seconded.
(2) The discussion may concern first one and then another division of the motion.
(3) The discussion may concern the motion as it is amended.

The discussion of a motion will be most effective when the members of the group confine their remarks to relevant material only. Listen to what the other man has to say; he may have a point. Adapt your response in clear, concise terms. Be friendly. It would be most unfortunate if the heat of your emotions served only to defeat your good ideas.

In the event that the motion as seconded involves two concerns, any individual may request that the chairman divide the motion for clarity in discussion. The chairman may comply by making such a division, or a motion for division may be made and passed by majority vote. In the event that a motion is divided, remember that the purpose of division is to gain clarity. You are discussing each division as an aid to intelligent voting on the motion.

An amendment to the motion may be made at any time during the discussion. An amendment is simply an adjustment which makes the original motion more meaningful. It can not change the entire meaning of the original motion. The procedure is simple.

Mr. Jones: Mr. Chairman.
Mr. Chairman: Mr. Jones.
Mr. Jones: Mr. Chairman, I move that the motion be amended to read . . . .

The motion for amendment must be seconded and approved by a majority vote. If it is approved, the discussion then returns to the *original motion as amended.* Frequently amendments of motions and amendments of amendments result in confusion and a slowing of progress. Remember that the purpose of parliamentary procedure is to provide an orderly system. Take one thing at a time. The system is simple; individuals provide the confusion.

C. *Voting.* Voting on motions may be for one of three reasons:

(1) The group may vote for acceptance or rejection of a motion.
(2) The group may vote to postpone further discussion on the motion.
(3) The group may vote to refer the motion to a committee.

The vote on a motion may come at any time during the discussion. Ordinarily a discussion will run its course, and it becomes obvious that the group is ready to vote on the original motion. If, however, the discussion shows no signs of concluding, it may become necessary to end the discussion by a vote. The procedure is as follows:

Mr. Jones: Mr. Chairman.
Mr. Chairman: Mr. Jones.
Mr. Jones: Mr. Chairman, I move the previous question.

This motion requires an immediate vote. It must receive a two-thirds majority. It is a motion to end the discussion period. If carried, all discussion ends and a vote is taken on the original motion.

The vote to postpone further discussion of a motion (to lay the motion on the table) may be necessary due to more pressing matters or because more time for decision is needed. In either case the intent is to reconsider the motion at a later day. The procedure is as follows:

Mr. Jones: Mr. Chairman.
Mr. Chairman: Mr. Jones.
Mr. Jones: Mr. Chairman, I move the question be postponed until . . . . or . . . . postponed indefinitely.

This motion also may be made at any time during the discussion. The motion can not be discussed. It can be adopted by a majority vote.

The vote to refer the motion to a committee usually results when the group feels the matter can best be handled by a smaller group or by a particular interest group. It may also be that the group feels the motion is worthy of special investigation in which case a special committee may be appointed.

> Mr. Jones: Mr. Chairman.
> Mr. Chairman: Mr. Jones.
> Mr. Jones: Mr. Chairman, I move that the question be referred to . . . (an existing committee or a new committee) with . . . . instructions to report back . . . (specific time) *or* . . . power to act.

NEW BUSINESS

The gauge of a successful business meeting frequently lies in the quality of the new business. Here is where new ideas, new goals, and new procedures are tested. Here is where the life blood of the meeting is injected. Without new business the meeting becomes stagnant. Without new business the organization's progress is slowed. Without new business the day will come when there is no old business. Without either, the business meeting becomes a waste of time.

Your considered judgment is important to any business meeting. This is particularly true with new business. Follow the steps which will help your proposal:

(1) Carefully consider your proposal in advance of the meeting.
(2) Phrase your motion clearly and concisely.
(3) Having been recognized by the chair, state your motion effectively.
(4) Enter into the discussion of your motion in good spirit.
(5) If your motion meets with the approval of the group, support it enthusiastically until its objective has been fulfilled.
(6) If your motion is rejected by the group, accept their rejection with grace. Do not lose your value to the group by being a poor loser.

The parliamentary procedure followed for new business is the same as for old business. This procedure should be adequate for the less formal business meeting.

ADJOURNMENT

Ordinarily the informal meeting ends at the conclusion of the new business. Everyone has had his say and the business at hand has been cleared. The chairman's statement "The meeting is adjourned" or a motion for adjournment from the floor is the customary procedure.

"The meeting is adjourned" statement from the chairman is the most informal closing. It requires neither a motion or a majority vote. The group expects no more. They have concluded their business. It is obvious to all that the meeting need go no further.

A motion for adjournment is also common practice. It may be made from the floor at any time during the discussion. If such is the case, the procedure is as follows:

Mr. Jones: Mr. Chairman.
Chairman: Mr. Jones.
Mr. Jones: I move the meeting be adjourned.
Mr. Smith: Second.
Chairman: It has been moved and seconded that the meeting be adjourned. All those in favor say Aye (majority response). Those opposed say No. (no response). The meeting is adjourned.

The motion for adjournment is not debatable and must be voted on immediately. Adoption is by majority vote.

In the event that a fixed time for adjournment was previously determined by the group, the chairman is required to adjourn the meeting at that time. An extension of time is possible if a motion to that effect is made and carried by a majority vote.

Remember: parliamentary procedure is an *aid* to orderly discussion, but not necessarily an essential of orderly discussion. Use it when it is helpful. Adapt it to serve your purpose. The really important consideration is the progress of the business meeting.

—Apply the Principles

Parliamentary procedure should always serve as an *aid* to orderly discussion. Familiarity with the basic requirements, as discussed in the chapter, should lead to the order desired in your business meetings. Apply the principles suggested below.

(1) Think back to the last business meeting you attended. Was it an informal meeting? Was parliamentary procedure used in any detail? How could the meeting have been improved? Did the meeting accomplish its purpose?

(2) Plan a mock business meeting with a group of friends. Make it an informal meeting but include all of the parliamentary procedure discussed in this chapter. After careful preparation present your mock meeting before an audience. This is an effective way of teaching others some basic parliamentary procedure.

(3) Attend other meetings as a spectator. List the good features of the meeting. List the poor features. What could have been done to improve the meeting?

FORMULA O

$$PBM = \frac{BMA}{EP}$$

(*PBM*) *Participating in the Business Meeting* = (*EP*) *Effective Participation* in the (*BMA*) *Business Meeting Agenda.*

Now, apply the formula!

Acquaint yourself with the basic requirements of parliamentary procedure as outlined in this chapter. Use the check list below in preparing for and participating in your next business meeting.

The Business Meeting

THE CALL TO ORDER:

Correct procedure _____
Sustained meaning _____
Implications _____

CALLING THE ROLL:

Record of attendance _____
Existence of quorum _____
Social force _____

READING THE MINUTES:

Comprehensive _____
Accurate _____
Communication _____
Corrections _____
Additions _____
Approval _____

COMMITTEE REPORTS AND ANNOUNCEMENTS:

Communication _____
Procedure _____

UNFINISHED BUSINESS:

Motions _____
Seconds _____
Discussion _____
Divisions _____
Amendments _____
Voting _____

NEW BUSINESS:

Motions _____
Seconds _____
Discussion _____
Divisions _____
Amendments _____
Voting _____

ADJOURNMENT:

Procedure _____
Vote _____

---

appendixes

A

discussion

questions

CHAPTER 1: WHY SPEAK?

1. List five outstanding technologists in your field. In what ways has effective speaking been essential to their success?
2. How much of the art of winning friends and influencing people is dependent on good bread-and-butter speaking?
3. Are you influenced more by *what* a person says or *how he says it?* Why?
4. How can speaking with others become pleasurable?
5. If your ability to speak was suddenly impaired physiologically to the point that you could not be understood, what effect would it have on your career?
6. In what way does speech reflect the technologist's personality?
7. What makes a subject worth listening to?
8. What differences do you note between experienced and inexperienced speakers?
9. Why is it essential that the technologist put particular emphasis on the listener?
10. What dollar and cents value can the technologist realistically place on good bread-and-butter speaking?

CHAPTER 2: THE KEYS TO EFFECTIVE SPEECH

1. What particular adaptations are required in the bases of good speech when a technical topic is discussed with a lay audience?

2. List some superior speech topics from your area of specialization. Why do you consider them superior?

3. What are the implications in the statement "A superior topic requires superior material"?

4. Why must the technical man give particular emphasis to clear organization?

5. List as many reasons as you can why a listener might not react favorably to a speech? What control does the speaker have over each reason listed?

6. How would you define "to communicate"?

7. Make a list of technical terms commonly used by the technical men in your area of specialization. What are the denotative meanings of these words? What are the connotative meanings of these words to the average man outside of your area? What are the implications of these differences to you the speaker?

8. When does practice _not_ make perfect?

9. You will do more impromptu speaking than any other type of speaking. How can you best prepare yourself for this type of daily speaking?

10. Why is gaining a favorable response the main objective of good speaking?

CHAPTER 3: ALERT YOUR MENTAL ATTITUDE

1. Discuss the part that self-confidence plays in improving your ability to communicate effectively.

2. Illustrate the fact that the speaker's attitude often does _not_ reflect the speaker's personality and character.

3. When is performance tension a good thing?

4. List as many reasons as possible why the technical man need not fear his listener. Discuss each.

5. Why does listener-concentration rather than self-concentration aid in lessening performance tension?

6. Recall several instances when you felt that your listener was not interested in listening to you. How do you account for _your_ attitude in each of these instances? What specific attitude changes might have helped _you?_

7. List several technical topics which you would hesitate to discuss even though you feel well informed on them. Account for your attitude in relation to these topics. How might you overcome these attitudes?

8. What does being thoroughly prepared involve?

9. Why should speaking be regarded as an opportunity?

10. How might you capitalize on a forgetting situation by turning it into a favorable response situation?

CHAPTER 4: UNDERSTAND YOUR LISTENER

1. What will you do in your next speech to destroy the art and science of "O" filling?

2. Name and discuss the kinds of listeners the technical man most commonly contacts.

3. Discuss the most interesting speaker you have recently heard. Why did he interest you the listener?

4. List five technical topics that are of interest to you. Why would *you* want to listen to them?

5. It is well known that the listener thinks more slowly than the speaker. What are the implications to both the speaker and the listener in this situation?

6. What effect might derogatory remarks have on the listener?

7. Why is it best to get your listener to agree with you early in your speech?

8. Summarize the ideas of a speaker just heard. Does the speaker agree with your summary? What had your listening missed or ignored? Why?

9. Discuss the ways in which the modifying factors influence the basic drives.

10. The listener, the speech, and the speaker are all influenced by the occasion. Why?

CHAPTER 5: DEVELOP YOUR PURPOSE, SUBJECT, AND MATERIAL

1. It has been said that speech subjects drawn from direct experience are generally more satisfactory. When is experience *not* the best teacher?

2. What is the difference between the general purpose and the specific purpose?

3. List several technical topics on which you are well informed. What might your general purpose be for each? How might your specific purpose change for each of these topics in talking to the following listeners: your co-workers, the local PTA, your social affiliation, your national association.

4. Why might the inclusion of humor be of particular importance to the technical man in communicating a technical topic?

5. List ways of helping to insure a favorable response to a technical report.

6. Why not reverse the order of the steps on the persuasion ladder to read: (1) to actuate, (2) to convince, (3) to stimulate?

7. Why did the title *How to Win Friends and Influence People* help to

launch the sale of several million copies of that book? Suggest some new superior titles.

8. List some technical subjects which you are confident will attract certain groups of listeners. Justify your confidence.

9. Why is it dangerous to support *only* your point of view in giving a speech to persuade? When should you support the opposing point of view?

10. What are the best sources of material available to you?

CHAPTER 6: ORGANIZE YOUR SPEECH

1. Why are the organizational purposes—the Five E's to Effectiveness—considered essential to good organization? What are the possible consequences of organization *without* purpose?

2. Discuss the possible ramifications of a poor introduction. Consider the listener, the speech, and the speaker.

3. Discuss some of the most effective introductions you have heard. Why were they effective? In what ways did they engage the listener? Did the occasion contribute to the effectiveness?

4. How can the speaker best insure that his listeners are aware of his main headings? Why is it that frequently a listener can not summarize the major points of a speaker's speech?

5. Why is the organization of material dependent on the listener? Discuss organizational changes needed when the same topic is discussed first with a technical audience and then with a lay audience.

6. Why must the speech to inform as well as the speech to persuade be concerned with enlightening, encompassing, and enthusing the listener? Why is it important that the speech to inform be made to interest, concern, and excite the listener? Discuss these aspects in lectures you have heard in school.

7. How does enlisting the support of the listener in the speech to inform differ from enlisting the support of the listener in the speech to persuade? Is one more objective than the other? Which speech would depend more on appeal?

8. List some famous quotations which would be particularly applicable as conclusions to specific technical topics. Why are they applicable? What relationship would they have to your purpose sentence?

9. What are the values of outlining a speech after you have spent considerable time in organizing your material?

10. Discuss the six steps in making a full-sentence outline.

CHAPTER 7: MAKE YOUR INFORMATION CLEAR

1. Why might one group of listeners feel that your information was clear while another group might feel just the opposite?

2. Why is audience analysis a prerequisite to the clarification of information?

3. Why is simplicity the modern keynote? What are the advantages? What are the dangers?

4. What are the implications of the statement "There is nothing new under the sun"? Do the implications provide a key to the speaker in the clarification of his information?

5. Discuss several ways of clarifying a new technical achievement for a lay audience. Illustrate your ways.

6. Discuss the make-up of a visual aid for a specific speech. What type of visual aid would you prepare? What would you include? How would it be composed? What effect would it have?

7. Discuss ways and means of making your own visual aids. Consider the use of paint, crayon, tape, cut-outs, photographs, metal, wood, and so forth.

8. Differentiate among the nine ways available to help simplify, amplify, and support a speech idea.

9. Discuss a recent speech which you have heard. Was the information clear? Why, specifically? Was some of the information not clear? How, specifically, could it have been clarified?

10. Consider a technical project you are now concerned with in your daily work. List several comparisons which would help to clarify your work to a friend unfamiliar with your field.

CHAPTER 8: MAKE YOUR INFORMATION INTERESTING

1. Differentiate among the eight tools of interest. Illustrate each.

2. Why are the tools of interest called psychological devices which attract attention?

3. When does the novel become the familiar? What are the implications of this to the speaker?

4. Why do sensory appeals help to make information interesting?

5. List four technical cencepts. Suggest ways of applying sensory appeals to each. Illustrate.

6. Give an example of the animate. Heighten your example with a sensory appeal. Do the same with the remaining seven tools of interest.

7. The attention span of a listener is brief even for the most interesting speech. Why, then, should the speaker be concerned with the tools of interest?

8. How can the speaker best compensate for momentary attention lapses on the part of the listener?

9. It is difficult to find examples of sensory appeal in the technical literature in your field. How do you account for this omission?

10. Discuss a recent lecture which you have heard. What tools of interest were utilized? What sensory appeals were used? How might the information given be made more interesting?

CHAPTER 9: LEARN TO PERSUADE

1. Select a topic you are presently concerned with in your daily work. What aspects of your topic will involve persuasion? What logical proofs will you use to support these aspects? What emotional appeals will you tie to your proofs?
2. What is meant by illogical emotional appeal? Why must it never be used?
3. Why is ethics of importance in persuasion? Cite and discuss some examples of unethical persuasion.
4. What part does colorful language play in persuasion? Discuss the implications in terms of the language used by some of our national leaders.
5. Why does the listener remain the most important element of the speech triangle in persuasive speaking?
6. Discuss ways of gaining personal prestige as a speaker. What effect can this have on your ability to persuade?
7. List those TV commercials which are least annoying to you. Why are they least annoying? What elements of persuasion account for your reasons? What can the speaker learn from your reasons?
8. Define and discuss the term "propaganda." When is it good? When bad? Cite billboard examples. What principles can be applied to the speaking situation?
9. What basic changes in attitude have you experienced during the past few years? What influenced these changes? What factors were primarily responsible for retarding your change in attitude? In retrospect what might have been done to hasten this change?
10. Review the five organizational purposes of any speech: to engage, to enlighten, to encompass, to enthuse, to enlist. The success of these purposes is dependent on the methods used. What methods would you use in the speech to persuade which you would not use in the speech to inform? Why?

CHAPTER 10: BE VISUALLY FORCEFUL AND DIRECT

1. Frequently we are surprised when we *see* radio announcers whom previously we had heard only. Why? Cite some examples.
2. Television has forcefully renewed our attention to the importance of the visual aspects in the speaking situation. Why and how?
3. Discuss the implications of Ralph Waldo Emerson's statement, "What you are speaks so loudly, I cannot hear what you say."

4. Why should we tolerate excessive movement in the beginning speaker? Does the beginning speaker tend to be inhibited? Does excessive movement free the body for later control? Is performance tension a factor?

5. What are the dangers of prepared movement?

6. How can purposeful spontaneous movement best be insured? Performance tension frequently is manifested in spontaneous movement lacking in purpose. What can be done under these circumstances?

7. It has been said that the speaker cannot lie to an audience. What are the implications of this statement in terms of the visual aspects of the speaking situation?

8. Differentiate among the criteria of good bodily action—purposeful, forceful, direct, genuine, interpretive.

9. What specifically might you do in your next speaking opportunity to insure a good first impression?

10. Any posture while speaking is acceptable if it contributes to the communication of your ideas. Do you agree or disagree with this statement? Why?

CHAPTER 11: BE VOCALLY DISTINCT AND PLEASANT

1. The "voice beautiful" *can* be a block to effective communication. When is this true? What are the implications of your answer in terms of your own vocal improvement?

2. List and discuss the ways in which vocal improvement can result in increased speaking effectiveness.

3. It has been said that the "vocally-alive" speaker is also "physically-alive." Discuss the implications. How does one affect the other?

4. Discuss the vocal aspects of some radio announcers whom you have never seen. What type of person do you assume he is? What type of personality do you assume he has? How do you imagine he looks? After you have answered these questions, inquire into the real identity of this announcer.

5. Speculate on the part that voice has played in the success of various political candidates for national office. In what instances was voice probably not a difference? In what instances might it have made a difference?

6. Discuss the criteria that should be used in determining correct pronunciation. What attitude should be taken toward regional speech?

7. When is a forceful voice a soft voice?

8. Illustrate vocally some examples of forward placement. Why does forward placement have the best carrying power?

9. List and discuss some reasons why vocal improvement is of *particular* importance to the technical man.

10. Why is vocal improvement a slow process? How best can the technical man discipline himself for vocal improvement?

CHAPTER 12: PREPARING THE ORAL TECHNICAL REPORT

1. Differentiate among the three kinds of technical reports.
2. Discuss the general procedure followed in preparing a critical report. How does this procedure differ from the preparation of a summary report or a fact-finding report?
3. Why is "being interesting" secondary to the "transfer of information" in a technical report? On the other hand, what can be done to stimulate and maintain interest?
4. Suggest criteria that might be helpful in determining the quantity and quality of summary information.
5. How do you know what your listener *wants* and *needs* when organizing your oral report?
6. *Effective* oral reading is comparable to *effective* bread-and-butter speaking. Discuss the implications of this statement.
7. People in responsible governmental positions are being forced to read their speeches more today than was the case a decade or two ago. Why? What are the implications of your reasons as concerns the reading of the technical report?
8. This chapter stresses four factors related to reading a manuscript. Discuss each factor.
9. Why is eye contact of paramount importance in oral reading?
10. List and discuss the reasons why effective oral reading is of particular importance to the technical man.

CHAPTER 13: HOLDING THE INTERVIEW

1. Differentiate between an interview and a conversation.
2. Differentiate among the three types of interviews—application, sales, and professional.
3. Discuss the experiences that you may have had in any of the three types of interviews. What mistakes did you make? What were your strong points and why? What were the results of the interview?
4. List the criteria you would be concerned with in a job application interview. What do *you* want to know about the company policy, the personnel, the wage scale, the retirement benefits, and so forth?
5. Jobs are won and lost on the basis of the interview alone. What is the significance of this truism in terms of your ability to communicate?
6. Why is the interview an excellent example of the need for effective bread-and-butter speaking? Why is the term "bread-and-butter" particularly applicable here?

7. How might the organizational purpose—the Five E's to Effectiveness—be adapted to the interview situation? Illustrate the fulfillment of each of the five purposes.

8. Name a particular company which interests you. What do you know about this company that would be helpful to you in an interview? What other factors must you become informed about?

9. The listener is the most important element of the speaking situation. When should the interviewer be the listener? When should the interviewee be the listener? In either case how can you adapt to your listener?

10. Discuss the responsibilities of the interviewer and the interviewee. When should you share the responsibilities of the other? When would this type of sharing be dangerous?

CHAPTER 14: CONFERENCE SPEAKING

1. What is a conference?

2. What are the advantages of the conference method? What are the disadvantages of the conference method?

3. Differentiate among the three kinds of thinking—random, intentional, and reflective.

4. Why is reflective thinking the key to conference success?

5. Discuss Dewey's five steps in reflective thinking. Why are these five steps particularly suited to the technical man?

6. What is the value of the conference outline? In what way is the suggested outline particularly suited to the technical man?

7. Discuss the qualities of a good conference discussion leader.

8. Good bread-and-butter speaking is essential to good conference participation. Why?

9. What can the individual participant do to discourage and prevent the "pooling of ignorance" in a conference discussion?

10. Discuss other types of discussion such as the round table, the panel discussion, the symposium, and the forum. When would each type be preferable?

CHAPTER 15: PARTICIPATING IN THE BUSINESS MEETING

1. What can you do personally to improve your participation in a business meeting?

2. What can you do to improve the participation of other members of a business meeting?

3. What can and should be done to prevent a breakdown in the progress of a business meeting?

4. What can be done to promote greater attendance at your next business meeting? How can your ideas be best promoted?
5. What can be done to improve the reading effectiveness of the minutes of a meeting?
6. At what point might parliamentary procedure defeat its purpose. What can be done if this happens?
7. Why is new business considered the life blood of any meeting? What is your responsibility in this matter?
8. Discuss the motions which are not subject to discussion. Why are they not subject to discussion?
9. What is the purpose of amending a motion? What are the rules concerning amendments?
10. Discuss ways of making a business meeting a more stimulating and effective gathering.

speaking

effectiveness scale

| Listener _____ | Speaker _____ | |
| Subject _____ | Date _____ | |

Criteria	Score 1–5	Comments
MENTAL ATTITUDE Self-Confidence _____ Listener concern _____ Speaking personality _____		
LISTENER ADAPTATION Basic Drives _____ Modifying Factors _____ The Occasion _____		
PURPOSE, SUBJECT, MATERIAL Appropriate _____ Limited _____ Clear _____ Sources _____ Fair ___ Representative _____		

| Listener _____ | | Speaker _____ |
| Subject _____ | | Date _____ |

Criteria	Score 1-5	Comments
ORGANIZATION Engage ___ Enlighten ___ Encompass ___ Enthuse ___ Enlist ___		
INFORMATION CLARITY Explanation ___ Statistics ___ Definition ___ Testimony ___ Illustration ___ Examples ___ Restatement ___ Comparison ___ Visual Aids ___		
INFORMATION INTEREST Sensory Appeals ___ Novel ___ Language ___ Real-Concrete ___ Self-Interest ___ Humor ___ Animate ___ Controversial ___ Familiar ___ Uncertain ___		
PHYSICAL ACTIVITY Purposeful ___ Forceful ___ Direct ___ Genuine ___ Interpretive ___		
VOICE Forceful ___ Pleasant ___ Distinct ___ Interesting ___		
General Effectiveness		

sample
speech

SOME THINGS THE WORLD SHOULD UNDER-
STAND ABOUT "H" BOMBS*

THE DANGERS INTRINSIC TO MEN'S POSSESSION OF NUCLEAR POWER

By THOMAS E. MURRAY, *Commissioner, United States Atomic Energy Commission, Washington, D.C. Delivered at the Golden Jubilee Dinner of Fordham Law School, New York, New York, November 17, 1955*

A major purpose of these remarks is to make a proposal that has long been one of my principal objectives as an Atomic Energy Commissioner. The proposal itself may strike some of you as rather dramatic; but the premise of the proposal is coldly factual.

This factual premise is the present possession by man of a new kind of power. Since the turn of the century scientists have progressively penetrated the secrets of nuclear energy. More recently technology has succeeded in releasing this energy on a tremendous scale. To a much more limited degree it has also succeeded in harnessing it. Man's knowledge of this new power and his ability to use it are no more than rudimentary at the moment. But technical progress is going on with a rapidity that is breathtaking.

Anything one might say about this new technological development

---

* Thomas E. Murray, "Some Things the World Should Understand About 'H' Bombs," *Vital Speeches*, Vol. XXII, No. 4, (December 1, 1955), pp. 107–110.

would inevitably be an understatement. All the revolutionary changes brought about by the Industrial Revolution pale almost into insignificance before the visions of the future opened by the Nuclear Revolution. The trouble is that these visions are not all lightsome. The future is bright with promise. It is also dark with danger.

I choose tonight to speak of the dangers intrinsic to man's possession of nuclear power. I would prefer the more pleasant topic now called "Atoms for Peace." But I remind myself, and you, that the essential conditions for the peaceful use of the atom is—peace. And peace has not yet been achieved. Over our age there still hangs the fateful unresolved dilemma: will it be war or peace? The process of trying to make peace goes on—precariously—perilously. But all along the lengthy and tortuous path to peace nations will constantly meet the temptation to war. It would be idle to pretend that this temptation has already been resisted, once for all.

The United States has done one important thing to deter our enemies from yielding to this temptation. We have built up an arsenal of atomic weapons, to which we have added hydrogen-thermonuclear-weapons. There was no prudent alternative to this course of action. The policy was necessary for our own security and that of the free world.

However, our quest for security has led us to a strange end. Presently we are no longer secure about the one thing that always in the past was secure. Amid wars, pestilences, and famines mankind has always been assured of one thing—that there would be a mankind living here on earth, until the day on which man's temporal history would be terminated by an act of Almighty God. We no longer have this elementary security. Man now has the power to put an end to his own history. In its effort to protect the freedom of the world America has invented nuclear weapons capable of destroying all human life. The avoidance of one danger has thrust us into a more radical danger.

The new danger does not lie in the sheer fact of man's greatest technological achievement—the release of nuclear energy. Rather it lies in the fact that we do not understand or realize the danger inherent in this achievement. And when I say "we," I mean "we, the people." It is true that a handful of men—in science, in the military, in government—do understand that we have in our hands a power of limitless destruction. But the fact that only a handful of men possess this understanding is itself a dangerous thing. I have long been persuaded, and have often said, that an essential insurance against the dangers inherent in nuclear weapons is an America-wide public and a world-wide public that fully realizes the cosmic dimensions of this danger.

Only a bare beginning has been made toward the creation of such an informed public. True there has been considerable talk about the implications of nuclear warfare. But the slow process of educating the people in the new habits of thought proper to the age of the Nuclear Revolution has not been adequately furthered by public policies. From the beginning our atomic weapons program had to be shrouded in secrecy in the interests of national security. But we have been too slow in realizing that the interests of national security also demand broad public information. Our problem has been to strike a balance between the requirements of secrecy and the no less stringent need of wise publicity. We have not yet solved this problem. Let me give but one example.

I refer to the tragic incident of the Fortunate Dragon. This was the Japanese fishing vessel that was caught in the radioactive fallout from one of our thermo-nuclear tests at our Pacific Proving Ground in March 1954.

Before these 1954 tests took place a policy of almost utter silence had been established. The decision was made to issue only two statements—first an announcement that tests were to be held, and then a short guarded statement at their conclusion. However, the inscrutable Providence of God, our Father, decided otherwise. Radioactive dust settled on the Fortunate Dragon, some 90 miles downwind. You remember the results. The news about the potential hazard of radioactive fallout from thermonuclear weapons burst out of secrecy. Twenty-seven Japanese fishermen announced to the world the first fateful news about the lurking catastrophe that may possibly lie in wait for all of us. In this instance the official policy of secrecy proved inept. When the secret came out, through the wrong channels, the shock to world opinion rivalled in its own way the blast of the H-bomb itself.

True, information about the radioactive fallout problem was subsequently released to the public early this year and further information has since followed. But there is still more that must be explained to the public.

The fact is that the first thermonuclear explosion in 1952 shattered all previous concepts of that central element of warfare which is called "power." Let me enlarge a bit upon this fact, because it forms the proximate premise of the proposal I intend to make.

In World War II the power of a bomb was its explosive force, the force of a blast, accompanied by heat and followed by fire. The atomic bomb, of the kind unfortunately dropped on Hiroshima, was indeed a bigger bomb, thousands of times bigger than the biggest high explosive bomb; it was a "blockbuster," this was a "city buster."

Then came the thermonuclear explosion of November 1st, 1952. This device taught us, not only that we had a new weapon, but that we had a different kind of weapon. We had unleashed a different kind of power.

The thermonuclear bomb crosses the threshold into a separate category of power by reason of the sheer force and reach of its blast. Its explosion is so tremendous that it must be reckoned as a different kind of explosion. But this is not the more important difference. The thermonuclear bomb not only blasts and burns more acreage, more buildings, more people; it also releases dangerous radioactive fission products into the atmosphere. True, the "A" bomb also releases these fission products, but on a small scale. However, the atmosphere contamination that results from large thermonuclear explosions is serious. In fact, it is so serious that it could be catastrophic. A sufficiently large number of such explosions would render the earth uninhabitable to man. This is plain fact.

This is why I say that large thermonuclear weapons represent an entirely new kind of power. Their potential destructiveness is so different from the destructiveness of "A" bombs that these new weapons do not belong in the same category—not by any stretch of the imagination.

Let me be more specific. One of the products released by any nuclear explosion is a substance that is called radioactive strontium. Unlike ordinary strontium, this strontium gives off beta radiation which is one of the three kinds of radiation emitted by radium and its decay products. Prior to the atomic age there was no radioactive strontium in the atmosphere or the soil.

Of the radioactive strontium released in an explosion of a large thermonuclear weapon some falls to earth rather quickly over thousands of square miles and some is shot up into the stratosphere. From thence it settles down, diffusing throughout the whole envelope of atmosphere that surrounds the earth. Rainfall speeds its descent but it comes down slowly; only a fraction of it is deposited on the earth during the course of a year. Hence, the contamination continues to be deposited on the earth for years after the blast of the explosion has died away.

From the earth's soil radioactive strontium passes into food and then into the human body where it is absorbed into the bone structure. Here its beta rays, if intense enough, can cause bone tumors. We know that there is a limit to the amount of this strontium that the human body can absorb without harmful effects. Beyond that limit danger lies, and even death. The problem has been to fix the limit.

It is still an unsolved problem. In the course of a year the estimates have changed almost wildly. A year ago the public was informed that the radiostrontium presently in the soil would have to increase a million times over before increased frequency of bone tumors from this cause could be recognized. Recent statements have revised that figure drastically and significantly downward from one million to ten thousand. Not long ago a figure of one thousand was made public. Whatever figure is agreed upon it will be lowered some—perhaps only a little—as the radiostrontium already in the atmosphere slowly settles to earth.

In any event, there is a limit to the tolerable amount of radiostrontium that can be deposited in the soil. Consequently, there is a limit to the number of large thermonuclear explosions that the human race can withstand without harmful bodily effects. This is a crucial point to remember when there is talk of an all-out-nuclear war.

There is another aspect to the insidious destructiveness of thermonuclear weapons. The radioactive products they release have an effect on human genetics. The sheer fact of this effect is certain. The new power we have in hand can effect the lives of generations still unborn. But beyond the fact itself there are many uncertainties. I have long felt and continue to believe that all possible assistance and encouragement should be given to all those geneticists upon whose competence we must depend for badly needed information about the genetic effects resulting from nuclear explosions.

Even this brief description of the new kind of power now at our disposal gives rise to many questions.

In view of the new dimension of destructiveness that large thermonuclear bombs create, in view of the fact that their effects persist for years after their use against an enemy, what are the limits to their use in a large scale war? On whom should we depend for such decisions? Are not we, the people, involved right up to the hilt of our common safety? Indeed we are.

How then shall we create a wide public understanding of what is really meant when we speak of "Atoms for War."

This public understanding cannot be created unless we revise our past policies of secrecy. Our possession of a new category of power confronts us with an unprecedented situation. We ought not therefore to be bound by precedent—especially when adherence to precedent has been proved useless or damaging, as in the case of the Fortunate Dragon. Here I come to my proposal.

There is much need today for creating a better understanding of America. This process is going on in certain areas—political, diplomatic, cultural—at all sorts of meetings, at the summit, on the slopes, at the bottom. What I propose therefore is another meeting for the purpose of making known a still hidden aspect of America. I propose a "Meeting at the Summit"—this time at the "Atomic Summit"—in order to explain to the world American power, which is the power of the free world.

I propose that we convene this meeting at our Pacific Proving Ground at the island of Eniwetok—and there detonate a large thermonuclear weapons before an audience representative of all the peoples of the world. History has seen many dramatic events. This one might outrank them all, because the earthly destinies of mankind are bound up with the whole meaning of the event.

What peoples should be present? Certainly the Soviet Union, Communist China, and the European satellite countries; certainly our own allies of the free world; certainly all the countries composing the United Nations. Indeed the invitation should be altogether general; this drama should be staged literally before all the nations of the world.

The group present would be small, even though its numbers, in my opinion, ought to run into the thousands. But this small group would be immensely influential.

It would include men who participate in the making of public policy in all nations. These are the men who in the first instance must come to a full personal understanding of the meaning of nuclear energy. They would, I should hope, later meet to talk together about war and peace, and about one essential condition of both, that is, the control of nuclear energy. All of them would talk more realistically and more fruitfully after their experience of witnessing a large thermonuclear explosion. They would come away from this experience utterly convinced, as I was, that humanity has entered a new age, in which certain old ideas about peace and war have become obsolete, useless and even dangerous. This experience could not fail to influence men in high positions in their work of national policy-making and international negotiations. So true is this that I cannot help wishing that the Meeting of the Atomic Summit on Eniwetok had preceded the Meeting at the Summit in Geneva. If it had, there might presently be more substance to the "spirit of Geneva." The spirit of survival is a good hard core to sustain a spirit of conciliation.

A Meeting at the Atomic Summit would not, of course solve the problem of effective international control of atomic weapons. But the men at this meeting would see the problem itself dramatized in all its urgency. At the very least therefore this meeting would create the climate of urgency so necessary.

In addition, at the meeting there would also be the press who would be prepared to give the peoples of the world a fresh vision of the new kind of power that frail man now wields. If this meeting were properly staged, with all the seriousness that attaches to life and death, the impact on world public opinion would be immeasurably great. It would be the impact of the Fortunate Dragon raised to the nth power.

The purpose would not be to strike terror into the hearts of men, but to implant understanding in their minds. The purpose would be to arouse all the forces of the human imagination, reason, and will. They are mightier than the physical forces of the atom. They are the spiritual forces upon whose vigor we set our hopes for a just and durable peace. These rational forces, resident in the human spirit, would be strongly stirred, if at Eniwetok we fulfilled our duty of explaining to the world the Nuclear Age into which we Americans have fortunately led the way.

The United States has recently stated its belief in the principle of inspection of armaments. We can right now give further proof of our belief in this principle, at least in a limited way. We can invite the whole world to view the end-result of the spectacular advances in our atomic weapons program. And this could be done without disclosing nuclear weapons technology.

Inevitably, the demonstration at Eniwetok would be a declaration of American power, a dramatic display of our ultimate resource of strength. It would not be a belligerent act. It would not be a threat of any American intention to start a war; there is no such intention. But it would be a statement, made to the senses and imagination, of the power we have to fight a war, if someone else were to start one.

During the past years all our efforts to bring peace to the world have been supported by a military strategy of deterrence. Many people still do not realize the effectiveness with which this strategy has saved the balance of power for the West. The arguments for the doctrine of deterrence, and for its continuing decisiveness have not yet been made sufficiently convincing. The spectacle at Eniwetok would make the case once and for all. An eyewitness view of the deterrent itself in action would bring ultimate conviction that against this kind of force an aggressive power would only hurl itself to destruction. In publicly dramatizing the price of war, we would likewise be dramatizing the international duty of peace.

Moreover, America presently needs to explain its arms superiority, in ultimate weapons of war. The Soviet Union has put abroad the idea that they have overtaken us in atomic and thermonuclear weapons. It is unfortunate that many Americans have swallowed this piece of Soviet Propaganda. It would be still more unfortunate if the Soviets believed their own propaganda. And it might be particularly disastrous if Communist China believed Soviet propaganda. The meeting at the Atomic Summit would go far to disabuse our enemies of any false estimates they may have of our superiority. In this respect, there is an important piece of self-explanation for America to do. Eniwetok would do it.

Furthermore, we have been trying to persuade the Communist world that its aggressive persistence in the use of force may lead to disaster. But we do not know just what picture the Communists, especially the Chinese Communists, have in mind when we warn them that disaster lies along the road of aggression. Are the Communist leaders, Russian and Chinese, familiar with the disastrous effects of an United States thermonuclear explosion? We cannot assume that they are. What they would see at Eniwetok would leave no doubt in their minds with regard to the meeting of disaster, as disaster is possible in this Nuclear Age.

The spectacle at Eniwetok would therefore be a show of force—a declaration of American power—a demonstration of the strategy of deterrence. And it would be something more profound than this. It would be an even more important piece of American self-explanation. It would illuminate our grasp of the principles of justice. It would manifest our belief that force always stands in the service of justice and that the use of force must be measured according to the dictates of justice.

Renunciation of force as a means of achieving national or ideological goals is an inherent dictate of the ethical order which America, and all civilized peoples, consider to be binding. America has made this renunciation of aggressive force. With us it is a first principle in the moral order and a cardinal policy in the order of politics. No nation need fear any aggressive use of force by the United States. We have made this clear.

Our national sense of justice has also obliged us to make it equally clear that an aggressor nation does have to fear retaliatory action on our part. We cannot permit the order of international justice to be violated with impunity. This too we have made clear.

But a further piece of self-explanation is still needed. We have yet to make it clear that our retaliation against unjust aggression will be moderated by the principles of justice. In this respect the dramatic spectacle at Eniwetok would do a service. It would prove to the world that we understand the force at our command, in all its dreadful destructiveness. It would therefore prove that when we speak of retaliation, we have a rational grasp of what the word concretely means in terms of death and disruption. In further consequence, the demonstration of our retaliatory power would itself be an assurance that we shall not use this power irrationally, recklessly, or irresponsibly. The fact is that our understanding of the destructive potential of nuclear weapons puts us under self-imposed restraints of a moral order. We accept these restraints because we accept the existence of an order of justice, established by God, to which all human action, including the action of war-making, is subject.

On the surface, Eniwetok would be a brilliant demonstration of America's technological strength. More profoundly, it would be a demonstration of our spiritual strength, our sense of justice. It would show our hatred of injustice, which has led us to develop the power that may be necessary to resist injustice. It would declare our intention of vindicating by force the order of justice, if a lawless aggressor should attack it. Finally, it would manifest our inner disposition to be governed by the dictates of justice in measuring our use of force for the defeat of unjust aggression.

You have heard my proposal for a Meeting at the Atomic Summit, and my reasons for making it. You and I know that we must not expect too much from such meetings. But you and I also know that their importance is considerable. I have no illusion that an international open meeting at Eniwetok would by itself resolve the still unresolved dilemma; will it be war or will it be peace? I do not promise that it would prevent war, still less that it would give us peace. But I do know that prevention of war and establishment of peace depends on one all-important thing—a return to fundamentals.

Prominent among these fundamentals is the fact of power. I have therefore proposed that we display to the world at Eniwetok the fact that a new kind of power has entered history and has inaugurated a new era of history. An experience of this fundamental fact of power would by itself be most salutary in the cause of peace. And I should hope that additionally this experience would impel all the peoples of the world to return to things even more fundamental than the realities of human power.

All forms of human power over physical nature are in their own way participations in the almighty power of God, whereby the universe is ruled. Christian man is no Prometheus, stealing fire from the heavens against the will of the gods. The God we worship, the God of Abraham, and the Father of Our Lord Jesus Christ, has not set His will against man's possession of fire—or of nuclear energy. It is His positive will that man should have dominion over nature and control of its forces. This is fundamental. It is likewise fundamental that God wills man to use all his power for God's own purposes, which are always creative, never destructive. Freedom, justice, peace—these are God's purposes. His own omnipotence is set in their service. In their service too man must place his present share in God's omnipotence—that is, his possession of the secret of nuclear energy. These are the fundamentals to which a meeting at the Atomic Summit—at Eniwetok—might impel the peoples of the world to return.

index